I0825174

MATISSE IN MOROCCO

MATISSE IN MOROCCO

A JOURNEY OF LIGHT AND COLOR

JEFF KOEHLER

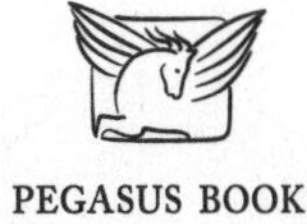

PEGASUS BOOKS
NEW YORK LONDON

MATISSE IN MOROCCO

Pegasus Books, Ltd.
148 West 37th Street, 13th Floor
New York, NY 10018

First Pegasus Books cloth edition June 2025

Interior design by Maria Fernandez

Library of Congress Cataloging-in-Publication Data is available.

ISBN: 978-1-63936-909-6

10 9 8 7 6 5 4 3 2 1

Printed in the United States of America
Distributed by Simon & Schuster
www.pegasusbooks.com

For my daughters,
Alba and Maia

CONTENTS

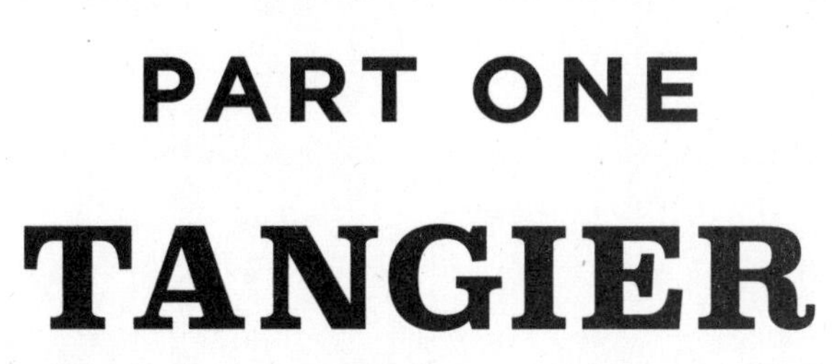

PART ONE

TANGIER

1

Standing on the breezy deck of the SS *Rindjani* in Edwardian traveling gear—frock coat, heavy overcoat, leather leggings—on a clear winter morning, Henri Matisse gripped the railing and scanned the watery blue horizon toward the North African coast.

The ship was one of Royal Rotterdam Lloyd's weekly scheduled passenger and mail services between the Netherlands and the Dutch East Indies. Launched in 1906, the *Rindjani* could carry 163 passengers (sixty-eight of them in first class) on the three-week-long run via the Strait of Gibraltar and Suez Canal, making a dozen stops to disembark and embark passengers along the way. When the ship had called in at Marseille three days earlier on its way back to Rotterdam from Batavia (present-day Jakarta), Matisse and his wife, Amélie, boarded for the leg to Tangier.

From Marseille, the *Rindjani* followed the French and then Spanish coastline south. Along the largely treeless tip of Andalucía, as the mouth of the Mediterranean narrows sharply and the currents surge in the Strait of Gibraltar, the ship headed for the tip of Morocco.

Set on the last bay of the Mediterranean at the very northwestern edge of Africa, Tangier was Morocco's chief port and known as its "European capital," as it was home to all its foreign consulates. The city's winter climate was considered among the finest in the Mediterranean and the large international diplomatic community made it a safe destination.

"We have had a quiet crossing, we have eaten well, slept well," Matisse wrote to his teenage daughter, Marguerite, from aboard the ship as they neared North Africa. At 9:00 A.M. on January 29, he told her, "On a slightly rough sea but of the purest blue, the boat glides without rocking or pitching. The horizon on the left [towards Morocco] is bordered by a few clouds on the right by the mountains of the Spanish coast that we have not lost sight of since the Balearic Islands." Under command of Captain T. Bakker on the bridge in his starched white uniform with polished brass buttons, the 460-foot-long (140 m), double-masted ship was even set to arrive that day a few hours early.

But such upbeat sentiment belied the anxiety behind Matisse's myopic, agate-blue eyes that were intently watching the horizon.

It was the beginning of 1912. Matisse was forty-two and not yet mid-career. While today he is one of the greatest, most influential, and most valuable artists in the world, with virtually unparalleled global popularity and blockbuster exhibitions, such widespread appreciation, commercial success, or even financial security, were still some years away. That winter when he boarded the *Rindjani* for Morocco, he had yet to find lasting admiration among the public, respect among his peers, or much recent praise from critics.

His brightly hued fauve ("wild beast") paintings had brought him instant notoriety when displayed at the 1905 Salon d'Automne. Spearheading a short-lived but significant movement that would also include André Derain, Georges Braque, Maurice de Vlaminck, Kees van Dongen, and his close friends Charles Camion and Albert Marquet, Matisse was known as the "fauve of fauves."

The fauves revolutionized painting with their non-naturalistic use of strong colors and fierce, visible brushwork. Exploding centuries of academy tradition—Derain equated the colors on their paintbrushes to "sticks of dynamite" that "exploded into light"—Matisse represented what he saw with an emotional reaction: vivid, raw reds and yellows, hot pinks, and acid greens seethe off the canvases with expressive forcefulness. Respecting no boundary, colors broke free.

The reaction to their radical works displayed at the Salon was vicious. "Here all description," wrote one French newspaper, "all reporting as well as all criticism become equally impossible since what is presented to us here—apart from the materials employed—has nothing whatever to do with painting: some formless confusion of colors; blue, red, yellow, green; some splotches of pigment crudely juxtaposed; the barbaric and naïve sport of a child who plays with the box of colors he just got as a Christmas present."

But among the avant-garde, the audacity and inventiveness were groundbreaking.

The focus of controversy at the Salon was Matisse's *Woman with a Hat* of his wife Amélie, which was greeted with more hostility than any other painting. Turning back with a wistful look, Amélie wears an oversized hat topped by what appears to be pieces of fruit. The canvas's unfinished quality and unsettling, discordant colors were shocking. The painting disregarded the convention of a portrait having mimetic qualities defined in its etymology: portrait, from *pour trait* or *trait pour trait*, literally "feature by feature" or "line by line." And if outer beauty was the traditional reflection of inner beauty, then what was he saying about this woman, his own wife no less?

Leo Stein called the canvas "a thing brilliant and powerful, but the nastiest smear of paint that I had ever seen," and reported that "visitors howled and jeered" at it. On the last day of the Salon, he and his sister Gertrude bought the painting anyway, and afterward asked to meet the artist.

Matisse became an important part of the Saturday evening salon at 27 rue de Fleurus, the Left Bank home of *Les Stein*—the quintet of Californian Steins (plus, later, Alice B. Toklas)—where his most revolutionary early paintings—*Bonheur de vivre* (*The Joy of Life*), *Blue Nude* (*Memory of Biskra*), *The Green Stripe*, and a rare self-portrait, his 1906 fauve *Self-Portrait in a*

Striped T-shirt—would join *Woman with a Hat* and hang alongside works by Picasso, Cézanne, Renoir, and Gauguin. Tastemakers who did more to support the Parisian avant-garde than anyone else at the time, the Steins became Matisse's first major patrons.

It didn't last. With Picasso's 1907 *Les Demoiselles d'Avignon* and the rise of cubism, Matisse was quickly usurped by his Spanish rival a dozen years younger. Gertrude and Leo Stein stopped buying Matisse—*Blue Nude* (1907) was their last purchase—and ardently championed the prodigious Spaniard. Picasso and his fellow cubists were hailed as heirs to Cézanne and the trailblazers of European art. The fauve movement was soon over. After hitting a high point in the spring 1907 Salon des Indépendants, it began to dissolve. Most of the original members followed Picasso and his lead, and works by the likes of Braque and Derain, two of the key fauves, showed that they, as Gertrude Stein put it, "had become Picassoites and were definitely not Matisseites."

Matisse's fall from vanguard leader had swiftly eroded to the point of derision. Not many years before, he had been in the wheelhouse guiding Paris's daring art scene. But by the time he sailed for Morocco, the Parisian avant-garde considered him passé, a figure of ridicule to be jeered at in public. Picasso's band of merry followers who hung out at the Lapin Agile cabaret in Montmartre painted anti-Matisse graffiti on posters around urinals in the hilly neighborhood, shot rubber-tipped darts at the portrait of his daughter that Matisse had given Picasso, and dipped the tail of a donkey in the brightly colored paints associated with the fauves, switched it against a canvas, and sent it to the spring Salon as truly authentic "wild beast" art.

More disparaging than such petty taunts were critics like André Salmon, who knew Matisse well. "Henri Matisse's taste has been very much praised. Though undeniable, it is second rate. It is a modiste's taste, whose love of color equals the love of chiffon." It was something decorative and done with feminine skills, unlike the work of the deeply masculine and innovative Picasso. A Moscow newspaper had just echoed the sentiment during Matisse's recent Russia visit: "But in the final analysis, Matisse is a *cravate*, a colored necktie, in the words of Pablo Picasso, his opposite. He is beautiful but not profound."

And while some in the art establishment argued the *beauté* of Matisse's paintings was only on the surface, others went further and questioned if they contained any at all. "It was Matisse who took the first step into the undiscovered land of the ugly," wrote an American critic in 1910. When some of his works showed in the United States at the Armory Show in 1913, *the New York Times* reported: "We may as well say in the first place that his pictures are ugly, that they are coarse, that they are narrow, that to us they are revolting in their humanity." In Chicago, faculty and art students—art students!—protested and held a mock trial for "Henry Hairy Mattress" on the Art Institute's south portico: "You are charged with artistic murder, pictorial arson, artistic rapine, total degeneracy of color, criminal misuse of line, general esthetic aberration, and contumacious abuse of title." He was found guilty, and copies of three of Matisse's paintings were burned in effigy.

The years of continual battle and criticism were exhausting and had taken a toll on his confidence. To the last few Salons, he had submitted little. In the spring 1911 Salon des Indépendants, the reaction to *Manila Shawl* had been so intense that the deeply stung Matisse took the painting down after five days and left *The Pink Studio*, with the paint still wet, hanging in its place.

At the 1911 Salon d'Automne, he exhibited only two pieces that an unimpressed Louis Vauxcelles noted were "sketched in a quarter of an hour." Matisse's close friend and fellow painter Georgette Agutte interpreted this paltry showing as a deepening lack of confidence. "Your two sketches, so fresh and so delicate in tone, seem a concession to public opinion; in this large room, they are as if lost, one would like to see them in a small private room, but there, you must have these large admirable paintings which catch the eye, impose themselves and would decorate this entire large room on their own," she tactfully wrote. She was referring to two new works that were sitting at the moment in his studio, *The Painter's Family* and *The Blue Window*. "Good Lord, what can you fear? Oh! the poor decorators, compared to these paintings, what a pitiful effect they would produce!" She urged him to not bow to the critics and to display bolder pieces, like his just-completed *Interior with Aubergines*, which she had seen. "The press? But what does this mean? Why worry about it, war is a hundred times better than indifference." With a final supportive nudge, she added, "you must dare to show everything."

By the time Matisse departed for Tangier in 1912, most of the few ardent early supporters had publicly turned on him, even ones who were personal friends like Apollinaire and Salmon. Gertrude and Leo Stein, his first important patrons, hadn't bought anything in five years. Just a very small loyal band of clients remained—Agutte and her husband Marcel Sembat; Michael and Sarah Stein; and, most importantly, a pair of Russian patrons, Sergei Shchukin and Ivan Morozov, who had purchased most of his canvases these last few years.

It took an enormous amount of courage to carry on, especially now that he was unaccompanied in his artistic path. "Matisse is alone," André Salmon put it quite straightforwardly a few months later in his book on French painting. No longer part of a group, Matisse had to endure the mocking and disparagement on his own. In his review of the approaching spring Salon, Apollinaire would soon write, "Matisse's influence appears to have disappeared almost completely." Conversely, he noted, "Picasso's influence is the most profound."

Originally, the Matisses had planned on going to Sicily. But they bought tickets to Tangier instead on something of an impulse and abruptly departed France with no fixed date of return.

Neatly packed in Matisse's traveling trunk were paints and brushes, palette knives, rolled canvases, and everything else he would require in Morocco. He had three commissions to fulfill for the two Russians, though these were not the sole purpose of the trip.

In order to continue toward his own artistic true north and not be pulled aside by other powerful magnetic forces, Matisse needed to get away from Paris. He had enough internal distractions in trying to push ahead and didn't need external ones adding to that noise of self-doubt. It was a deliberate distancing of himself from the dominating, inescapable face of cubism, which had engulfed the Parisian art world, and the arrival of futurism, which was having its first group exhibition in Paris less than a week after his departure at the same gallery that represented him. In Tangier, he could meditate on his evolving work. He needed to find his own way ahead and advance his own distinctive vision.

He desperately needed to work well. For that, he required good, steady light. Albert Marquet, his gifted pal from the École des Beaux-Arts and fellow ex-fauve, had spent the previous August and September painting in Tangier. Coming away with a series of fine oils, he urged Matisse to head there for its distance from Paris and for its fine light. Plus, the weather would be warmer. It had been cold in Paris—the Matisses had just gone ice-skating with Agutte and Sembat—and the night before their departure the temperature in Paris fell well below freezing.

The *Rindjani* cleared the tip of Morocco and steamed past the stout Cape Malabata lighthouse. From the deck, Matisse and Amélie watched the ancient whitewashed city appear, in the words of another traveler fifteen years before, "like a white dove brooding on its nest." The ship entered the semicircular Bay of Tangier, a wide arcing expanse limned with golden sand, and the dazzling city hovering over the sea revealed itself in full: "All is white, perfectly white, so that the whole seems cut out of an immense chalk rock," the traveler had written. A trio of lithe minarets tiled with enameled faience rose above the dense tiers of flat roofs that climbed upward like an amphitheater toward the looming kasbah citadel with its belt of crenelated walls and heavy battery of guns.

Tangier was to be both a refuge and a place for inspiration. Along with escaping the pressures of Paris, in Morocco Matisse could reflect on and be inspired by Islamic art traditions. He had been exploring the varied art history of the Muslim world for the past decade and felt that it could be a key to his path forward. It was such ancient traditions that help, as he later put it, "jump the ditch."

2

At the very northwestern edge of Africa, Tangier is a crossroads, a meeting point of two seas, two continents, and various cultures, a gateway and a bridge, a welcoming, even tolerant, place. The country's oldest and most cosmopolitan city, it was where East and West nearly touch. Out Matisse's hotel window, he could clearly see Spain, just nine miles (15 km) away.

Founded in the seventh century B.C.E. by Phoenicians in a strategic position at the narrow mouth of the Mediterranean, Tingis (as it was soon known) became a flourishing imperial colony under the Romans, whose ruins are scattered around the city. Roman supremacy ended in the fifth century C.E., and Tangier was, in turn, under control of the Vandals, Byzantine Empire, and then Christian Visigoths.

After the death of the Prophet Muhammad in 632, Islam swept westward from the Arabian Peninsula, through the Middle East and Egypt and across North Africa. By 707, the north of Morocco had been conquered. In 711, Arabs and their Berber foot soldiers used Tangier as a port of embarkation in their conquest of the Iberian Peninsula. Muslims brought to Tangier a new religion, a new language, and new traditions. For centuries, the city was ruled by a string of powerful Moroccan dynasties. By the fourteenth century, Tangier was, alongside Barcelona, Marseille, and Genoa, one of the great ports of the western Mediterranean.

Tangier was soon a key target in Portugal's colonial expansion. The Portuguese conquered the city in 1471 and set about converting the city's main mosque to a cathedral and fortifying the city's walls and towers. It was "a city with walls of bronze and with magnificent palaces of gold and silver," the sixteenth-century French writer F. Élie de la Primaudaye enthused, "the royal house of the Kings of the West, the mother of the cities of the Maghreb, the most beautiful and the most ancient."

The Portuguese controlled Tangier until 1661, when they included it in the dowry of the Infanta Catherine of Braganza in her marriage to the English king, Charles II, who called it "a jewel of immense value in the royal diadem." While the English strengthened the kasbah's defenses and built a stone mole (jetty) in the port, they were besieged in continual attacks by Moroccans and lost many men in skirmishes. By 1684 the English had had enough and abandoned the city—though not before spending five months systematically destroying the huge mole that had reached, with considerable expense, 1,436 feet (438 m) in length and 110 feet (33.5 m) in width, as well as the city's fortifications that they had constructed over the past two decades. They didn't want the Moroccans or any European rivals to benefit from their labors.

After three centuries of European rule, the city passed back to Moroccan control, becoming part of a vast sultanate that stretched south from the Mediterranean into the Sahara and west from the Atlantic to the border of what is today Algeria.

It was still an independent sultanate when Matisse sailed to Tangier in early 1912. But it didn't look likely to remain so for much long. The French, who ruled neighboring Algeria and Tunisia, had been increasing their presence in the country over the last few years and were pressing to complete their control of North Africa.

Tangier was a major commercial center on one of the world's busiest maritime routes. At the end of the nineteenth century, 1,750 vessels a year were calling into its shallow port. Along with Matisse's Dutch vessel, there were two French passenger ships, a Spanish passenger ship, and a British cruiser that also arrived into port that same day.

After the *Rindjani* dropped anchor offshore in early afternoon, passengers and luggage had to be ferried to the newly built pier by launches, the only vessels capable of navigating the shallow bay. "The average tourist is utterly overwhelmed at the confusion encountered at the landing-stage," the recent American consul-general wrote in 1914, "and is apt to think that a revolution is in progress, or that he has fallen among Ali Baba and his forty thieves." Boatmen, touts, and hotel agents argued as they fought for the luggage of disembarking passengers.

The Matisses made their way through the quayside chaos (and cattle from the interior waiting to be loaded onto flat-bottom lighters for the Ceuta- and Gibraltar-bound cargo ships anchored in the bay), paid their pier dues, and passed under the pale, stone arches of the customs house, where inspections were known to be lenient and passports not required. With their formalities completed, they exited the side of the stout, brick building. Porters loaded their luggage onto mules, and they climbed the gentle ramp from the harbor, passed under Bab al-Marsa gate and into the ancient walled old city of Tangier.

"*Bâlak, bâlak!*" shouted the mule driver to get people to make way as they jostled among cosmopolitan crowds of men in cinnamon-colored hooded burnouses and Jewish ones in black kaftans and maroon tarbush fezes, straw-hatted Europeans, men from the Rif Mountains in calf-length, emerald green *djellabas*, and veiled women in all white.

After a few minutes the Matisses reached Jamaa el-Kebir (the Grand Mosque), distinguished by its lofty brick minaret and ornate entrance portal with radiating geometric motifs, interlacing green patterning, and carved and painted wooden canopy, and turned right, ascending the medina's widest and straightest street to cross the old city in its entirety on wobbly sea legs.

Passing carts selling oranges, tangerines, and the last of the year's pomegranates, noisy café terraces, and veiled women sitting on the ground selling disc-shaped loaves of bread for a penny, they reached Souq el-Dahkal, the "inner souq" or market, known generally by foreigners as the Petit Socco. Edged by government buildings, banks, and the English, German, and Spanish post offices—each of the four major powers had their own; the French *poste* was behind the mosque—the slender square was the heart of Tangier. Just ahead was the Spanish Cathedral of the Immaculate Conception and, immediately beyond it, an alley that led to the main synagogue; there were seventeen synagogues for Tangier's significant Jewish population.

Tangier was a melting pot. The 1911 Baedeker's guide lists Tangier's diverse population at 46,270, with 25,000 Muslims, 12,000 Moroccan Jews, and 9,270 foreigners, including 7,000 Spanish. (Morocco's total population was about eight million.)

Along with its advantageous location, a decision in the eighteenth century helped to create the city's makeup. In 1782, the sultan wanted to gather all diplomatic representatives into one place, and selected Tangier as the seat of European consulates. During the nineteenth century and into the twentieth, as the sultan remained in the imperial cities of Fez and Meknès, Tangier acted as the diplomatic capital, home to every foreign embassy and consulate in Morocco. In 1821, the US Legation and Consulate in Tangier's medina became America's first diplomatic property.

The Matisses continued up rue des Siaghins, named for the resident silversmiths. Besides silverwork, nearly every jewelry stall bought and sold gold and currency. Among the Spanish and French shops with plate-glass windows were niche-size and open-fronted ones where merchants reclined among goods within reach of an outstretched hand—dates from the Saharan oases, raisins, and flattened dried figs strung on twine, tubs of fermented butter called *smen* and different honeys, cones of sugar, roasted nuts, cakes of soap, cooking pots, candles, and colorful sandals embroidered with shimmering golden and silver thread. Shod hooves clattered on the cobblestones, water-sellers rang their brass bells, and mule drivers flicked their switches and yelled *"Bâlak, bâlak!"* to get their animals through the crowded street.

Passing, finally, under the double arch of Bab al-Fahs—the gateway to the interior of the country, the name means "hinterland" in Arabic—and out of the dense old city, the Matisses cut between rows of vegetable stalls and emerged onto the Souq el-Barra, the "outer souq" or Grand Socco, where the city's legendary open-air market gathered twice a week.

Above this broad and gently sloped field stood the Hôtel Villa de France, where the Matisses were going to stay.

From the bottom gate, a path inset with smooth river stones curved up through the terraced gardens with huge palms, purple bougainvillea, roses, and blooming mimosa, and around to the porticoed main entrance on the side of the three-story building.

While extremely close to Europe, Tangier remained remarkably remote and distinct, and seemed to Westerners upon arriving as something extraordinary. Disembarking a week later and making the identical walk from the port to the Hôtel Villa de France, where she was also staying for the winter to paint, the Australian artist Hilda Rix captured her breathless feelings in a letter to her mother and sister dashed off just after entering the hotel:

> Oh my dears if only I could give you an idea of everything here—we came up from the boat with our luggage loaded on donkey back and we passed slowly up hill through crowded streets full of wonderful people—up & up past queer little cubby hole shops, under quaint arches to the foot of the open hill called the Soko where, joy for us, the big market was in full swing. 'Twas like walking through an Arabian nights story, so wonderful were the costumes of the seething mass of people—so many different races with varying complexions,

> some very dark, some clear white, & some with transparent gold skin—all with different headgear of white and gorgeous colours—Oh oh the thrill of it all.

Especially for Amélie, who had only been outside France a few times, including for their honeymoon trip to London in 1898 and briefly to Italy in 1907, the introduction must have seemed intense.

Matisse was no doubt struck by the scenes around him that were unfamiliar and exotic en route to the hotel, but he was also looking upward to the sky.

The clouds that he had glimpsed from the ship that morning had continued to gather, darkening the sky over Tangier. Winds swirled, and fat, pregnant drops of rain fell as the Matisses made their way across the city. By the time they reached the hotel, it was pouring rain. For the painter, nothing could have been more distressing.

It was still coming down heavily the next day. And the next one, too. "We got caught in the rain here, a real flood," he told his daughter on January 31. "It seems it could go on for a whole month."

Accompanying the rain was wind, knocking out the telegraph and keeping the mailboat riding at anchor in the bay unable to offload. When the bay was rough, a blue flag was flown on the quay and the price of landing was doubled. When the authorities raised the yellow flag, meaning stormy weather, prices were negotiable if landing was even possible.

The wide-mouthed Bay of Tangier is the only protected anchorage on the southern side of the Strait of Gibraltar. But it is open-mouthed and faces northwest, which means that while offering good protection from the strong eastern *chegui* wind that blows in summer, during the rest of the year, when the winds frequently come from other directions, it can be fully exposed.

In the days after Matisse's arrival, the churning sea crashed against the ramparts and waves raced far up onto the sand along the corniche. "On Friday [February 2] a gale of exceptional violence blew from the S.W. at high tide the sea broke heavily on the beach and carrying away a large quantity of loose ground and made an inroad, which only the lull on Saturday prevented from being dangerous to buildings along the seafront," the city's twice-weekly English newspaper, the *Al-Moghreb Al-Aksa*, reported, "Bathing sheds and everything movable was swept away. . . . A part of the esplanade in front of Mr. Petri's buildings was undermined by the breakers and, as a result, fell in."

The rain refused to relent. To his friends back in Paris, the frustrated Matisse fired off angry missives. "Shall we ever see the sun in Morocco?" he wrote on a postcard to Gertrude Stein. "Ever since we arrived eight days ago," he moaned to the painter Henri Manguin, "it's been a downright flood. Shall we leave again? What a misadventure!"

As the one who persuaded Matisse to go to Tangier, who had expounded on the prospect of good, steady light, Marquet received numerous pointed notes.

"Ah my friend! What an adventure! We arrived Monday at 3 o'clock, today it is Saturday as the other [card] said, and we've only seen it raining without ceasing, on the contrary harder and harder," he wrote on the back of a postcard to Marquet that showed some camels from a caravan in a courtyard. "I don't know what that means, nor do the people from Tangier either. They have never seen it. They are much more surprised than me because it had been going on for more than 15 days when we arrived. Good Lord, what to do! Going back would be ridiculous but it seems logical. The light is like in a cellar."

On a second postcard, of a gate inside the kasbah, he continued: "While I am writing to you, the rain is coming down harder than ever. You've certainly never seen it rain as hard in all your charming life." Even if he said he didn't blame his old friend, he did in a way. "Goodbye old pig, no hard feelings, since you are not responsible for anything that goes wrong."

Across the very bottom of the card, Matisse added, "Ah, Tangier, Tangier! I wish I had the courage to get the hell out."

3

Matisse was not a natural traveler. He had a delicate disposition, and was vulnerable to periods of deep depression, severe anxiety, and panic attacks. Nervous energy radiated from him. According to Matisse's future son-in-law, Georges Duthuit, "his inability to relax, his killing labor, his absolute incapacity, if only for the space of a tear or a smile, to sit down with his neighbor" profoundly marked his character.

Compounding this, Matisse was frequently prone to lengthy bouts of insomnia. During sleepless nights, Amélie would read to her husband until dawn broke or he had dozed off. (Often, when she thought that he finally had succumbed to sleep, she would quietly put the book down only to hear him say, "Keep reading.") Traveling alone in Spain the previous winter, he had experienced a crushing spell of sleeplessness. "I went for a month and a half like that, with no sleep," he later explained. "When I dozed off, I woke up immediately in a state of panic. I was tired, I was completely worn out." Finally, in Sevilla, it caused a physical and emotional breakdown. "My bed shook, and from my throat came a little high-pitched cry that I could not stop." Ill and feverish, he dosed himself with laudanum.

In his cabin aboard the *Rindjani* on the way out to Tangier, he had slept well. But his insomnia returned the first night in the hotel. As wind and rain rattled the wooden window shutters of their corner room, Amélie tried to comfort her husband.

Amélie hadn't traveled with him to Spain the previous winter. He was supposed to be gone a month but it was twice that long before he returned. Her letters reflected her unhappiness with him. At one point during his lengthening absence, she was so angry that she moved out of their home, requiring family intervention to get her to return.

Rather than staying in France this winter, though, Amélie accompanied him to Morocco, leaving the three children behind. Their two boys—Jean, who had just turned thirteen, and eleven-year-old Pierre—were with relatives, while seventeen-year-old Marguerite, Matisse's daughter from his previous partner, was left in charge of the household in Issy-les-Moulineaux on the southwestern outskirts of Paris. Marguerite had few friends there, few neighbors, and little to do. There was a psychiatric hospital down the hill and at night she would lay awake listening to the movements in the trees around the villa and the branches rasping the windows. "Boredom by day," she wrote to her father and Amélie in Tangier, "terror at night."

Amélie's dedication to her husband was steadfast and she did what was needed so that he could concentrate on his work. Their relationship had been founded knowing that she would undertake this particular role.

Matisse married Amélie Noellie Parayre, a handsome, dark-haired woman from Toulouse with large, wide-set eyes, in January 1898, less than three months after being seated next to her at a wedding banquet in Paris. The day before that wedding banquet, he had decided to separate from his partner, his ex-model Camille Joblaud, and left her and their young daughter Marguerite in Belle-Île, off the rugged coast of Brittany, to attend the ceremony alone. The twenty-eight-year-old Matisse was the best man, and Amélie, three years younger, the bride's maid of honor.

It was a quick romance, more pragmatic than ardent. Matisse knew she would never supplant his truest passion. "Mademoiselle, I love you dearly," he warned Amélie after becoming engaged, "but I shall always love painting more."

Amélie accepted that life with the struggling painter would be one of self-sacrifice and austerity, and she embraced her role with loyal, single-mindedness, never doubting the value nor importance of her contribution. A few months after marrying, she moved into Matisse's apartment-cum-studio on quai Saint-Michel to live quite literally among his art (and true love). Besides serving as his frequent model, she ran the studio, kept the other models happy, and washed out his brushes each evening. Amélie offered stability and support, both emotional and, at the beginning of their marriage, financial. While her husband could not sell a canvas, she ran a small milliner's shop. For three years, Amélie's hats were the family's main source of income. Years later, their close friend Charles Camoin praised Amélie's devotion to her husband and his art, telling the French writer Raymond Escholier, "His marriage was a happy one for him—Madame Amélie Matisse, exceptionally devoted, working to leave him free to paint! Charming, courageous, and full of faith in her husband's talent."

While Matisse captured his wife's captivating eyes and arching brows in his numerous portraits of her, the canvases generally tend not to highlight her handsome, dignified beauty that is glimpsed in photographs of her. Nor do published comments about her looks from Gertrude Stein reflect the reality. With her husband, Amélie had been a regular at the Steins' Saturday salon on rue de Fleurus and knew the entire clan. In her most famous work, Stein described Amélie in rather offensive terms. "She was a very straight dark woman with a long face and a firm large loosely hung mouth like a horse," Stein wrote in her gossipy, self-serving, and relationship-severing 1933 book *The Autobiography of Alice B. Toklas*. "She had an abundance of dark hair."

In a supplemental pamphlet to the Parisian magazine *transition*, an experimental literary quarterly distributed largely through Sylvia Beach's Shakespeare and Company bookstore, that collected numerous grievances and inaccuracies in Stein's work, Matisse defended Amélie in a curious and somewhat tentative rebuttal. "Madame Matisse was a very lovely Toulousaine, erect, with a good carriage and the possessor of beautiful dark hair that grew charmingly, especially at the nape of the neck. She had a pretty throat and very handsome shoulders," he wrote. "She gave the impression, despite the fact that she was timid and reserved, of a person of great kindness, force and gentleness. She was generous and incapable of calculation in her gestures of kindness."

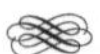

Throughout his life as a painter, Matisse's obsessive drive to work never wavered. He was very much a follower of the sculptor Auguste Rodin's motto: "*Travailler, toujours travailler.*" (Or, as Gertrude Stein put it in *The Autobiography of Alice B. Toklas*, "Matisse worked every day and every day and every day and he worked terribly hard.")

Yet now in Tangier, stuck in his hotel under rainy skies, working as he had hoped—and required—was impossible. The rain also ratcheted up the pressure on his insomnia and his headaches.

Painting was his obsession but also sanctuary, and he found refuge in intensely working. It was a remedy for his nervous anxiety, or at least distracted his attention from it. Virtually confined to his corner room, he at last set to work. There was little else he could do. A week after arriving, he wrote to his daughter, *"J'ai commencé un bouquet d'iris bleus."*

Irises were blooming on the hills outside Tangier, and women carried massive bundles of the bluish-purple flowers on their heads into the city to sell in the open-air market that gathered below Matisse's hotel. They were even growing in the hotel gardens.

Matisse was well-acquainted with irises, which grow across the northern hemisphere. The flower's name comes from the Greek meaning "rainbow," reflecting the wide range of colors found among the species. Irises had been part of the French heraldry, with the stylized fleur-de-lis depicted on the country's traditional royal coat of arms. For Matisse, the flowers were something familiar to ground him in this new place.

In *Vase with Irises* (see figure 1), a bouquet of lush irises sits on a mahogany-colored wooden dressing table, with an oval mirror reflecting the blooms that Matisse rendered in a pinkish-purple and yellow with emerald green stalks. As the flowers are fragile, the painting was likely done in just a couple of sessions.

Measuring nearly 4 feet tall by 3½ feet wide (118 x 101 cm), it's a large canvas, and while the dark tones from the deep charcoal gray wall might suggest a bleakish atmosphere, there are hints of brightness in the reflection of yellows and turquoise-green in the rococo mirror, the gaps of untouched primed canvas between the flower petals that radiate white, and the warm reddish-brown wood of the dresser. As well, the purple shade of the irises themselves is brighter than reproductions tend to indicate.

Such still lifes were not fashionable then among Matisse's leading contemporaries. A few of his predecessors had done stunning versions. Manet, in the last year of his life, his legs in agonizing pain and dying of complications from syphilis, had painted eighteen graceful floral still lifes in 1883. Apart from the obvious symbolism of the flower being temporal, the bouquets, done with a delicate and expressive brush, contain no wistfulness, sadness, or traces of melancholy. In May 1890, in the last year of his life, Van Gogh painted four bouquets of spring flowers just before checking himself out of the psychiatric hospital in Saint-Rémy-de-Provence. Two were of irises, one of which Matisse likely saw. For two weeks in the fall of 1907 and again for nearly a month in early 1908, the version with the white vase, white background, and green surface that today hangs in the Metropolitan Museum of Art in New York was on display at the Paris gallery where Matisse held a contract, the Bernheim-Jeune.

For Matisse, alongside a way to distract his anxiety, the flowers were simply ravishing to look at, and he took joy in their freshness and colors.

That pleasure shows, and the painting feels almost playful. The flowers are dazzling and very much alive. There is not a single fallen petal on the dressing table.

Vase with Irises is one of the most stunning floral still lifes of his entire career, and certainly the finest work he had done yet outside of France.

Yet despite this surprisingly promising start—not just in the success of the picture but that he had done it so quickly—Matisse wanted to leave the foul weather and return home immediately.

As the rain continued and Matisse remained hotelbound, he began working on another still life, this time of a wide bowl of oranges sitting atop the night table by his bed.

Oranges and lemons were in season and found in abundance in markets, in kitchens, and on dining room tables after lunch and dinner. Famous for its citruses, Tangier lends its name to a small, sweet variety with thin, brilliant-orange peels. Matisse piled a dozen or so pieces in a wide bowl and set them on his night table, over which he had draped a silk brocade embroidered with bouquets of peonies. The brilliant orange and yellow fruit are outlined in black, and the leaves are done in thick smears of green paint. Peachy, pale pinks color one wall and also the cloth with peonies that cascades off the night table.

Large and nearly square (just over 3 feet by 2½ feet, or 95 x 85 cm), *Basket with Oranges* (also commonly called *Still Life with Oranges*) is a gorgeous still life that thirty years later Picasso would buy and hang in his studio (see figure 2). (It is now at the Musée Picasso Paris.) To mark the gesture, Matisse would send Picasso a box of oranges as a gift each New Year. Picasso owned a personal collection of stunning pieces he cherished and admired by Cézanne, Miró, Rousseau, Balthus, Modigliani, Braque, and Derain. But this bowl of oranges by Matisse was the finest of the bunch.

Françoise Gilot certainly thought so. In spring of 1943, when the twenty-one-year-old Gilot went for the first time to Picasso's studio, the piece she immediately noticed was not by the sixty-one-year-old Spaniard who would, three years later, become her partner for a decade and would have two children with. "Black blinders were drawn over most of the windows, and it was relatively dark, rather like the den of a wizard, but I was dazzled by the *Still Life with Oranges* by Matisse which was prominently displayed," she wrote in her book about the friendship between the two artists. "I was struck by the fact that the main part of the painting, the basket of fruit itself, with strong colors and dark outline, seemed still to belong to nature. What set it in the realm of intangible poetry was the boldness of the pink, magenta, and ultramarine tablecloth. The competition between the green, the cadmiums, the diverse fuchsias, the strong darker red and intense blue created on ascending scale, an exultation." Picasso's secretary, Jaime Sabartés, was not amused when she blurted out praise for a rival's canvas to him, but the young Gilot reiterated it to Picasso himself. "Picasso was very amused, I think, by this outburst, which for once was not intended for himself, but he was gratified when I added that only an artist of his caliber could afford to place such a masterpiece among his own works, in the center of his atelier."

This wasn't the first version of the still life, though, and was nearly not the last one. Matisse fiddled and changed the canvas over the next weeks. He was struggling at the time, with his work and with his state of mind.

"Dismayed by the weather which has been cloudy and rainy for 2 days, I have hardly slept last night, and this morning, although tired, I would start working if it was not for the rain," he wrote to Georgette Agutte in mid-March. "Let me add that I would like to paint a still life with oranges which had been finished and I found lovely, but thinking it was not enough, I started it again by destroying it, and now because of the weather, I am probably going to waste it: I had carried on however, in an attempt to inject an intimacy that I am researching at the moment and it was promising."

Matisse included two thumbnail sketches. While the first is closer to the final picture, the second, the more intimate one to which he alludes, is narrower and much more tightly cropped, with less wall and no sign of the night table. "I prefer the [wider] composition opposite, it is more graceful but, but this one here [the tighter composition] will be stronger I hope." Evidently, he didn't do that tighter one as the final version that Picasso eventually acquired is the earlier wider view.

The still life might have radiant colors, and the oranges more dazzling than any of Cézanne's peaches or Zurbarán's lemons, but it also exudes a deeper sense of claustrophobia than the painting of the irises. Vertical bars (from the headboard of the bed or the back of a wooden chair) run behind it and others along the folds of the plummy-purplish curtain, while green bars horizontally cross the gold and red patch between those two sections like thin slats of window shutters.

This mood is more explicit in a sketch of the painting he included in a letter to Gertrude Stein's older brother Michael and his wife, Sarah, in Paris. In a rather faithful rendering of the finished canvas, the bowl of fruit and cloth are tightly framed on three sides within a prison of vertical bars.

Such a reading is not fanciful conjecture. The memory of being utterly miserable after arriving in Tangier never lessened, and he would remember it as such for the rest of his life. Seeing the painting again after many years brought it all back, Matisse later told the critic Pierre Courthion, "and in front of it I relived the moment when it was made and I said to someone who was there: 'I gave birth in pain!'"

When Picasso took Gilot to meet Matisse for the first time, in the late winter of 1946, she wanted to know more about *Basket with Oranges*, which with she so admired. Gilot "mustered the courage to inquire directly of the master how he had succeeded in expressing so much *joie de vivre* in a work of art," she wrote. Matisse answered that "the explosion of joy in the painting . . . had nothing to do with his personal feelings at the time;

on the contrary, when he had created it he had been entirely penniless in Tangiers and had been seriously contemplating suicide."

Matisse had wondered if it would be the last painting he would ever make. "Transcending personal doom," Gilot wrote, "his masterpiece might in fact have been his swan song."

4

Matisse came relatively late to painting. Born on the last day of 1869 in his grandparents' two-room weaver's hut with a beaten earth floor in Le Cateau-Cambrésis, a rural village in northern France, Matisse spent the first twenty years of his life on this low-lying plain near the Belgium border. A largely flat, nearly treeless expanse of broad fields, distant horizons, and villages that huddle around churches with high, sharp steeples, the area was marked at the time by smoking chimneys and factory effluent of textile mills and beet-sugar refineries.

When Matisse was just eight days old, his family settled in Bohain—today officially called Bohain-en-Vermandois, population five thousand—some ten miles (fifteen kilometers) south through gently undulating fields, taking over a hardware store on the main street. His father handled seeds, grains, and tools, while his mother took care of the paint counter.

Matisse was a sickly kid, and it soon became evident that he wouldn't be running the family business. In 1887, after finishing school in nearby Saint-Quentin, he was sent to Paris for a year to study to be a lawyer's copying clerk. Back in Saint-Quentin, he went to work in a law office.

Matisse only turned to painting at twenty following an attack of acute appendicitis—perhaps coupled with a breakdown—and a lengthy post-surgery convalescence in his parents' home above the store. When his mother gave him a paint set, he bought a book titled *La manière de peindre* (*How to Paint*). It was something new and unknown to him. Up to that point, Matisse had paid slight attention to art. He had seen few of the Old Masters in person, knew scant about modern movements like impressionism, and likely little of Monet or Renoir. "But the moment I had the paint box in my hands," he later recalled, "I felt that this was my life."

Once recovered and back to work in Saint-Quentin, Matisse enrolled in painting classes without the knowledge of his disapproving father. He attended these before work (it was a mere minute's walk from his office), painted during his lunch break, and when done for the day he would hurry home to his rented lodgings to paint in the remaining light. Live models or even painting from nature were prohibited at the conservative art school; students worked only from classical busts and decorative motifs. (Textile design was one of the main subjects taught there.) When one of the young teachers set up a rival academy on the edge of town to offer those forbidden modern elements at lunchtime, Matisse enrolled there, too. Painting consumed him. He was making up for lost time. "That was the seed; it was bound to grow—the bud had to blossom," he said in 1941. "Before that, nothing interested me. Since then, I've hardly given a thought to anything else, just painting."

Within a year he left for Paris to fully pursue his art, scandalizing his family and angering his father, who supposedly yelled as his departing son, "It means starvation, you'll see, you'll starve in the streets."

In Paris, repeatedly failing the entrance examination for the École des Beaux-Arts, he studied with the symbolist painter Gustave Moreau, who eventually arranged for him to be accepted into his studio at the Beaux-Arts in 1895. There he met other students who would be important, loyal friends throughout his life, including Camoin, Marquet, Derain, Manguin, and Georgette Agutte. Agutte had been admitted as a "free student" (*élève libre*) in 1893 and was the lone woman at the school. The École des Beaux-Arts only officially began admitting women in 1897.

Agutte's father, a painter and student of Camille Corot, died in an accident the year that Agutte was born. When she joined Moreau's studio, she had been working largely as a sculptor. Abandoning this for painting, she discarded much of her past training. Agutte was strongly inspired by colorists and symbolists, namely Corot and Delacroix. Current theories on colors in painting was something close to her. She had married the art critic Paul Flat in 1888, and in 1893, the year she joined Moreau, Flat began publishing Delacroix's journal for the first time. Flat annotated the entries and wrote the introduction of a work that would be highly important to generations of artists. It would propel Paul Signac to write his deeply influential 1899 treatise *D'Eugène Delacroix au néo-impressionnisme* (*From Eugène Delacroix to Neo-Impressionism*), which drew heavily on long journal passages of Delacroix's color theories.

Matisse may have lacked a traditional early artistic education or the precocious talent of many of his fellow students—Camoin had entered the École des Beaux-Arts in Marseille at sixteen and went to Moreau's studio in Paris after winning a prize for his drawings; Marquet moved to Paris in 1890 at fifteen to study at the École des Arts Décoratifs and joined Moreau at the Beaux-Arts in 1897—but Matisse had an unusually rich visual imagination from his upbringing among textiles.

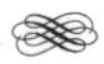

It wasn't in a Paris atelier where Matisse found his identity as a painter, but six hundred miles (one thousand kilometers) southeast, on the Mediterranean. At the beginning of 1898, he and Amélie honeymooned in London—in part at Camille Pissarro's urging to see the luminous paintings of J. M. W. Turner in the National Gallery—and then traveled to Corsica, the French island just north of Sardinia.

"I am in a wonderful place where I will probably stay for a very long time. (I don't dare say 2 years)," he wrote to Marquet on the last day of February 1898, two weeks after arriving. "Amazing place. Almond trees in bloom among silver olive trees and the sea, blue, blue, so blue that you could eat it. The dark green orange trees with fruits that are like mounted jewels, the tall eucalyptus trees with variegated foliage like rooster feathers and dark blue. And behind almost always high mountains with snowy peaks." It was a revelation. "I was quite dazed by it all; everything shines, everything is color and light," he later said.

Matisse may not have stayed two years on Corsica, but he did remain until the end of July (by then Amélie was pregnant). In those six months he made fifty-five paintings. He was in a spell.

Not everyone was impressed by the resulting canvases, though. His Belgian friend Henri Evenepoel—who had been with him in Moreau's studio and whose works would posthumously be associated with the fauves (Evenepoel would die in 1899 of typhoid at twenty-seven)—thought the Corsica paintings were done "as if by an epileptic and crazed impressionist!"

No matter. Matisse was twenty-eight, beginning as an artist, trying to find a way ahead with his art, and the impact of his time in the Mediterranean was profound, even incalculable. He found a paradise of blue skies and saturated colors that had been unknown to him in northern France or in Paris. "They did not alter his disciplined mentality, but they swelled his imagination," Janet Flanner wrote in *The New Yorker* in 1951 when a major retrospective of the artist opened at the Museum of Modern Art. "The sun and its scintillating colors gave him his painting climate, which thereafter he carried with him on his palette."

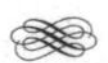

Matisse's breakthrough came at the 1905 Salon d'Automne, where he exhibited outlandishly colored paintings along with similar radical fauvist works by Derain, Camoin, Vlaminck, Marquet, Manguin, and Jean Puy. Already thirty-five, Matisse was the oldest of the fauves. Camoin and Derain were a decade younger, and Braque nearly thirteen years his junior.

The reaction to their works was vicious, with one critic likening them to "a pot of colors flung in the public's face." The French president Emile Loubet refused to open the exhibition at the Grand Palais because of Room VII, where the colorful paintings hung. With an Italianate bust of a child in the center of the gallery, critic Louis Vauxcelles famously quipped, "*Donatello parmi les fauves.*" ("Donatello among the wild beasts.") Soon the offending room was known as the "*cage aux fauves*" ("cage of wild beasts"), giving name to the nascent movement.

The first of the twentieth century's newfound art movements, fauvism broke not just with traditional methods of representation, but also with impressionism and postimpressionism, taking another leap in the liberation of color. Responding to nature with bold, vibrant, and nonnaturalistic colors, often straight from the paint tube, unmixed, and applied in gestural brush strokes, fauvists offered an electrified response to nature on the canvas. The colors and expression of a painting matched not the subject itself but the artist's experience of the subject—not the scene of fishing boats in the small harbor but a visceral reaction to seeing it. The sea could be red, trees could be blue, and the face of a woman could be rendered in about every shade but skin tone.

Particular ire in the 1905 Salon was directed at *Woman with a Hat*, Matisse's jarring portrait of his wife whose face is splotchy with greens, blues, yellows, and reds. "There were a number of attractive pictures but there was one that was not attractive. It infuriated the public, they tried to scratch off the paint," Gertrude Stein wrote of the canvas. "People were roaring with laughter at the picture and scratching at it."

At such moments, Amélie was at her finest and fiercest. "As for me, I'm in my element when the house burns down," she said of handling the response to the portrait. She posed for her husband's other radical early portraits, including *The Green Stripe*, which had a strip of pea green bisecting her face.

This was complicated, revolutionary art that even someone as savvy as Gertrude Stein—the very epitome of avant-garde—acknowledged was not easy to grasp. "It is very difficult now that everybody is accustomed to everything to give some idea of the kind of uneasiness one felt when one first looked at all these pictures on the walls," she wrote in *The Autobiography of Alice B. Toklas* of the works by Matisse, Cézanne, and Picasso that hung in her Paris home. "Now I was confused and I looked and I looked and I was confused."

Stein was keenly aware of their impact and understood that something completely new was happening in painting. She fully understood the power of these works. Fauvism would last just a handful of years (by 1908 most of the associated artists had moved onto other styles of painting), but its expressive and unbridled use of color heralded a shift toward abstraction, and its influence would be strongly felt for decades in successive waves of avant-garde art.

Scandal alone didn't buy food or tubes of paint. Matisse needed to sell canvases. While he served out a learning process with both rigor and conviction, it was a struggle for even marginal financial security. By 1912 he had yet to achieve it. The two dozen years he had been painting were marked with little certainty and plenty of anxiety. "In spite of everything, the amount of happiness one experiences when one succeeds does not equal the unhappiness one feels when one fails," he said toward the end of his life. It was a period when unhappiness frequently beset him and seemed to often outweigh everything else.

But when the idea of going to Tangier came about, his caution dissipated with his need to work well. Work—even the potential of it—took all priority. Matisse couldn't stop himself.

The spontaneous decision to winter in Morocco was financially risky. Less than a decade before, Matisse had been unable to sell a painting, and the memory of years of deep financial stress clung to him, a feeling, a fear—like hunger—that never fully dissipated.

In 1908, with the financial and logistical support of friends, including the Steins and Hans Purrmann, a German painter who oversaw the day-to-day running of the studio, Matisse had opened an academy that would eventually welcome over a hundred students, including many Scandinavians and a number of Americans. While it offered some steady income, Matisse found that he was spending too much energy in his time with the students. He was an artist and not a teacher, he saw, and had to prioritize his own art. Académie Matisse was short-lived and closed in the summer of 1911. Since then, the family's sole income came only from his art, a terrifying thought for Matisse.

Unfortunately, he was not going to Morocco on a *bourse de voyage*, a travel bursary from one of the official artistic institutions that was common at the time for French painters in North Africa. And while Tangier was, according to guidebooks, "decidedly cheap" compared to Algiers, Cairo, or other popular wintering spots in North Africa, Matisse was paying his own way, although he could little afford it. Just weeks before leaving for Morocco, he had signed a contract to purchase the villa in Issy-les-Moulineaux that they had been leasing for the past few years. Using their savings, he put nearly a third down; the remainder was due in five years.

Commissions from Shchukin and Morozov were allowing him to make the Tangier trip. He needed a "souvenir" of Morocco for Shchukin, of which Matisse felt freedom to do any subject. For Morozov, he had to paint a pair of landscapes that had been ordered a few years before and still not yet done. In September, Matisse had promised Morozov he would complete them that winter.

Yet traveling to North Africa to fulfill these commissions was fanciful justification. Previous trips abroad had yielded little in terms of tangible work. He returned from two months in Spain the previous winter with just a pair of still lifes, "work of a nervous man," Matisse later called them. (The sympathetic and supportive Shchukin bought them both anyhow.) During a trip to Algeria in 1906 Matisse made just a single canvas, a small, hastily painted street scene, and in a month during the summer of 1907 in Italy—visiting Venice, Ravenna, Padua, Siena, and Florence, where he stayed with Leo Stein in his hillside villa above the city—he painted nothing at all. Why would it be different this time in Tangier?

Yet much about the city drew Matisse to come for the winter. Perhaps a stay here would be the catalyst he needed. It certainly had been, he knew, for his great predecessor Eugène Delacroix.

5

Nearly eighty years to the day before Matisse's arrival in North Africa, Delacroix traveled to Tangier and spent six months in Morocco with a diplomatic delegation led by Count Charles-Edgar de Mornay. At the behest of the French king, it was to meet the sultan of Morocco. Having invaded neighboring Algeria in 1830, France was seeking cooperation from Morocco in asserting and maintaining control. Delacroix went along to record the mission in his sketchbook.

The prodigiously talented artist was thirty-three and restless for adventure, with two Orientalist masterpieces behind him, *The Massacre at Chios* and *The Death of Sardanapalus*. As the second choice for the mission, Delacroix had to cover all of his own expenses except for the journey out to Morocco. The investment paid handsome dividends. The trip became the lynchpin to his development as one of France's greatest artists.

Departing from the port of Toulon near Marseille, the tedious thirteen-day journey was so rough that the ship was blown past Tangier, through the Strait, and out into the Atlantic. It managed to track back and land on January 25, 1832.

As soon as he stepped ashore, Delacroix was overwhelmed by what he encountered. "I've just arrived in Tangier. I have rushed through the town. I am quite bewildered by all that I've seen. I can't let the mail boat go—it's leaving shortly for Gibraltar—without telling you something of my amazement at all the things I've seen. . . . One would need to have twenty arms and forty-eight hours a day to give any tolerable impression of it all," he hurriedly wrote to a childhood friend. "At the moment I'm like a man in a dream, seeing things he's afraid will vanish from him."

Life in and around Tangier enthralled, inspired, and energized Delacroix. He carried a green-covered notebook with him everywhere, and sketched continually—leaning against doorjambs, in the spacious gardens of the Swedish consul, squatting on roof terraces in the medina, even resting his pad on the saddle of his mule. With an anthropological eye, he did hundreds of watercolors annotated with detailed notes, and filled seven sketchbooks with drawings, many highlighted with fluid touches of watercolors. Charging horses, lounging muleteers, and people milling in the market, shopkeepers in their cubbyholes, pupils leaving the Quranic classes at the madrasa, and even the sultan himself crowd the pages of his *cahiers*. "This place is made for painters," the young artist wrote from Tangier.

Unlike his esteemed contemporaries Messrs David, Ingres, and Corot, Delacroix did not pass a formative period in Italy. In fact, he never went to Italy at all, something virtually unheard of at the time for any serious painter. After Morocco, Delacroix didn't need to go. "Rome is no longer to be found in Rome," he wrote in one of his last letters from Tangier. Antiquity was alive around him. "I have Romans and Greeks on my doorstep: it makes me laugh heartily at David's Greeks, apart, of course, from his sublime skill as a painter." His friends back home would never believe it from his inadequate sketches, he told them. "There's nothing finer in classical art. Yesterday a peasant came by, got up like this [a sketch]. And this was what a wretched Moor looked like, begging for a handful of coppers a couple of days ago. All of them in white, like Roman senators or Greeks at the Panathenaean festival."

For Sir John Drummond Hay, who served as Britain's Envoy Extraordinary at the Court of Morocco from 1845 to 1886, and whose father was the consul in Tangier during Delacroix's visit, the city felt almost biblical. "Here at once, in a three hours' sail from Gibraltar, you are transported, as if by enchantment, a thousand or two thousand years back, and you find yourself among the same people and the same style of living as you read of in the Scriptures," he wrote in his memoirs. "The Bible and the 'Arabian Nights' are your best handbooks, and would best prepare you for the scene."

From the start, Delacroix constantly worried that he would never capture everything, and what he could get down in his notebooks wouldn't be of much use later. "I'm even sure that the considerable sum of curious information that I shall bring back from here will be of little use to me," Delacroix wrote after being in Tangier for about six weeks. "Away from the land where I discovered them, such particulars will be like trees torn from their native soil; my mind will have forgotten its impressions, and I shall disdain to give a cold and imperfect rendering of the living and striking sublimity that lies all about one here, and staggers one with its reality."

Delacroix was in Morocco longer than expected, as the delegation's meeting with the sultan had to be delayed because of Ramadan, the holy month of fasting and abstinence. In Meknès, where the French made a ten-day journey on horseback for their regal audience, Delacroix wrote, "The picturesque is here in abundance. At every step one sees ready-made pictures, which would bring fame and fortune to twenty generations of painters."

Such abundance of material threatened to overwhelm the young artist. "But I am learning by experience that one's sensations are dulled in course of time," he wrote after two months in Morocco, "and the picturesque stares you in the face so much all around that one ends by becoming insensitive to it."

In June, six months after their arrival in Tangier, the delegation set sail for home, calling in at Oran and Algiers en route to France. Along with his precious notebooks, Delacroix was carrying a large variety of souvenirs. The hundred or so objects included musical instruments, earthenware pieces, and weapons (saber, cartridge belt, powder bags) that would both jog his memory and appear in his paintings. There were numerous pieces of clothing, too. The local dress captivated Delacroix. "I plan to bring back enough sketches to give some idea of these gentlemen's appearance," he wrote to his friend Henri Duponchel, director of the Paris Opera. "Moreover, I shall bring back actual specimens of most of their articles of dress. I'll gladly ruin myself for this purpose, and for the sake of the pleasure you will get from seeing them."

The clothing had talismanic powers for the Frenchman, noted the Algerian novelist Assia Djebar. "From this place through which he had passed, Delacroix brings back some objects: some slippers, a shawl, a shirt, a pair of trousers. Not just trivial tourist trophies but tangible proof of a unique, ephemeral experience. Traces of a dream," Djebar wrote in *Women of Algiers in Their Apartment*, her lyrical collection of stories named after Delacroix's famous painting. "He feels the need to touch his dream, to prolong its life beyond the memory, to complete what is enclosed as sketches and drawings in his notebooks. It's the equivalent of a fetishist compulsion augmented by the certainty that this moment lived is irrevocable in its uniqueness and will never be repeated."

It wasn't. Delacroix never returned to North Africa. But the single visit was enough for a lifetime. For decades he recycled his sketches, souvenirs, and experiences into large canvases. Around eighty of his paintings have Moroccan themes. He even drew upon his sketchbooks for canvases set elsewhere. It was testimony to the massive impact that the visit had on the young artist, who was forever changed.

Matisse was familiar with Delacroix's Moroccan canvases and his North African sketchbooks. He acknowledged the importance of Delacroix to his own work, and a link was frequently drawn between the two Frenchmen.

But, perhaps wanting to appear more independent late in his life, Matisse dismissed following in his predecessor's footsteps to Morocco. "About Tangiers: it's interesting you were there, just where Delacroix went," the Swiss art critic Pierre Courthion said to him during a rare extended set of interviews in 1941, done in Lyon following a series of risky surgeries for intestinal cancer and three months recovering in hospital solitude. At seventy-one, Matisse was for the first time looking back over his life as an artist and taking some public measure of it. "Delacroix was the last thing on my mind," Matisse retorted. Taken aback, Courthion said, "The last thing when deciding on your travels, by all means, but I know you have always been fond of him." Matisse didn't say anything more, and, according to the transcripts, the conversation moved on.

Perhaps Matisse's statement surprised Courthion because just moments before the artist had told him that what he had found in Tangier was "as in Delacroix's paintings. In short, Delacroix's pictures are an accurate representation of the Moroccan landscape from Tangiers to Tetuan." Matisse stressed the point, adding that he had seen one precise view from the kasbah that Delacroix had put it in a certain painting.

While Matisse may not have gone *because* of Delacroix, his illustrious predecessor's works *were* clearly on his mind.

Matisse knew that he would find the "ready-made" subjects that had so enthralled Delacroix, and, with their seemingly tangible link to the past, enchanted Western visitors. (After visiting Morocco in 1917, Edith Wharton wrote, "To touch the past with one's hands is realized only in dreams; and in Morocco the dream-feeling envelopes one at every step.")

But Matisse didn't go for such exotic or historical scenes, which is perhaps why he pushed back so forcefully against the implication of Courthion's comment. There was something else that overwhelmed Delacroix while in Tangier that particularly interested Matisse: the light.

At the Salon of 1845 in Paris, Delacroix caused a sensation when he displayed *The Sultan of Morocco and His Entourage*, a magisterial painting of Moulay Abd al-Rahman on his stallion among a crowd. In whites, pale ochers, and some reds of their dress, the large group of men stand before the stout city walls. A luminous blue sky offsets the vivid green parasol raised above the proud and poised monarch. "In spite of the splendor of its hues," noted the young art critic Charles Baudelaire, "this picture is so harmonious that it is grey—as grey as nature, as grey as the summer atmosphere when the sun spreads over each object a sort of twilight film of trembling dust."

Tangier's sumptuous light thrilled Delacroix. In a letter from Tangier, he praised "the rare and precious influence of the sun, which gives intense life to everything."

Another nineteenth-century visitor equally struck was the writer Pierre Loti. Matisse had read Loti's popular travelogue *Au Maroc* (*In Morocco*). In the spring of 1889, Loti traveled on horseback from Tangier to Meknès and Fez as part of an official French mission to visit, at the behest of the ambassador-designate Jules Patenôtre, the court of the sultan. Like Delacroix, Loti tagged along to chronicle the journey, though capturing with words rather than images "a vast, silent, wild country, all flooded with light"—dazzling, diaphanous light. "Although one distinguishes with extreme sharpness the slightest details of every object, the least crack in every wall," Loti noted, "they are separated from us by vaporous mist that lends a vagueness to their bases, and renders them almost vaporous. They look as though they were suspended in the air."

That filter, which draws out intense colors while reducing their contrasts, lent balance and rhythm to Delacroix's broad and vibrant palette, and acted as something of a springboard for the lyricism of the canvases that followed.

"C'est l'un des premiers ambassadeurs de la lumière du Maroc," said Abdelaziz El Idrissi, the director of the Mohammed VI Museum of Modern and Contemporary Art in Rabat and co-curator of the museum's 2021 exhibition

on Delacroix's stay in Morocco: Delacroix was one of the first ambassadors of Morocco's light. Other artists came in his footsteps.

The most determined among them was Matisse. And also, initially, the most disappointed. Matisse found no hints of this celebrated light upon his arrival in Tangier, just rain and bleak skies.

6

For two weeks, the rain did not relent. Matisse watched anxiously through the corner room's windows waiting for the elements to change.

He certainly did not expect such inclement elements and awful light. Pushing open the tall window shutters of his room, he looked out at the leaden sky after another night in Hôtel Villa de France. Gusts whipped up off the bay. Rain showers soaked those dashing along the muddy streets below, and rivets of water ran down through the hotel's terraced gardens.

Putting his health, family, and finances at risk, Matisse had made a heavy gamble on coming here. He saw the trip was a complete failure, and certainly regretted the impulsiveness at choosing this destination. He was in a panic. If he could, he would return to France. But gale winds and churning seas made leaving problematic.

He remained largely stuck in his hotel.

There were half a dozen hotels in Tangier recommended in the 1911 edition of Baedeker's *The Mediterranean: Seaports and Sea Routes*. The Hôtel Continental, opened in 1872 on a spur above the port and favored by Americans, and the Hôtel Cecil, along the corniche, were the most expensive. Also suggested by the guide were Hôtel Villa Valentina along the rue de Fez leading out of town, Hôtel Bristol on the old city's Petit Socco among consulates, post offices, and café terraces, and the Matisses' hotel, the well-established Hôtel Villa de France, a favorite among international diplomats, minor British aristocracy, and clergy visiting St. Andrew's Church. The Villa de France was, another guidebook at the time noted, "preferred by most visitors making a long stay at Tangier, partly owing to its superior position."

Built in 1880 as the residency for the head of French diplomacy before being transformed into a hotel, the stout, three-story Hôtel Villa de France was set among terraces of well-tended gardens and protected by high walls and wrought-iron gates. Goats and donkeys grazed along the outside of the walls on weeds and stiff, aromatic grasses. There were mosaics around the spacious grounds, wide verandahs for sitting, and ornate ceilings in the dining room where the Matisses took their meals. The flat rooftop offered unbroken views.

"The Villa de France had once a high reputation, and held undisputed sway in the estimation of tourists as the one Tangier hotel, its name having been familiar to every traveller in Morocco for half a century almost," noted the seventh edition of the English guide *Mediterranean Winter Resorts*, published in 1914, somewhat exaggerating the length of the hotel's history and fame. "Of late years it has gone through vicissitudes, but still holds its own as the favourite sojourn of invalids, artists, and literary people."

Among the artists it drew were a handful from Matisse's artistic circle in Paris. Camoin had lodged at the Hôtel Villa de France in 1905. In 1910, the Dutch-French artist Kees van Dongen, another of the fauves, stayed, and then exhibited some of his Tangier paintings at the Galerie Bernheim-Jeune in June 1911. Van Dongen convinced Marquet to go, and Marquet stayed there the summer before the Matisses arrived. Gertrude Stein and Alice B. Toklas had come to the hotel on a recent summer visit and recommended it to the Matisses as well.

But mostly the hotel attracted a very different type of traveler and catered to a more conservative clientele. The week the Matisses arrived, the hotel hosted the large annual meeting of the British and Foreign Bible Society.

Ads ran for weeks beforehand in the English-language Tangier newspaper stressing that all were welcome to attend.

The Hôtel Villa de France's staid tone and quiet decorum made it a fitting choice for Matisse, who was no artsy bohemian, and generally avoided such types. He favored well-cut suits, carefully chosen silk shirts, and fine ties. In Montmartre, his small, gold-rimmed spectacles had helped earn him the nickname "The Professor," though he looked closer to a provincial doctor, pharmacist, or banker.

His close friends knew his humor, comic impersonations, and self-deprecating wit, but with strangers Matisse was deeply reserved, even stiff, and frequently described as shy. His neatly trimmed sandy-red beard and receding hair, his conservative suits and ties, and the grave, measured manner with which he spoke added to the respectable impression he presented. For some of the hotel's non-French-speaking guests, a lack of English combined with his natural reticence accentuated Matisse's seemingly aloof manner.

Until the 1930s, Hôtel Villa de France remained one of the city's best hotels and was even considered by some to be among the finest along the southern Mediterranean.

Madame Matisse did not share such an opinion. (Nor did the *Mediterranean Winter Resorts* guide, which felt that it had been slipping by the time the Matisses checked in.) She found the hotel small, dirty, and expensive, but, she wrote to Marguerite, their room had "a superb view." While Baedeker's guidebook did not reward the hotel with a star, it did highlight the panoramic vistas from the rooms.

The Matisses' corner *chambre* had two tall windows with slatted shutters. One looked north out over the dense medina and towering fortified kasbah and across the Strait to Spain. The other window, on the front side of the building, faced the sweeping curve of the Bay of Tangier and distant Cape

Malabata lighthouse. The city's Ville Nouvelle was under construction, and its growing grid of semi-orderly streets and still-empty lots radiating from the old city were situated largely out of sight from the Matisses' windows.

The view from *chambre* 35 was of an ancient city that appeared little changed.

❧

One of the few new buildings Matisse could see out his window was St. Andrew's Anglican Church. Less than a decade old, it was not yet enveloped with tall trees. The wall of the compound stood just across the street from the hotel's bottom gate.

Under the Diocese of Gibraltar, the Reverend John Hackett offered Sunday services in English from December through Easter at 8:00 A.M., 11:00 A.M., and 3:00 P.M., when chimes from the bell tower sent flocks of nervous, guttural pigeons darting from their perches and worshipers hurrying through the compound's cast iron gate, across the small graveyard with young cypress trees and growing number of tombstones, and into the church through the keyhole entrance on the side of the building. A row of high, open arch windows illuminated a triple-aisle nave with enough room for nine rows of wooden pews. Constance Wheeler had taken over as church organist the previous year and was accompanied that winter by her elder sister, Sybil, whose fine soprano voice carried up to the hotel. Apart from the wood floor planks and the wooden ceiling, the church was entirely white. Just before Matisse's arrival, the interior woodwork had been freshly oiled, and the building itself given a new coat of whitewash.

Sultan Moulay Hassan I had gifted the parcel of land to Queen Victoria in 1883 for Tangier's British community to erect an Anglican church and sent skilled artisans from Fez to decorate the building. While the first sermon was delivered in 1894, all of the final details were not in place until 1903. With a tall, crenelated church tower adorned with geometric interlacing and arches around blind keyhole windows at the top like a minaret, and the glazed, Fez-made tiles in the traditional green of Islam covering the roof, it looked from Matisse's window like a mosque.

And indeed St. Andrew's was in many ways more akin to a mosque than a church. Wedged between two Muslim cemeteries, it had an altar aligned to Mecca, a recessed, arch-shaped niche on the wall behind the altar that appeared like a mihrab (indicating Mecca's direction), and an abundance of Islamic decorative motifs. Along the nave ran soaring, deeply incised horseshoe arches some twenty feet high and thirteen feet wide (6 x 4 meters) and festooned with floral decoration and Arabic inscriptions. Fez artisans did the stucco work, intricate polychrome cedar ceiling above the chancel and the altar, and Quranic wall texts in interlacing Arabic calligraphy. These included PRAISE BE TO GOD FOR THE GRACE OF ISLAM repeated five times and ALL KNOWLEDGE BELONGS TO GOD—HE WHO HAS THE POWER AND THE GLORY, as well as extracts from the Quran in the scallop-edged arched frames around the reredos. Carved in sculpted plaster in the recessed niche behind the altar were numerous repetitions of the Nasrid motto, the final Muslim dynasty on the Iberian Peninsula who ruled Granada from 1232 until 1492: *Wa la ghalib ila Ala* (There is no conqueror but God).

St. Andrew's was (and remains) one of the most remarkable Christian churches in the world, and indeed unlike any Matisse had ever seen.

As the foul weather continued unabated, Tangier's sky remained steely and cold, and white gulls wheeled above the hotel on gusty bay breezes, Matisse set up his easel in front of the north-facing window of his room and worked during clearer moments to catch the view out over St. Andrew's to the kasbah. He made a pen-and-ink drawing, looking carefully at the view as he took it apart in his mind and reassembled it on a sheet of paper with swift, confident lines. It offered some release from the claustrophobia of the room and helped take his mind off his anxiety.

On his easel he placed a primed canvas just over 45 x 31 inches (115 x 80 cm). Holding in his left hand a square-cut palette with dollops of carefully separated paint, a couple of spare brushes pinched in his fingers, Matisse began *Landscape Viewed from a Window* (see figure 3).

Doing a window view was not new for Matisse. Such scenes were one of his leitmotivs. From the first in 1897, nearly one hundred works over his career have windows in them. "Windows have always interested me because they are a passageway between the exterior and the interior," he told an interviewer in 1951. The artist (and viewer) is on the inside looking out—inside but connected to the outside world. In 1905, in the picturesque fishing village of Collioure near France's Mediterranean border with Spain, he painted the first of his "open window" paintings, the small but explosive fauvist masterpiece *Open Window, Collioure* (usually just called *The Open Window*), with its dazzling, impasto salad of splashy, thickly smeared colors.

In his Tangier hotel room, Matisse dabbed his wooden palette with fewer (and less outlandish) colors than for that infamous predecessor. Dominating the center of the picture is the green-roofed St. Andrew's Church surrounded by deep blues (cooled with some black) and forest greens. The walls of the kasbah rise up in the distance. Across the lower right foreground runs a zigzag of gold, a sunlit path with an indistinct figure on a donkey following a second animal. (This isn't an anachronistic touch. The first automobile—a French-made Delaunay-Belleville—wouldn't arrive in the city until later that year. The second was an American Dodge.) Matisse crudely captured the figure with a couple of choppy strokes of a brush loaded with white paint, and the animal in little more than four dark legs plus a neck and head. Two vases of flowers sit on the windowsill: a mauve pitcher with a handle on the left and, almost centered on the vertical canvas, a squat orange pot with red flowers. The leaves themselves are thickly outlined in dark brown and given some ribbing of the same color over bare canvas. The pots add a touch of warmth to the scene and draw the viewer back into the room. It is both a view and a scene of the artist looking at the view.

Matisse didn't finish *Landscape Viewed from a Window*, perhaps because of the weather. After two soaking weeks, the rains finally broke. While the surf remained high, the breezes from the west were light and the sky cloudy.

"Today's the first day it's relatively beautiful and pleasant. The barometer has moved up a quarter of the dial," he wrote to Marquet on February 11. Rising atmospheric pressure on the barometer usually means improving weather. He had taken a lovely two hour walk that day, he told his friend, "the only outing that has been possible since our arrival." He remained exasperated. "What a life we've led. If the sea had been calm, we would have left," he wrote. "I am very depressed by this setback. Morocco is beautiful, perhaps because I only know the grand socco [below the hotel]. But not this season."

Soon, though, he'd finally get a chance to see more, to experience what he had come to find, and any desire to immediately leave would dissipate. The following day, the *Al-Moghreb Al-Aksa* newspaper reported that the weather was, finally, "settling."

For the next ten days, the weather remained somewhat unstable—darting clouds, sporadic showers, misty wind—with daytime temperatures between 52° and 60°F (11° and 15°C). But it was good enough to venture for walks along the beach, across the Marshan plateau that ran from the northwest edge of town, and through the pine-covered hills. In the ancient city itself, Matisse explored the jumble of lanes in the medina with bread ovens, tunneled passageways, and dead-end alleys lined with painted flowerpots.

It was in the fortified kasbah, in the upper part of the old city above the medina, where he found an abundance of new motifs to sketch.

7

With commanding views over Tangier's city, port, and long curl of bay, and out across the Strait of Gibraltar to Spain, the kasbah had been a citadel and seat of power since the reign of the Berber Almohad empire in the twelfth century. The stout walls were built, rebuilt, and restored over various stages of the city's history, with the oldest predating the Almohads. They once enclosed a vast amphitheater and stout governmental buildings, but over time a dense neighborhood spread within the kasbah's walls, and then spilled down below into an expanding medina.

The most direct way for Matisse to reach the kasbah from his hotel was via its upper gate, Bab Kasbah. Carrying painting materials, portable easel, and collapsible stool, he crossed the edge of the Grand Socco and went through the Bab al-Fahs gate into the old city. But rather than turn into the twisting lanes of the medina, he could follow rue d'Italie that ran downhill along the outside of the old city. On the right-hand side of the road were recently built apartment blocks in grand Spanish style with ornate balconies, wrought-iron balustrades, and decorative brickwork that were home to mostly Spanish residents; on the left, where the road flattened briefly and the Cine Alcazar was soon to open, were new apartments housing mostly Italians from Genoa. From here, the street was known as rue du Télégraphe Anglais and passed the English telegraph building and climbed steeply up parallel to the walls toward the decorated keyhole arch of Bab Kasbah at the high end.

Once inside the old citadel with canon batteries topping the crenelated walls, he turned right and followed lanes so narrow that he could touch both walls by extending his arms. Within a few minutes he reached a marabout, a traditional domed tomb of a saint, that was, like mosques, off-limits to non-Muslims. It was built in 1845 for Sidi Ahmed Bugudja, a rich and generous landowner who died penniless after dedicating his later life to teaching the Quran.

Matisse made numerous drawings in wiry lines done with swift, fluid economy as he began to get a feel of the shapes and crenelations of the building. On a small prepared canvas board (8½ x 10¹³⁄₁₆ in; 21.5 x 27.5 cm), he made a painting of the marabout, rendering the white walls of the tomb in cool, purplish-blue and green, with a few touches of pinks and yellow. Catching some late afternoon sun, only a piece of the dome in *The Marabout* is white; the rest remains in blueish shadow. The colors are vivid and delicate, surprising but also somewhat literal.

Two decades before, Pierre Loti noted the shift in colors that takes place in the afternoon: "Tangier, which appears at a distance, looking at this hour like a scattering of cubes of stone on the slope of a mountain; its whitenesses, in the gathering dusk, turns into an icy blue." Rather than the cherished "golden hour," it was a blue one, "like snow at twilight," as Truman Capote later described it. "We have blue shadows that seep from the sky, from the sea," the contemporary Tangier painter Abdelaziz Bufrakech recently put it, and they stain the whitewashed buildings with their hues.

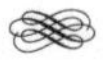

Carrying on, Matisse would pass the seventeenth-century Kasbah Mosque, with its elegant octagonal minaret decorated by ocher corner brickwork and inlaid tiles, and emerge onto a broad square that held the palace, tribunal, treasury, and prison. A short distance ahead was the Bab al-Assa gate that cut through the kasbah's southern wall. Just through the arch, a pair of flat platforms flanked the steps down, extending like a short hem above the medina. It was a popular viewpoint and offered a perfect place to set up an easel.

From the broad left flank, Matisse painted the city as it fell steeply downward in a jumble of flat white roofs toward the choppy bay. Seen at the Musée de Grenoble where it hangs, the first impression of the small *View of the Bay of Tangier* (see figure 4) is how Matisse caught the intensity and transparency of the light radiating off the landscape, for him more important elements than any actual topographical configuration.

On an unprepared canvas, he made a quick pen-and-ink sketch of the vista and then painted in the geometric grid of houses with dabs of blues and whites. The architecture of the city, then, is largely intimated with the lines but not actually rendered, and most of the medina's density is of unpainted, textured canvas between the dashes of paint. A number of veiled figures in white and black move along the narrow street that cleaves into the dense old city; they are not clustered together but move individually. He included the brick and green-mosaic-tiled minaret of the mosque on Aissawa Square and flanking palm tree, and, in the foreground, the marabout of Sidi Ibn Raisul, whose smooth white dome gets a blush of mauve. In the churning greenish-blue bay, a dozen boats depicted by simple black dashes ride on anchor. A thick and threatening band of charcoal clouds hovers above jade-green and bluish-gray hills refreshed by the recent rains. The stormy weather might have largely passed but it wasn't completely gone.

In the Musée de Grenoble's files, an annotated *constat d'etat* (condition report) records fingerprints toward the bottom of the picture. Looking at the painting in the gallery with that knowledge, what is largely inconspicuous suddenly becomes glaringly obvious: four fingerprints, three together and one a little to the right. It seems as if perhaps another squall was approaching, and Matisse hastily grabbed his painting materials, easel, and wet canvas, and dashed for the hotel.

Matisse was unaccustomed to working *en plein air* in such busy spots. He seemingly felt awkward sketching or painting in public in Morocco and also likely found the curiosity of the locals disruptive. While appearing serious, even grave in character, he was not above mocking his position as an outsider and out-of-place Westerner. He made a quick pen-and-ink sketch of himself sitting jauntily on a rickety camp stool with a small paint box balanced on his knees and brush in hand. Wearing a frock coat and straw hat, his glasses askew, he is painting the marabout in the kasbah on a portable easel as two fully veiled women pass, one who has stopped and stands just behind him to look at what he is painting.

This wasn't the only time he depicted himself in such light. On a colored postcard of the covered passageway at the entrance to the sultan's palace in the kasbah that he sent to Marquet, he added a quick sketch of himself sitting against the wall with a paint set on his lap as he captures a small group of men in traditional robes lingering in the shaded passageway. This was Matisse as the artist-as-tourist, both immersed in the city and remarkably distant from it as he captures it.

On the slope just below his hotel was the hectic Socco el-Barra, literally "Outer Market." This was one of the appeals of staying at the Hôtel Villa de France. "Its position is healthy and open, on an elevated site just outside the Soko," said a guidebook at the time, "and it possesses at its gates a wealth of Oriental colour in the artistic sense, owing to its proximity to the native market (Soko)."

This Socco was the easiest place in the city for visiting artists to find the "ready-made paintings" of Delacroix. Along with the market, the uneven, slightly sloped patch of land was also where traditional *moussems*—tribal gatherings from the nearby regions to celebrate Islamic festivals—took place. The highlight of these were the fantasia, short but stirring synchronized galloping of horses that ended, abruptly, with simultaneous firing of the riders' muskets. It was also where departing caravans assembled. In 1832, Delacroix mustered here when the French mission set off with its vast entourage of grooms, soldiers, and numerous horses and mules for the royal city of Meknès and an audience with the sultan.

While merchants came every day to sell goods, Thursdays and Sundays were market days and the field transformed into a vast, boisterous souq. "There is nothing so noisy as an Arab market, and the uproar at this one was enough to make one's head split!" wrote the French author Alexander Dumas after a visit to Tangier's market in 1846 at the height of his fame. At dusk, storytellers, musicians, snake charmers, and acrobats took over the slope.

The Grand Socco had changed little between Dumas's visit and Matisse's. Ladies from the Rif Mountains in wide-brimmed straw hats sold garden produce, fresh herbs, eggs, and chickens raised in the *bled* (countryside). Other merchants stood behind barrels of oranges and tangerines, stacks of firm winter melons, and mounds of grayish sea salt that felt damp in the hand. Among produce and livestock were tents with veterinarians and blacksmiths, barbers and street dentists, and plenty of hot food for the hungry from dozens of small cooking sheds.

"*Bâlak, bâlak!*" was continually heard from mule drivers steering heavily laden charges through the haggling crowds of men in hooded, chestnut-brown burnouses and veiled women dressed in white, their faces largely covered. Gray donkeys carried baskets of charcoal held into place with twigs and primitive string nets and camels loaded with carpets, straw mats, and baskets moved along the edges. "Occasionally," wrote Dumas, "a camel would stretch out his long, snaky neck and utter a high-pitched scream, quite unlike the sound made by any other animal."

Most painters visiting Tangier spent their plein air sessions working in the Grand Socco. "The Grand Sok or Great Market is a mass of good material for the pencil and brush, and pictures abound on every hand," wrote the painter Robert E. Groves in the popular British monthly art magazine *International Studio* a few years before. "The native barber in his quaint tent, the fruit and vegetable-sellers with heaps of delicious and brilliantly-coloured produce, the bread-sellers, sweetmeat vendors, snake-charmers and story-tellers; the numerous kinds of livestock—fowls, turkeys, donkeys, horses, mules and camels—and the wonderful variety of costume are of the highest value as subjects for the artist."

Hilda Rix, who arrived a week after Matisse and was also lodging at the Hôtel Villa de France, heeded such standard advice. Her outdoor scenes were done almost exclusively in the Grand Socco, where, echoing Delacroix, she extolled its "wonderful picturesqueness, every way one turns the head there is a new picture."

Twenty-seven and unmarried, Rix was talented, elegant, and cosmopolitan, part of an artistic, upper-class traveling set. While few women ventured so independently to Morocco at the time, Rix enjoyed the freedom that her class, economic level, and unmarried status conferred. After her father had died five years before, Rix traveled to Europe with her mother and sister, Elsie, dividing her time between London, Paris, and, for the past few summers, Étaples, an artist colony on the French coast near Calais.

Traveling to Tangier with a small painting party from Étaples, Rix left France about the same time as the Matisses, but took a different route, heading down through Madrid, Córdoba, and Algeciras, where the group planned to make the crossing to Morocco. But the poor weather forced them to travel further south to Gibraltar for a shorter—but still very rough—crossing to Tangier. She stayed at the Villa de France for two months, departing a week after Matisse. Rix returned to Tangier and the Villa de France in early 1914, this time accompanied by Elsie.

A tall woman wearing a broad-brimmed sun hat held in place with colorful scarves, Rix was highly conspicuous in the Grand Socco. Photographs of her sketching there show curious onlookers and staring kids standing very close. Such crowds made oil work virtually impossible in the Socco, and she generally sketched with pencil and crayon and then completed her pictures back at the hotel.

While in her letters she frequently refers to what she was experiencing as dreamlike, fantasy, and out of the Arabian Nights, on her sketchpads and canvases she offered more realistic depictions of Tangier as she sought to faithfully capture daily life of the market and its people, as exotic and unfamiliar as it all was to her. The clothing and dress particularly caught her interest. In an illustrated letter to her mother and sister, she wrote, "See how most of them are covering their faces—They have mostly cream draperies & perhaps orange waistcoats and little tight mauve green trousers—(tight at ankle)." Such attention to detail is present in her drawings and paintings as well.

As her biographer, Jeanne Hoorn, makes clear, Rix didn't consider herself an Orientalist. She spoke out against it and rejected many of the staples of the genre: there is no violence in her pictures, no battle scenes or charging horses, no odalisques or anything remotely erotic. She wasn't capturing Morocco in terms of fantasy but attempting to accurately illustrate what she was personally witnessing in the Socco.

Yet at the time, this style of depiction was fashionable for Orientalist works, and her Tangier efforts garnered Rix her first solo show. In November 1912, Galerie J. Chaine & Simonson in Paris showed forty-five of her works, most of them from Morocco. The critic in the French edition of the *New York Herald* praised the scenes that had been captured on the spot. "This artist has the ability to make life-like images in remarkable compositions bringing outstanding realism and accurate impressions that capture the 'types' to be found among the Moroccan people." After the exhibition, the French government purchased for the Musée du Luxembourg the pastel drawing *Grand Marche, Tangier*, which depicts two Berber women in red-and-white striped cotton dresses and large hats in the souq. The long-running director of the museum was Léonce Bénédite, founder of Société des Peintres Orientalistes Français (Society for French Orientalist Painters). At the society's exhibition of 1913 at the Grand Palais, Rix showed twenty-nine works done in Tangier.

Like most artists in North Africa, Rix was looking for subjects to capture and present for the consumption of others in the West. This fit neatly into the experience of "the colonial process of extracting resources," wrote North Africa expert Barnaby Rogerson. "Instead of phosphates and olive oil they sought colors, subjects and images with which they could enrich their studios back home." Pictures of harems and cavalrymen, they found, sold well, as did water sellers and camels in the souq. This was the Orient of "types" that buyers back in the West wanted, and that critics tended to praise.

Matisse had no desire to capture (or extract) any of this. Despite over sixty published sketches that Matisse did around Tangier, not a single one appears to have been done in the Grand Socco. It was one of the places, despite its proximity to his hotel and wide range of subjects, where he completely avoided working. He shunned the classic Orientalist themes—the harem, ceremonial "fantasias" of galloping horses, and sultans in magnificent dress—or even the popular ones of the orange sellers in the souq or village women with straw hats offering bouquets of irises.

Matisse remained most interested in Tangier's light and how it affected color. And finally, after some weeks in the city, he was at last experiencing it. On the first of March, a suddenly enthused Matisse wrote to Manguin, *"Le beau temps est venu. Quelle lumière fondue."* "The good weather has come. What melted light."

8

As the days cleared and the barometer steadied, Matisse explored the peninsula around Tangier on foot, mule, and horseback. Outside the city, on the verdant peninsula, heather stood as tall as a horse, dense thickets of gum rockrose with papery white petals clustered along the slopes, and, in the underbrush, rabbits and wild boar were plentiful. Amélie frequently joined him on these excursions.

Tangier's rich vegetation struck Matisse, and, although not generally a landscape painter, he needed to complete Morozov's outstanding commission for two of them. In September, he had written to the Russian apologizing for the delay and promising to finish them that winter. Working in a public spot in Tangier would be impossible for him, he realized, and sought a secluded, private place to paint.

With the intermediary help of longtime Tangier resident Walter Harris—the legendary reporter for *The Times*, British agent, and friend of the sultan who had settled in Morocco in 1887 when he was twenty-one—Matisse received permission to work in the private gardens of Villa Brooks, a vast property owned by an Englishman named John Brooks. Scion of Tangier's most prominent British family, he was the son of John Hay Brooks, who had been largely responsible for the construction of St. Andrew's Church, served as its treasurer and chaplain's warden for two decades, and had an active role in the designing and decorating of the church; the grandson of Sir John Hay Drummond Hay, the long-serving British consul in Tangier who acquired the villa and adjoining land in the mid-nineteenth century; and great-grandson of Edward Drummond Hay, who had served for fifteen years as the British representative in the city, including during Delacroix's stay. After buying the property, Sir Hay Drummond Hay had it planted out in English style, with curving pathways, plane, eucalyptus, and myrtle trees; orchards of oranges and lemons; and large flower beds. In his letters, Matisse, with an almost nonexistent level of English, called it "Villa Bronx" or used the French phonetic spelling "Broux." In Moroccan Arabic it was known as Senya al-Hashti (Spring of Hashti).

Less than fifteen minutes on foot from the Hôtel Villa de France, the Brooks's estate began at the edge of the largely Spanish neighborhood of San Francisco—named after the Franciscans and home to the Spanish Catholic mission, hospital, and consulate—and comprised a swath of low hills. "It was immense, field after field as far as the eye could see," Matisse later recalled. He wasn't exaggerating. It spanned nearly thirty-eight acres (sixteen hectares).

Today, elderly neighbors wistfully remember "Park Brooks," the last section of the estate that was finally buried by buildings in the early 2000s. The flowers and trees have disappeared under a jumble of apartment buildings, leaving only the faintest reminders in a car repair shop called "Brooks," the "Lavage Broox luxury car wash," and "Pharmacie Brook's." A pair of stout trees that once marked the entrance to the villa now stand in the middle of a traffic intersection. The villa itself, a blend of neo-Moorish and neoclassical styles, opened as an upscale restaurant in 2022 with the lavish interior seemingly untouched.

Buttoned up tight in his suit jacket, Matisse walked with Amélie to Villa Brooks, knocked at the gate, and waited for one of the Moroccan workers to let them in. From one of the outbuildings that he rented to store his gear, he took out his canvas, paints, and easel. Avoiding the more familiar plants and flowers, he headed for the masses of palms, aloes, and acanthus to set up his easel in the dappled shade. "I worked in a spot planted with big trees, their canopies opening high above me. The ground was covered in acanthus. I'd never seen acanthus before," he vividly remembered three decades later. It made an enormous impression. He knew them only from the drawings of Corinthian capitals as a student at the École des Beaux-Arts. The deeply jagged, spiny leaves—acanthus means "thorn"—were enormously popular in the Greco-Roman world, and appeared on columns, pediments, and cornices, decorated temples and buildings, and scrolled around fountains, planters, and pottery. "I found them magnificent. Green acanthus were much more interesting than the ones in the École! I was thrilled by the sight of these big, tall trees, and down below, the acanthus, so rich and sumptuous that they were scarcely less interesting than the trees."

A dark photograph shows him painting on a portable easel in white shirtsleeves, with a snug vest and flat-peaked English cap. (The handful of family photos taken in Villa Brooks that have been published tend to be somewhat underexposed, perhaps because Matisse forgot the instruction manual to the new camera, purchased in the Au Bon Marché department store in Paris for the trip. He asked his daughter to find it at home and mail it to him.)

To not impinge on the painter, the owner banished himself from the section where Matisse was working. Matisse described him as "*morose*." Ten years before, Brooks's parents had died in a scandalous murder-suicide in their Scottish manor outside Edinburgh—his father shot his mother sleeping in bed twice with a rifle and then shot himself in the right temple. Along with only imagining how Brooks himself felt, it divided the British community in Tangier. A plaque in St. Andrew's Church in their memory reads, with added italics, THIS TABLET IS ERECTED BY *SOME MEMBERS* OF THE CONGREGATION IN GRATITUDE FOR THEIR UNITED AND UNTIRING LABOURS, OWING TO WHICH IN A LARGE MEASURE WAS DUE THE FOUNDING AND MAINTENANCE OF THIS CHURCH.

Thirty-four and still unmarried, Brooks was considered something of a misanthrope and rich recluse. His garden was generally closed to visitors. Matisse was an exception.

⁂

In Villa Brooks, Matisse was, at last, experiencing Tangier's particular light. "After having seen the rain fall for fifteen days and as many nights, we relish the good weather and the vegetation which is completely luxuriant," he wrote to his close friend and fellow fauve, Charles Camoin. "I have started working, and I am not too displeased, although it is very difficult; the light is so soft, it is something completely different from the Mediterranean."

Under Matisse's brushes, the garden slowly came alive, though certainly not with ease. He struggled to adjust to this hybrid of African and Atlantic light and was overwhelmed by what he was finding in Tangier. "How new [the light] is, too," he told Manguin, "and how difficult it is to do with blue, red, yellow, and green."

Over a layer of pink, Matisse painted the garden a translucent blue; over deep blue, he painted the sky translucent pink. There is no figure to provide a sense of scale, but one isn't needed to capture the grandeur. Offset to one side, a mighty tree tinted plummy magenta draws in both tones, and fuses the work together, while giving the scene an overriding sense of verticality and towering height.

During Tangier's winters, the sky often clears in the late afternoon, the clouds lift, and the low sun saturates the colors. In radiant pinks and lavenders, as the foliage shifted from emerald to blues, Matisse captured that elusive moment when everything pauses—pauses and waits a beat in suspense for something to happen.

Once called *Park in Tangier*, it is now generally known as *Moroccan Landscape* (*Acanthus*) or just Acanthus from the leafy plants that flourish along the ground (see figure 5). It is not a lonesome landscape he depicts, nor a sentimental one that might easily adorn a room. Done on the same size canvas as the window view, it is a *paysage décoratif*, or decorative landscape.

In an interesting coincidence that Matisse was likely unaware that eighty years before Delacroix had frequently sketched in the same garden. It belonged at the time to the Swedish consul and was known as the "Swedish garden." In 1848, Sir John Hay Drummond Hay bought it from the Swedish consul, who happened to be his father-in-law.

"The garden of the Swedish consulate was the closest to the city walls. That is where we spent a great part of our days," Delacroix wrote. While in Tangier, he saw Edward Drummond Hay and the Swedish consul, Julius Lagerheim, nearly every day. Referencing an unpublished memoir by Lagerheim, the translator and editor of Delacroix's notebooks from his trip to Tangier described the garden at the time in this manner: "Criss-crossed by paths shaded by vines that led to a high point with a view of the sea and the market, and enclosed by a wall and a hedge of canna reeds, it contained hundreds of trees such as oranges, pomegranates, figs, chirimoja, dragon blood trees, palms, acacia, and so forth, as well as northern European species—apples, pears, cherries—including a fir."

Among the people that Delacroix sketched here was the gardener, Ali, who belonged to the Issawa (or Aïssaouas) religious sect. According to the Swedish consul, Ali "was wild when he had eaten kif during their festivals, but otherwise was a calm and quiet man. He regretted that he belonged to this sect but could do nothing about it." This sect were the "convulsionists" of which Delacroix made three paintings, including one of his most famous works, *The Fanatics of Tangier.*

In his letters and journal, Delacroix made numerous references to the Swedish garden. "I go for rides in the surrounding country, which I find infinitely delightful, and I enjoy moments of delicious idleness in a garden by the city gates, under a profusion of orange trees in full bloom and covered with fruit," he wrote about a month after arriving in Tangier. "Amid these lush natural surroundings I experience feelings like those I had in childhood. Perhaps some vague memory of the southern sunshine which I saw in my earliest youth is astir within me." But being in the garden also brought up certain self-doubts. "Anything I may accomplish will be insignificant in comparison with what might be done here," he continued. "Sometimes I feel quite baffled, and I'm sure I shall bring back only a faint shadow memory of it all."

Working in the same spot, Matisse was beset by anxiety and insomnia. "The great interest that Morocco gave me as well as the works that I made there cannot make me forget the anguish that I experienced in expressing my feelings in painting. I was obliged to split myself; to leave a crazy man, doubting himself, in order to gain a few moments of calm that would allow me to work," he later said, referring to working on *Acanthus*. "My sensations in front of nature gripped me and I could only free myself from them by a strenuous effort. At that time, I couldn't sleep."

He confided to Agutte how he was struggling with his painting, his state of mind, and his sleeping in Tangier. "I tend to express my sensations much later. I always have to work so hard to organise them. I don't produce much, but nevertheless I live only for that, I think only of that, always and so much, that it prevents me from sleeping," he wrote to his dear friend and fellow painter in an unguarded, heartfelt letter. "There is within me a work of deduction that I am not conscious of, but which however makes me exhausted. So during the day if I do not settle down with a paintbrush, I regret it, and by night I don't always sleep, often without knowing why. I am always surprised when a great perceptiveness comes to me suddenly, after a night when I only slept for a few hours. How much I admire you," he told her, "you receive an impression and you can express it straight away."

The letter runs seventeen pages. Full of details of his ongoing work in Tangier, it included eleven thumbnail sketches, many annotated with specifics on colors. Agutte was an artist who showed at the same progressive Salons as Matisse, exhibited at the same galleries, and was judged by the same critics, and he treated her with equal respect.

That year, André Salmon praised her in his book *La Jeune peinture française*: "And [how] could we take no interest in the fine efforts of Mrs. Georgette Agutte? That artist is moving toward a severe style, without consenting to the dangerous emotional restraint that keeps us from fully enjoying [the Nabis painter Félix] Vallotton, whom she resembles, however. The sense of color, at once brilliant and limited, is not the least appealing sign of Mrs. Agutte's orderly but always picturesque talent." A decade later, the critic Francis Carco would compare her nudes to those of Matisse. Working from live models, they had a strong sense of volume. "While Mr. Henri Matisse asserts himself as a graceful, tenderly sensual creator of beautiful bodies which he penetrates with a soft light, Georgette Agutte, virile, interprets, under blunt lighting, coarse, muscular forms," Carco wrote in his 1923 book *Le Nu dans la peinture* (*The Nude in Painting*). "She always took pleasure in modeling, in preference to soft carnal curves, the signs of strength."

Matisse and Agutte had been close for nearly two decades, sharing their art and their passion for flowers and music. The house in Bonnières-sur-Seine of her and her husband, Marcel Sembat, was not far from Issy-les-Moulineaux, and the Matisses saw the couple frequently. Importantly, Matisse and Agutte both understood the difficulties in being artists and offered each other needed support over the years.

Still, in his letter, Matisse was aware of being absorbed in his own struggles. "Can I send you this letter, with all this rambling chat?" he wrote. "I let myself go on, writing about everything I'm tormented. Please accept it as a token of friendship, and don't judge me too selfish for talking only about myself."

For six weeks, Matisse worked and reworked *Acanthus* and the canvas shows the battle scars. Art historian Rémi Labrusse likened it to "*un chantier*" (a construction site), a painting that had "no magic, no prestige, but a complete frankness, cards on the table, where the work is defined" as the viewer looks at it. The presence of Matisse the painter is strong as his fight and struggle on the canvas, giving the work its exceptional power. *Acanthus* offers clues in "understanding a painting through painting," according to Labrusse, and achieves "a specifically modern definition of the Western image: that of an image under construction, which must be simultaneously experienced and kept at a distance in order to understand it."

Matisse had finally jumped the ditch. Or at least *a* ditch. And though he didn't consider the painting fully done, Matisse felt he could move on.

After languishing over *Acanthus*, Matisse quickly completed two other stunning landscapes in Villa Brooks. While almost exactly the same size, they were distinct in construction and coloring. Both required significantly less effort to complete.

Periwinkles (Moroccan Garden) is lighter, more pastelly, more sinuous (see figure 6). Curving arabesques that ring and play off each other fill the pulsating canvas—the sloping green land, some leafy emerald foliage, puffy gray clouds shaded with black, and, governing the painting, a forking, ruddy cinnamon colored tree with a smaller, darker one wrapped in vines beneath it. A path that cuts across the bottom corner and in a gash in the center is the color of wet hay, and done, Matisse told Agutte in a list of color annotations beside a thumbnail sketch of the painting in his lengthy letter, with ocher and yellow. Spiraling up from the turquoise-toned shrubbery are periwinkles with fifteen star-shaped mauve blossoms. In the top half of the canvas, an eerie sky glows in a soft orangish-red tone made by blending vermilion with white.

The pencil marks of the original sketch remain visible on the canvas, lines that Matisse largely ignored as he applied paint with far more spontaneity than in *Acanthus*. It's more free-flowing and more confident.

Even more luminous is *The Palm* (or *Palm Leaf, Tangier*). Its original title when it was sold by Bernheim-Jeune in 1912 was *Matin du mars prés de Tanger*, or *March Morning Near Tangier* (see figure 7). From a point of view looking slightly downward, perhaps off a small knoll, a terra-cotta path runs like a prominent scar up the center of the gardenscape toward a black-trunked bay tree heavy with leaves and coiled in ivy. Brush marks swirl through the dense, deep-turquoise ground cover, while glimpses of pale-blue sky show at the very top. Dominating the image is a fan-shaped palm frond with nearly two dozen brilliant leaflets exploding outward. "Leaves as big as swords," as he described them to Agutte. Foot-long and largely over a white background on the canvas, Matisse painted these with quick, often single strokes. For emphasis, he scratched lines in the leaflets with the wooden tip of a brush through a section of gray, gouging deep marks down to the textured canvas.

There are few bright hues in the picture. Yet perhaps nowhere in Matisse's entire oeuvre do colors glow in such splendor. With a sense of freedom, of openness and jaunty optimism, it's far from the cramped feeling of the still lifes done in his hotel room or even in the tense *Acanthus*.

In mid-March, two days after his lengthy letter to Agutte, Matisse sent a postcard to Gertrude Stein. "Painting is always very hard for me—always this struggle—is it natural? Yes, but why have so much of it?" he wrote on the back of the card. "It's so sweet when it comes of its own accord."

As for the struggle, he was likely referring to *Acanthus*. He had labored over it, erasing areas and adding colors and motifs as he constructed the image, and felt, despite working on it for a month and a half, that it continued to lack something, that it remained unfinished. But *The Palm* came much easier. It had come on its own accord. He did it "in a burst of spontaneous creation," he later said, "comme une flamme"—like a flame.

It was exactly what he needed.

Hanging near *The Palm* at the National Gallery in Washington, DC, is Matisse's iconic 1905 fauve masterpiece *Open Window, Collioure*, with bright paint so thick, so urgent, that it could have been applied with the tip of an index finger (see figure 8). This and *Woman with a Hat*, the startling portrait of his wife, were the two most significant paintings displayed at the infamous Salon d'Automne that launched fauvism onto the art world.

Decades later, Matisse called the movement "the exaltation of color": "Fauvism at first was a brief time when we thought it was necessary to exalt all colors together, sacrificing none of them." As Michel Puy wrote in the first extended essay on the movement, "Their harmonies no longer sing, they roar; they don't caress you, they jump at your throat. The fauves are aggressive and can leave no one indifferent. One has simply to accept them or to turn away from them in horror." The shrieking reds and pinks and whites of those works from Collioure, the small Mediterranean town near the Spanish border where he made his first fauve works, feel like a violent assault.

For Matisse, the more strident colors of fauvism had evolved into these subtler, seductive tones on the trio of Villa Brooks canvases. In Tangier, he was reapproaching nature with a different palette, one that was softer and offered more joy. It was less exalted than whispered, exhaled in the spirit of delight rather than an urgent shriek. He was offering a more convincing version of Arcadia. Nature wasn't quite so shocking. It had become, under his brushes in Morocco, sensuous.

9

What interests me most is neither still life nor landscape," Matisse wrote in 1908 in "Notes of a Painter," one of his few formal artistic statements, "but the human figure." He was keen to paint a model in Tangier.

As well—and certainly not inconsequentially—Shchukin, his main patron, had recently developed a clear preference for figurative works. Matisse had just received a not-so-subtle reminder of that when Shchukin rejected *The Red Studio*, his landmark canvas and the subject of its own blockbuster show at the Museum of Modern Art in 2022. Just a few days after arriving in Tangier, Matisse had written to the Russian about the painting and included a colored illustration to help convince him to accept it. "Yesterday I received your letter from Tangier of February 1 and also the watercolor for the big red painting," Shchukin responded. "It must be very interesting but I now prefer your paintings with figures, mainly the portrait of your family," he wrote, referring to the recent *Painter's Family*.

In conservative Morocco, though, getting a model to sit was extremely difficult. The very act of making an image of a living human (or animal) figure was considered prohibited in traditional Islam. Intricate geometric patterns, interlaced arabesques, and abstracted ornaments from the natural world became the principal motifs in North African art rather than the figure. Even if Matisse was most interested in figurative representation, he found in Islamic art new ways of looking at space and perspective, as seen so clearly in *Painter's Family*, which looks like a Persian miniature.

Finding sitters was an issue that portrait painters visiting North Africa all faced. "Everyone says it's absolutely impossible to get models here," Elsie Rix wrote from Tangier in 1914, when she accompanied her sister, Hilda, on her second winter painting sojourn. "You get them to promise and they won't come or they come only for the first sitting then are bored and won't turn up again for any money. Or maybe their friends and relatives hear and tell [them] they'll go to perdition and they become ashamed and won't turn up."

Matisse's own shyness and reticence with strangers added to the challenge. In a letter to Tangier not long after his arrival, Agutte urged him to draw portraits of locals. "But it is really difficult to ask them to pose for me—they always fear that their religious friends might know about it, and the few miscreants ready to pose are not interesting," Matisse wrote back. "A few days ago, I saw the nicest male face one could dream of, that of a young man of the mountains, a face with an extraordinary expression, somebody out of a Perugin painting—more profound—I tried to ask them to pose for me and my request was badly rejected." He was most likely referring to a man from the nearby Rif Mountains.

In another letter, Elsie Rix noted how often Hilda's figures were out of necessity composite. "Mother you can't think how tremendously difficult it is for her to get the Arabs. They dodge away & hide or get into their burnous & so quite alter themselves. Sometimes she has to use about 10 people for one man."

For Rix, working in the Socco among the crowds was part of the thrill and excitement, both in feeling immersed in the daily rhythms of the vibrant city, and in the element of "game" she found in trying to capture people. During her second stay, Rix was asked to write a letter from abroad for *International Studio* magazine about painting in Tangier, and she detailed some of the lengths artists went to sketch locals. "Of course many subterfuges have to be employed to keep the victim unsuspecting, but unhappily some one in my audience invariably recognises my prey and calls to Mohammed or Absolam that he is being captured on paper. Sometimes the said Absolam only looks sheepish, wriggling, alas! out of position, or sometimes completely disappearing," she wrote. "If one feels that there is a resentful spirit growing one gracefully melts away."

Foreign artists seeking subjects found this to be a nearly insurmountable barrier. During his 1832 stay, Delacroix wandered around Tangier without too much trouble. That changed as soon as he took out his sketchbook. Locals, considering him a harbinger of bad omens or possibly a spy, accosted and even attacked the young man. "I am gradually insinuating myself into the customs of the country, so as to be able to draw many of these Moorish figures quite freely," he wrote to friends two weeks after arriving. "They have very strong prejudices against the noble art of painting, but a few coins slipped here and there settle their scruples."

This comment carries a whiff of braggadocio, and certainly makes it appear easier than it actually was for him, considering the tricks he employed to surreptitiously draw people, namely women.

Delacroix's sketchbooks are filled with images of Moroccans from all classes—muleteers, young cavalry soldiers, gardeners, grooms, the sultan. Nearly all are men. Women couldn't be bought off with a few copper falus (or even silver dirham), or, as they went covered in public, be quickly drawn from the shadows of a doorway where he would hide.

The Frenchman sketched with unusual speed, capturing key details in swift, confident strokes. Matisse liked to repeat to the students at his academy, "Delacroix said one should be able to draw a man falling from the sixth floor while he was still in the air."

Deviously, and deeply against local mores, Delacroix followed paths up through the terraces of the medina where he could spy down on the flat roofs shielded only by short, serrated walls, at risk of being stoned or shot at, he said. "The Moors are fantastically jealous, and it is on these terraces that their women usually take the air or visit one another," he wrote to his friends back home. This was the private domain of women where they moved around wearing only haiks—wraps loosely pulled over the head but with their faces remaining uncovered. Here he could stealthily watch them hanging out their laundry, lounging on carpets, saying prayers, or just carrying on with daily life. That simple act of reaching up to hang a piece of clothing became, in such chaste circumstances, sexually charged, as it revealed not only the woman's face but also the shape of her figure.

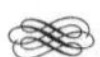

If Matisse found getting a male model during his stay difficult, a female one was virtually impossible. Along with cultural taboos on posing, there were added sexual connotations for women. Muslim women did not pose. And prostitutes were only available to an extent. Superstition meant that they often refused as well. "The greatest hindrance to my painting in Morocco was the natives' belief in the Evil Eye," wrote the Royal Academy society painter Sir John Lavery, who spent sixteen consecutive winters in Tangier beginning in 1904. ("Mr. John Lavery, the eminent artist, arrived on Saturday to take up his residence here during the season," *Al-Moghreb Al-Aksa* prominently reported about a week after the Matisses had disembarked.) "All of my Moorish sitters believed I possessed it and, no matter what their morals might be, jibbed against being painted. They were certain it meant being damned." Even Walter Harris, the ultimate connected foreign resident who had lived in Tangier for a quarter century, was only able to get a few aging women from a brothel for artists who asked for his help.

Despite the prohibition and the difficulty involved, generations of Western painters visiting North Africa continued to insist on finding uncovered women to pose. "Veiled beauties are interesting (sometimes much more interesting for being veiled); but it does not serve our artistic purpose much to see two splendid black eyes and a few white robes," wrote the nineteenth-century English author and illustrator Henry Blackburn in his book on having a winter painting studio in North Africa. "However models we must have," he added.

Delacroix largely sidestepped the issue by painting those exempted from the restrictions of wearing a veil, namely Jewish women. In this, his circumstances in Tangier helped considerably. As Delacroix was not a paid member of the French mission, he didn't board with the French consul but instead rented a room at his own expense in the home of a Jewish *dragoman* (interpreter and guide). Through this contact the painter managed to attend a Jewish wedding, where he furiously recorded the elaborate steps in the ceremony, the behavior of the bride, the clothes, and every other detail he could fit onto the pages of his notebook. Almost a decade later, he translated that experience into his magnificent canvas *A Jewish Wedding in Morocco.*

During a three-day stopover in Algiers on the way back to France, Delacroix finally managed the exception when he was granted access to the private women's quarters of a house, the harem, likely from the port's chief engineer who arranged for one of his employees to take Delacroix to his home. Count Mornay, who led the expedition, reported that Delacroix was so excited when he was admitted to the harem that he had to be calmed with sorbets.

The intensity of the experience came through on page after page in his sketchbooks which became the basis for arguably his greatest painting, *Women of Algiers in Their Apartment* (1834), which Baudelaire, one of Delacroix's astutest contemporary critics, called "that most engaging and showy of his pictures. That little poem of an interior, all silence and repose." In the years ahead, many of the most avant-garde painters were deeply impressed by it. "When I speak to you about the joy of colors for the sake of colors, well, this is what I mean," Cézanne said of the large canvas that hangs in the Louvre. "These pale pinks, these rough cushions, this slipper, all this limpidity, I don't know, it goes into the eye like a glass of wine goes down the throat, and you are immediately intoxicated." Picasso, in rapturous homage, did fifteen paintings and more than seventy drawings of it over a two-month period in the winter of 1954–55. And Renoir, who late in life supposedly couldn't control tears running down his cheeks when he spoke of its light, told the dealer Ambroise Vollard, "*Les Femmes d'Alger, il n'y a pas de plus beau tableau au monde*": there is no more beautiful painting in the world.

Perhaps showing her desperation in getting a female model during her two Tangier sojourns, Hilda Rix accepted a unique opportunity, even if it was against the model's will. Rix did two Orientalist drawings in pastel of an escaped enslaved woman being held until her trial at the French consul—*An African Slave Woman* and, sitting against the wall on the floor, looking downcast and away from Rix, *A Negro Woman, Morocco*. "Well Hilda and I are now as I told you before in the tribunal," Elsie wrote to their mother as her sister worked beside her. "They have hung a cream burnous behind her head for a background. She has [is] a good type not really beautiful and [has] nothing in the way of clothes—save that the black handkerchief bound around her head has a red border & is interesting against her bronze face:—her dress is a washed out pink cotton jelaba with an old darned man's cream burnous on top." She wasn't, Elsie admitted, a perfect model. "They asked her if she would pose & she said yes—but she just curls up with fear every moment & doesn't know to stay still."

During two stays in Algeria in the early 1880s, Renoir handled the challenge of finding a female sitter by dressing up the children of French acquaintances in local costumes and darkening their hair as needed instead. Similarly, Rix dressed her sister in local clothes and painted her as a Moroccan woman.

Matisse, certainly, could have organized something similar and used one of the numerous Italian or Spanish women who lived in Tangier, or one of the city's many Jewish women, who were not required to wear haiks and mixed with men. During his stay, he visited a leading member of the large Jewish community and could have asked her for help. Or he could have even painted his wife in costume, as he had done numerous times, including for *La Japonaise: Woman Beside the Water* (1905), *Red Madras Headdress* (1907), and *The Algerian Woman* (1909), where Amélie's heavily rouged cheeks clearly acknowledge that she is dressing up.

But Matisse didn't want someone pretending. He didn't want a woman playing a role with its inherent artifice. He wanted a Muslim North African sitter.

Within a handful of years of Matisse's visit, this would be easier to accomplish. Following World War I, Tangier officially became an international city (or "zone"). While there was a representative of the sultan in Tangier called the *mendoub*, it was administered by a consortium of foreign powers until Moroccan independence in 1956. During this period Tangier acquired an unsavory reputation that would last into the twenty-first century. "It was one of the charms of the International Zone that you could get anything you wanted if you paid for it," wrote novelist Paul Bowles, a Tangier resident for over fifty years. "Do anything, too, for that matter;—there were no incorruptibles. It was only a question of price."

But when Matisse was looking for a Moroccan woman to sit for him that spring of 1912, it wasn't yet the case. Tangier was not yet a city where everything was possible, even for money.

10

The winter that Matisse traveled to Tangier, Morocco was undergoing one of the most volatile, charged moments in its history, and political events indelibly altering its future were reaching a feverish climax. For the last decade, the French had been increasing their presence in the country while fending off the colonial aspirations of other European powers in Morocco. France was keen—and poised—to take control.

In 1905, Kaiser Wilhelm of Germany came ashore in Tangier to give support to the sovereignty of Morocco's sultan. In a rousing speech on the grounds of the German legation (which later became the Mendoubia, the house of the sultan's representative who dealt with foreign powers), he backed Moroccan independence. To the French, it was a deeply provocative act against their intentions and growing influence in the country, and sparked a major international crisis. France began its final colonizing push in Morocco with the bombardment of Casablanca in 1907 and then committed significant troops to the garrison to protect French citizens. In the years since, Morocco's hope in retaining independence had dwindled and then was completely lost when Germany renounced any claims in North Africa in return for territories in Central Africa in the autumn of 1911, giving France a free hand with Morocco; German, England, or Spain would not interfere. The sultan and his viziers were resigned to falling under French rule.

On March 16, 1912, as Matisse was enjoying decent weather and steady light, a diplomatic mission led by Eugène Regnault, head of the French

Legation in Morocco, set out from Tangier for the royal court at Fez to present the sultan with France's mandate.

The caravan assembled on the grounds of the Grand Socco below the Hôtel Villa de France. Watching it gather, Matisse took note of the incredible amount of luggage. Regnault was not traveling with a small entourage—there were hundreds of soldiers, grooms, muleteers, cooks, and assorted hands, plus scores of pack animals—nor was he traveling light. The luggage contained 1,000 bottles of wine, 300 bottles of champagne, 34 bottles of cognac, and 576 bottles of Vichy water, 310 tins of potted meat, 21 terrines of foie gras, pasta, 440 pounds of potatoes, 100 pounds of dried vegetables, cheese, 100 pots of jam, 49 pounds of bonbons, plenty of coffee and tea, 54 packets of toothpicks, and, for the celebration, fireworks.

Mixing with French diplomatic circles, Hilda Rix met Regnault and his wife at a party and wrote enthusiastically to her sister about the preparations going on in the Socco. "The colour of their quaint saddles and trappings filling my artist's heart with joy. Just picture a tall white horse with flowing heavy white mane and tail, with high huge double pointed saddle, bridle girth, etc of wonderful flame colour."

Matisse and Amélie had the opportunity to ride with the caravan to Fez. The experience would have been uncannily similar to that of Delacroix and his official journey to the imperial court eighty years before. After considering it, Matisse decided against joining the ride. "As for us, we will not take advantage of this superb opportunity as I will be working and I have enough material with what I have seen here," he told Agutte in a letter two days before the caravan set off. "It is not much, but as you know, I am not greedy. I do not need much to fill my head, and I think that seeing more now would be pointless and would only get me tired."

When the caravan finally departed, Rix joined the cavalcade and rode out of the city on horseback with the troops as far as the outskirts. The column filed out of Tangier, passing alongside Matisse's hotel and visible from his corner room, raising a sustained racket of noise and dust. He was no doubt relieved to see it gone.

After a nine days' march along the piste—the interior had no paved roads nor motor vehicles yet; Morocco's infrastructure was significantly less developed than in neighboring Algeria—Regnault and the lengthy caravan entered the Imperial City of Fez. While residents of the mellah, the large Jewish quarter, turned out to cheer as the entourage strode through the streets, the reception in the rest of Fez was notably less enthusiastic. The sultan received Regnault, who, "with almost indecent haste," presented the ruler with the treaty and demanded his signature. In Paris's political halls, whose echoes reached Fez, there had been talk of "indirect rule." But the document Regnault carried surprised the sultan and his viziers. While offering the ruler religious authority and secular sovereignty, the agreement gave the French full control of executive powers. France would run Morocco's administration, judicial affairs, finances, and its army, and act as the sole intermediary between Morocco and every other foreign power.

On March 30, the sultan finally agreed to the Treaty of Fez. After two decades of mounting pressure, Morocco—the last independent country in North Africa—had become a French protectorate while Matisse was painting in Tangier. *L'Afrique française du Nord*—French North Africa—now stretched halfway across the crown of the continent.

Being a protectorate was different than being a full colony. It meant control by France without being a direct possession, having more autonomy with its own affairs, and receiving less European settlement. But such distinctions meant little at that moment. Morocco was now back under European rule after over two centuries as an independent and locally governed sultanate.

Tangier turned tense. The threat of impending violence against the new rule (and rulers) was perceptible.

Yet there is scant mention of these issues in Matisse's frequent letters to his family and friends back in France. A skeptic might see his attitude of caring about the weather but not the politics as that of a typical colonial and Orientalist painter.

But such reticence was typical of Matisse. "He lived through some of the most traumatic political events in recorded history, the worst wars, the greatest slaughters, the most demented rivalries of ideology, without, it seems, turning a hair," wrote Robert Hughes. "Matisse never made a didactic painting or signed a manifesto, and there is scarcely one reference to a political event—let alone an expression of political *opinion*—to be found anywhere in his writings." Or in his art. Creating places of comfort and refuge on the canvas, Matisse configured a world to make people feel good. Even late in his life, when ill, bedridden, and believing death was near, he continued to make only art that reflected a calming, private domain of pleasure and happiness.

After seeing his Moroccan paintings, Marcel Sembat—a socialist member of the French Chamber of Deputies and future government minister who understood the political implications of what was going on in Morocco, and a close friend of Matisse who knew of the personal and artistic struggles he suffered—would write: "Matisse keeps his sorrows to himself! He does not wish to broadcast them. He wants to offer others only peace of mind."

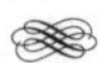

But it was another event on the very day of the treaty's signing and Morocco's capitulation to France that carried a much higher risk of destabilizing Matisse's work routine: his wife was packing her steamer trunk to return to France, leaving him alone in Tangier.

11

On March 31, the day after Morocco's sultan had agreed to the Treaty of Fez, Amélie sailed back to France on the SS *Ophir*, one of Royal Rotterdam Lloyd's weekly mailboats. Her stay had stretched for two months, much longer than anticipated. Her two young sons were still with family, and teenage Marguerite remained alone in Issy-les-Moulineaux. Amélie was as driven as her husband in prioritizing his work, but she could remain in Tangier no longer.

Parting onboard after he had seen her to her cabin, the two had a row—both were strong-willed and stubborn, quick to weep and quick to quarrel—and she departed on an angry note, something Matisse would brood over until he saw her again.

Matisse returned to the Hôtel Villa de France and to an empty room that smelled of turpentine, drying paint brushes, and cut flowers. The weather had been good, but, fittingly, that day was cloudy and rainy.

Matisse looked again at *Acanthus*, which he felt wasn't quite done, and immediately wrote to Amélie that he had "reconciled" with the canvas that had caused so much grief. "After examining it, I found what is harming it." It was two sun spots on the pine tree that broke the momentum of the lines, he said, adding in a quick sketch. "I'm going to glue paper over these two spots and paint them the same tone as the rest of the tree. These two blemishes removed, the picture has a lot of grandeur. This finding made me very happy," he wrote. "Why didn't I realize this earlier? I wouldn't have been so desperate before you left."

When away from his wife, he wrote to her daily, adding updates on his work with frequent thumbnail sketches to illustrate what he was explaining in the letter. These were also a way for him to work out problems. Even while apart, he made her a participant to his artistic struggles.

In this letter, he seems almost desperate to justify himself, and for her to comprehend his behavior. "You should realize that my fits of despair have always been followed by something better. I need to understand myself in order to be able to live. I accept that I can do interesting things almost unconsciously," he wrote. But he struggled in giving himself completely over to it. "I panic too quickly."

Beset by anxiety with her now gone, he couldn't sleep that night. The hands on his pocket watch crept toward dawn. His Dickens novel brought little relief. Amélie was not there to comfort him, to distract him, to lull him to sleep by reading softly aloud. Her departure left him, he later said, "*désorienté comme un enfant que laisse sa mère*"—disoriented like a child left behind by his mother.

The following day, he went to see a Russian doctor that the hotel manager Mademoiselle Davin recommended, and was prescribed much of the same regime he had been following: rest, hot baths, exercise, early nights.

"How bitterly I regret parting from you like that," he wrote to his wife of their quayside spat. "I'm following your voyage, you've only got another eighteen hours to go—but having to make such a long journey upset as you were when you left me—truly I curse myself."

Likely still angry at her husband, Amélie did not cable him as promised upon landing in Marseille. The distraught Matisse called the steamship company and eventually reached its director at home to get news of the ship's safe arrival.

Amélie's departure threatened to upset the delicate equilibrium that had allowed Matisse to work so well since the weather had cleared. Alone, he wondered if it had been worthwhile to stay on without her, and went to get information on the next departures for Marseille.

The same day that he saw the Russian physician and inquired about sailing for home, though, Matisse finally had a breakthrough in getting a model. He wrote with news that an "Arab girl" had been found to sit for him. Young, poor, and likely from the countryside, she was an outcast.

He could not, of course, bring her to his room at the Hôtel Villa de France. A different, secluded space had to be found. That problem was solved by the hotel's proprietor. "After lunch, Mlle Davin told me that I would work in the studio where Tranchant was and that then the young Arab girl could come without being seen," he wrote to Amélie, steaming back to France. Davin provided other painters with similar arrangements—Tranchat was the French painter Maurice Tranchat de Lunel—including Hilda Rix, at least during her second stay at the hotel, when she gave her use of a space for a studio. "It's small but it has a good light," Rix's sister, Elsie, reported to their mother.

Painting the Moroccan turned out to be as complicated as procuring her services. "Yesterday afternoon I would have liked to work with the young girl," he told his wife five days later, "but that was impossible for me, her brother was with her. It seems he would kill her if he knew she was posing."

But, he added, a young *groom* (bellboy) named Amido from the Hôtel Villa Valentina "was free and might pose." (Although slightly less expensive than his own hotel, the Villa Valentina, just down the rue de Fez from Matisse's Villa de France, had a starred recommendation in the Baedeker guide.)

In *Moroccan Amido*, the barefoot boy wears a white shirt and turquoise waistcoat with short, lilac jodhpur-like pants (see figure 9). Matisse used a long, narrow canvas measuring almost five feet high and two feet across (146.5 x 61.3 cm) that accentuates his slender physique and renders him nearly life-size. Amido appears loose-limbed and casual, with one hand on the leather satchel slung across his chest and the other down at his side and lightly resting on his thigh. His bare lower legs, large, narrow feet splayed on the floor, and exaggerated eyelashes emphasize his coltish youth.

Likely completed in a couple of sessions, the painting was done in a relaxed style akin to a watercolor sketch, with features captured in quick brushstrokes and overall warm tones. In much of the portrait, Matisse's drawn lines show through the thinned, brightly colored paint. There are no shadows, and only a hint of expression on the boy's face. Standing at a three-quarter angle, his head turned away from the painter with awkwardness in his averted gaze, he looks toward a window edged with a white and blue curtain. His hand twitching in a blur, the boy looks as if he would rather be somewhere else.

Moroccan Amido was the "souvenir of Tangier" that Shchukin had asked Matisse to do for him. It was his first portrait in Morocco.

Matisse, though, wanted to paint the "Arab girl." Any issues with her brother were, evidently, resolved by Amido, who began acting as an interpreter for the artist. It was agreed. Zorah would sit for him.

"What did Hamidou [Amido] say to this young woman who probably does not even know what a painting is," wrote noted Moroccan author Tahar Ben Jelloun in his lengthy essay, "Lettre à Matisse." "No museum; no tradition of visiting museums. In Moroccan houses at the time, paintings were not hung on the walls. Carpets, tapestries, embroidery were enough. Painting pictures was not part of the tradition in Moroccan society. Moroccans exercised their art differently, on utilitarian objects, on walls, those who had the means had part of the walls lined with blue, green, white, black zelliges. The ceiling wood was carved and then painted." Ben Jelloun, who moved to Tangier as a kid in 1955 and has set most of his novels in the city, imagined the scene this way once her brother had been mollified: "Hamidou must have said to Zorah: you're going to earn money without doing anything, just sit in a corner on the terrace and that's it; it's a foreigner, a Christian, someone who works with color. You will just have to sit down and watch him. You have to not move too much. He's a good person." Zorah, Ben Jelloun writes, is curious. "Why not?"

Yet even if Matisse managed to placate the brother, or simply disregarded the fraternal threats, the potential consequences for her posing were steep. Matisse would have been aware of risking the girl's reputation and her future.

But these concerns were secondary to the driven artist, and Matisse was soon at work on her portrait.

On a size twenty-five canvas (roughly 32 x 25 in; 81 x 65 cm), Matisse loosely sketched out the girl in pencil sitting on the ground with her legs tucked under her. With a dozen colors squeezed from tubes onto his palette—pale ultramarine, brick red, bluish-green viridian, bluish-hued alizarin crimson—he began filling in the colors, carefully leaving some primed canvas between each section.

Wearing a generous, billowing yellow gown with a wine-red hem, Zorah rocks back on her haunches, tilted slightly to the side, as if adjusting her posture; the tip of a bare foot escapes from under her generous robe. Her hands are clasped in front of her. Dark, center-parted hair shows under a bright pinkish headscarf and flows down her back. The pink of the scarf is the same color as the trim on the gown and of her frowning lips. Her face is oval and mask-like, with elongated, wide-set eyes with black pupils and sharply angled eyebrows. The left eye is a blur, and seems unfocused, giving her an expression of, at best, awkward resignation. She appears older than a "young girl" and lacks the youthful energy of Amido. The background is a scrubbed and splotchy pale turquoise, indistinct and lacking any context. Only her gown gives any indication to a regional location.

Matisse used a dozen colors, and only in a few places did he superimpose them, most notably her yellow ocher robe, where he rubbed in a bit of golden shading, added some touches of charcoal to the robe, and outlined the folds with alizarin crimson. Doing this from an original sketch took great skill and discipline. "This all or nothing is very exhausting," Matisse had complained the previous year when completing the similarly executed *Painter's Family* for Shchukin, and offered comparable comments in posts from Morocco. To paint like this was working without a net.

Conspicuously absent of any sexual suggestion, the girl is lost in the large, even masculine robe. It was a shift from the earlier figures that lounge naked in *Luxe, calme et volupté*, frolic in *Bonheur de vivre*, or the buxom, muscular woman before Algerian palms in *Blue Nude* (*Memory of Biskra*).

There was another key difference in this canvas. Matisse named her. He called the painting *Zorah en jeune* (*Zorah in Yellow*). And with that name, she became not an object, not a symbol, but a subject: Zorah.

12

By April, hawks and storks migrating north after a winter in warmer southern climes wheel above Tangier as they wait to cross the Mediterranean to Europe. Large groups of Griffon vultures sail across the Strait. Alpine swifts, bee-eaters, and rollers arrive on the peninsula in mid-April; babbitts, swarms of quail, and little bustards shelter in the maize fields outside the city in April and May; and, in the grassy valleys speckled with wildflowers, vibrant white egrets gather placidly among grazing cattle.

That spring there were early April showers and volatile clouds. Rain splattered the windowpanes of Matisse's room. Puddles and muck formed in front of the hotel and where the souq gathered. The days were lengthening, but the favorable weather was turning. Conditions were, *Al-Moghreb Al-Aksa* reported, "unsettled," a dreaded word for Matisse.

"Shall I leave on Monday? Shall I stay on?" he wrote on April 6 to Marquet, his favorite target for climate complaints. Tangier's spring weather was living up to its reputation as being trying rather than simply pleasant. "The light is superb, but the weather too variable. You'd think you were in an express train."

Tensions in the country now under French rule were rising to dangerous levels. Rumors flew around with talk of mutiny in the army and reprisals against foreigners. There must have been little else spoken about in the streets, on the terraces of Café Central on the Petit Socco or the Lion d'Or and Café du Commerce near the French post office, or in the traditional coffeehouses of the medina.

Yet Matisse was undisturbed. He remained unwavering in his singular drive to work. He had even begun to relax and sleep better. "I thought it right, having left you so tragically, to send you a telegram every morning to tell you if I slept well. As you know that with me everything depends on that, when you read 'slept well,' you are sure that everything is fine," he wrote to Amélie on the same morning of his letter to Marquet about departing. But now he wasn't even sure of when he might return to France. His plans were continually in flux. "Because I went back to see the garden of Broux. It's quite beautiful, the white bindweeds are beginning to bloom, the meadows are dotted with yellow flowers that you know, the acacias are in bloom, it's spring. If I'm in good shape, I'd better stay."

It was likely that same day that he painted *Zorah in Yellow*.

His mood was buoyant. After a string of obstacles, he had finally hit stride. The stunning portrait of Zorah was his finest work yet in Tangier. He kept postponing his departure for France.

A week later, though, Matisse was packing away his canvases, tubes of paints, brushes and palette knives, and the new textiles that he had picked up in Tangier.

It wasn't the political intrigue swirling around the city or fear of violence against Europeans that ultimately drove Matisse from Morocco, nor the lack of Amélie's calming presence, or even wanting a change of surroundings. "I'm getting ready to leave," he wrote to his wife a few days before departing. "I'm going from right to left, I'm looking at the country which is becoming increasingly more beautiful by the greenery that fills it."

Rather, it was the unpredictability of the sky and the variability of light, whose stability was everything to Matisse. For a successful picture, he needed to remain in the same state of mind for several days, and for light that he could depend on lasting throughout. It was changing too much, and too quickly. An easterly gale blew for four days. Some fair days and smooth seas followed before it began to rain again. The "express train" of weather and light with the coming of spring had finally exhausted his patience, but with the completion of *Zorah in Yellow*, plus *Vase with Irises*, *The Palm*, *The Moroccan Amido*, and *Basket with Oranges*, he felt he had been productive. He drew his Tangier sojourn to a quick close.

On Sunday, April 14, after making a drawing in Mademoiselle Davin's album at the hotel, Matisse, in his tightly buttoned jacket and carefully knotted tie, went with his trunk and valises to the port for the Marseille-bound SS *Tambora*, a new ship on Royal Rotterdam Lloyd's "Accelerated Regular Mail Service" between Rotterdam and Batavia.

The mood among the foreign community on the quay was strained. The previous week, a launch taking passengers to a ship in the bay had sunk, killing ten people as a horrified crowd watched helplessly from shore. The three children of the French Chargé d'Affaires had drowned. The bereaved man and his wife were traveling back to France.

On a fine day, with light westerly breezes and a calm sea, the *Tambora* pulled up its anchors and steamed out of the wide-mouthed bay. Black smoke billowed from its stack as it headed out into the Strait of Gibraltar and the white city of Tangier faded from view.

In the next day's issue of *Al-Moghrab Al-Aksa*, there was a brief mention of departing passengers on the *Tambora*. Listed among them was a "Mattisse." His arrival hadn't been noted in the local newspaper, but his departure was, even if his name was misspelled.

Delacroix's North Africa canvases were largely painted years after he left the region. He eventually did some eighty paintings with North African themes. "I began making something passing out of my trip to Africa only after I had forgotten all the little details and, in my pictures, retained only the striking and poetic side," Delacroix wrote. "Until then, I had been pursued by the love of exactness, which most people mistake for truth." Delacroix eluded this by reworking scenes. "This process of idealization goes on almost unknown to me, when I repaint a composition based on my imagination," Delacroix noted in his journal two decades after leaving Morocco. "This execution is based upon a perfectly idealized theme; the mass of details which slip in, owing to the imperfection of the memory, cannot destroy that simplicity, of quite a different interest, which has first been found in the expression of the idea." Never losing sight of what had originally interested him in the image, the essential elements ultimately remained. As one of Delacroix's famous phrases goes, *"La froide exactitude n'est pas l'art."* (Cold exactitude is not art.)

While Delacroix's celebrated *Women of Algiers* came just two years after his 1832 visit and *The Fanatics of Tangier* a relatively brief six years after, he painted *The Sultan of Morocco and His Entourage* in 1845, more than a dozen years after leaving Morocco, the masterful *Arab Rider* almost two decades later, and *Arab Horses Fighting in a Stable*, *Arab Horseman Attacked by Lion*, and *Arab Saddling His Horse* later yet. Even his two late masterpieces *An Arab Camp at Night* and *Arabs Skirmishing in the Mountains*, both done the year he died (1863), hark back to his North Africa trip over thirty years beforehand.

Unlike his predecessor, Matisse did not have to wait. Matisse was notoriously slow at painting, but here, in the two and half months he had lodged at the Hôtel Villa de France, Matisse, against significant challenges and early setbacks, produced a dozen paintings.

On other travels outside France—to Algeria, Italy, Spain, Germany, Switzerland, Russia, and later the United States and Polynesia—he was only able to complete preparatory sketches, or minor works, if any at all. No other trip abroad yielded such a number of canvases, nor anything of significance.

He also made numerous drawings—lively sketches largely in pen-and-ink but with a handful done in graphite pencil or charcoal. Most locations are easy to track down today. Putting himself (and the viewer) directly in the picture, they are more immediate responses by the artist as he was processing the new place and its motifs in preparation for painting them.

Before departing Tangier, Matisse paid a final visit to Villa Brooks. He walked through the verdant grounds among graceful yellow acacia and white trumpet bindweed flowers. The acanthuses were in full bloom. These hearty, creeping perennials lie dormant in autumn and winter and then burst up in whorls with dozens of purple flowers sprouting from tall spires. The changes thrilled him. The garden, he reported to Amélie, "is quite enchanting—all the flowers are there. There is especially a wisteria near the house which is a marvel. I made two drawings of it which will give you a slight idea. I was interested in the little, delicious flowers that are everywhere. I saw an iris, green-brown, with a golden yellow heart, which is quite captivating."

The visit to Villa Brooks wasn't only closing off the trip but setting up with new ideas. To his family, he wrote, "There came to me two ideas of pictures which I intend to carry out on my return."

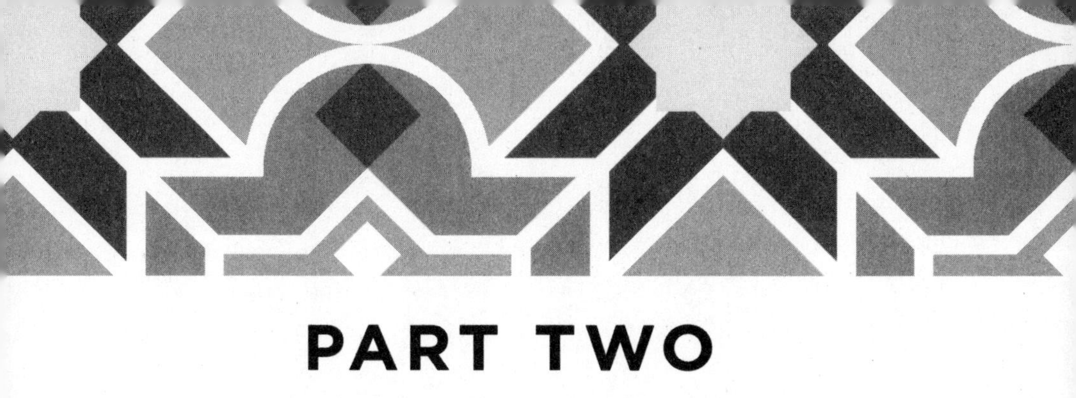

PART TWO

ISSY-LES-MOULINEAUX

13

Once home in Issy-les-Moulineaux, the new Moroccan canvases were unpacked, stretched, and framed, and some hung on the walls of the studio that occupied a corner of the villa's generous grounds. Colors vibrated from them: charged hues that both echoed and competed with the flowers in the well-tended gardens glimpsed through the studio's open double doors and large glass windows.

After the sprawl of Villa Brooks, Matisse found his garden to be "*tout-à-fait exigu*"—terribly cramped—yet he took enormous pleasure in it. With its lilac grove, fruit orchard, and shady bower of tall trees under which the family took tea around a pale-pink marble table, it was, according to Gertrude Stein, "what Matisse between pride and chagrin called un petit Luxembourg." Paths wove among apple, walnut, and lime trees, lilacs, narcissus, numerous varieties of creeping nasturtiums in flamboyant shades of yellows and oranges, peonies, white shrub roses, ferns, ivy, and a multitude of perennials. Flowers encircled a pair of ornamental ponds and lined the pebble-covered path from the house to the studio. Amélie was also a keen gardener and had planted these among the alley of pyramid-trimmed cypress trees for her husband.

"Here, come look at my garden!" Matisse had proudly told a Danish visitor that previous August. "Apart from Collioure, this is my favorite place to be. Isn't that flower bed finer than the finest antique Persian rug? Look at the colors, how distinctly they differ from one another yet blend together. Look at the gradient from the deepest of deep blues to this bold, bright color, lighter than and as luminous as the sky itself, and yet so intense and confident in its strength. Or that cactus flower. Its substance is like silk and velvet—see how it shines like a glowing ember against the grayish green background, like a spiderweb spun over thick, deep green silk! Have you ever seen such giant violets?" Matisse's enthusiasm was contagious, his pride immense, and his generous interest in the topic genuine. "In the spring, when all this bursts forth from the earth and travels the garden pathways like a lavishly decorated train," he continued, "I watch how all the spindly and pale sprouts drink power and color from the sun day by day. . . The intensity of these colors—in reality it is unattainable. At times I hold flowers directly up to my paintings—and how poor and dull all my colors seem then!"

Flowers were a personal passion for Matisse but also fundamental to his art. "The flowers often give me impressions of color that are indelibly burnt onto my retina," he once explained. "Later, when I stand palette in hand before a composition and know only approximately which color I should apply, a memory like that may appear in my mind's eye, and come to my aid, give me a clue."

It was not surprising, then, that his first painting upon returning to France was a small still life of pink geraniums. It was to a familiar floral anchor that he returned to again and again. The potted plant, with a single blossom, sits on a lavender and purple ledge backed by two other shelves of pots, seemingly in the garden's greenhouse. A step back from Zorah and the complexities and rigor of figurative painting, the small floral still life was an easing back into work in his Issy studio.

While lovely, *Pot of Geraniums* hints at a certain disappointment with the European spring that he found upon his return—the relatively pallid colors, the empty clay pots surrounding it, the mildew that covers the bottom part of the central pot. His palette held the same purples and greens he used in Morocco, but mixed in paler shades (see figure 10).

Matisse would need some time to readapt to Issy and the change in pitch of the duller northern light. It didn't take him long, though. In his studio that spring and summer, full of inspiration, new ideas, and energy from his stay in Morocco, a rejuvenated Matisse painted some of his best-known works.

Matisse had moved out to the southwestern suburbs of Issy-les-Moulineaux with his family two-and-a-half years before, in the fall of 1909. Located on a hill above riverside factories and chimneys about four miles (six kilometers) from the center of Paris, Issy-les-Moulineaux was largely residential and still sparsely populated. The spacious villa had views over farm fields and forests. Trains from Gare Montparnasse stopped at Clamart station, from where it was a fifteen-minute walk to the villa.

The entrance was along the route de Clamart (now the busy Avenue du Général de Gaulle) and marked by two stout pillars and an ornate wrought-iron gate. A path led toward the house's main entrance. Ivy-covered columns supported an elegant glass canopy that stretched out over the six steps up the front door. The three-story house had a wooden trellis covering the whole of the front façade and a tall weathervane sat atop the steeply pitched mansard roof.

"Matisse came to settle in Issy because he found Paris too polluted," his late grandson and future owner of the house, Claude Duthuit, explained. "Here was his breath of fresh air."

This is at best an incomplete reason for the move. He was also withdrawing from the pressures of Paris, where cubism, just a few years old, was tightening its grip on the avant-garde. There was also the practical element of needing space for the large panels that Sergei Shchukin had commissioned for his house.

Indeed, it was Shchukin's generous commission for *Dance* and *Music* and, at last, an impending contract with the Galerie Bernheim-Jeune, that finally allowed Matisse and his family to move to such spacious digs from their more cramped ones at the Hôtel Biron on Boulevard les Invalides. Previously the Sacré-Coeur convent and boarding school, Hôtel Biron had been subdivided in 1905 into lodgings that became home to a number of famous residents, including Auguste Rodin, Rainer Maria Rilke, Jean Cocteau, and Isadora Duncan. In 1909 the residents were forced to leave and the building began it journey to housing, a decade later, the Musée Rodin.

With Shchukin's money in hand, Matisse leased the villa in Issy. The four-bedroom house offered plenty of space for him and his wife and the three children. They took the adjacent lot as well, giving a total of around 50,000 square feet (4,617 square meters), or just over an acre. Matisse's atelier sat on that second parcel.

Part of the Shchukin's payment went toward an iron-framed prefabricated studio that could accommodate the commissioned panels. Measuring 33 x 33 feet (10 x 10 meters), or nearly 1,100 square feet, in size, with walls that reached over 16 feet (5 meters) high, the studio was boxy and ample. An offset peaked roof—the short side of glass, the other of corrugated sheet metal—offered airy spaciousness, and the fir wood paneling attached to an internal frame of metal girders a feeling of warmth.

Matisse was nearly forty years old and finally getting a studio designed to his specifications. He had been working in cramped spaces, often carved out of where he lived. But now he had what he desired—but also required. The studio's dimensions reflected the scale and ambition of the panels he was undertaking for Shchukin.

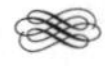

While not a hoarder like Picasso, Matisse surrounded himself with objects. Along with two enormous carved armchairs, a console with books, and a tall grandfather clock, his studio contained an eclectic collection of bric-a-brac. Crowding tabletops, lining shelves, and stacked around the tidy studio were pieces of pottery from Algeria and Spain, tiles from the Alhambra in Granada, Persian carpets, a sculpted figure from Java that fit in his palm, a primitive icon from Russia, large shells, ashtrays, and carved wooden sculptures from sub-Saharan African (he bought the first in 1906 and owned twenty within two years). These objects not only inspired the artist but appeared frequently in his paintings.

The most important items in Matisse's miscellanea, though, were textiles. From his traveling trunk, he pulled out the new pieces that he had acquired in Tangier.

He had begun amassing a collection as an impoverished art student in Paris, picking up snippets from second-hand stalls near Notre Dame, and continued to gather a large and eclectic collection throughout his life, buying tapestries, wall hangings, printed cotton pieces, Islamic embroidery, Algerian prayer mats, pieces from end-of-season sales of Parisian haute couture, and exotic gowns on his travels. The collection was continually being added to and renewed.

Striped, patterned, flowered, and nearly always sumptuously colored, these pieces fired his imagination and ended up on his canvases as table covers for still lifes, throws for sofas, and, most conspicuously, backgrounds to his reclining odalisques in the 1920s to create the illusion of Eastern luxury, splendor, and visual decadence. Some pieces appeared repeatedly over the years. A favorite length of blue toile de Jouy that he had spotted from the top of a bus in 1903 first appeared as a conventional table covering before eventually becoming the motif for an entire composition.

Matisse called the collection *"ma bibliothèque de travail"* (my working library) and took it with him from studio to studio, and even packed some for his travels. Among the pieces tucked into his luggage for Tangier had been the pale-pink flower-patterned French silk one that formed the center of *Basket with Oranges*.

Textiles were literally in the Matisse blood, as generations had earned their livelihoods at the loom. Coming from a northern industrial area in French Flanders that was a center of textile manufacturing, his deep connection with material began as a boy. His hometown of Bohain-en-Vermandois was renowned for producing high-quality, luxury fabrics—tulle, embossed and patterned velvet, and, most famously, silk in shimmering colors and original designs that were destined for Parisian fashion houses.

The town itself was without galleries or museums, had few public sculptures, and hardly a mural, and for children like Matisse, one of the few outlets for the visual imagination came through those rich, luxury silks woven in the dozens of ateliers around Bohain. It is either an irony or an impetus that out of this bleak landscape of beet fields, factory effluent, and smokestacks emerged Matisse's magnificent joy of colors and the greatest colorist since Delacroix.

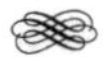

That spring back in Issy, he began an important new motif, goldfish, one that had yet to appear in his work. The first was *Les Poissons rouges*, or *Goldfish*, done on a large canvas. Governed by ovals and circles, the composition revolves around a cylindrical glass fishbowl sitting on a marble garden table. Luxuriant geraniums, orchids, and nasturtiums in soothing pinks and mauves, brilliant green spring foliage, and the curving armrest of a chair crowd around the tall jar. The stillness of the day is barely fazed by the slow, hypnotic movement of four jewel-like orange fish.

Idyllic, sumptuous in color, and comforting to look at, it is one of Matisse's most reprinted pictures. So accustomed to seeing small reproductions of it on greeting cards and refrigerator magnets, its large size (nearly five feet high, or 146 x 97 cm) is somewhat startling when standing before the original on the gallery wall at the Pushkin Museum in Moscow, staring quite literally eye-to-eye in the gaze of four fish.

He was working well, and rather than go to Collioure on the Mediterranean coast, as in many previous summers, he decided to stay in Issy. It was the first summer in a number of years that he remained in or around Paris.

The studio in Issy had abundant light, but it became stifling in the heat (and unbearable during a heatwave that second week of May). Matisse stood at his easel in light cotton work pajamas. At the time considered exotic leisurewear in Paris, he wore them for many years to paint, switching to woolen pajamas when the weather cooled.

The previous spring and summer had been productive for Matisse, and notable works included *Les Coucous, tapis bleu et rose*, a sumptuous still life of a tall vase of cowslips sitting on a piece of handwoven tapestry of dark blue with pink motifs that he had bought at an antique store in Madrid. (The canvas was acquired in 1981 by Yves Saint Laurent and Pierre Bergé and sold in 2009 at Christie's after the couturier's death for over $46 million, setting a world record price for a Matisse at auction.) This was followed by the large, landmark canvases of his workspace, *The Pink Studio* and, in a slightly different perspective and in rusty, ruddy-reddish, *The Red Studio*.

Now, with a pair of dogs lounging drowsily at his feet and flies buzzing around him, he delved into work with confidence and newfound inspiration from his winter in Tangier and did a number of magnificent new paintings of his workplace.

He completed two versions of *Nasturtiums and "La Danse,"* tall, flat scenes of the studio with an old preparatory version of his *Dance* panel dominating the background. The ring of movement of that previous work for Shchukin counters the stillness of a plant in a bulbous, reddish vase on a narrow, three-legged stand. Unlike the pink and red paintings of his studio done the year before that captured fuller views, these zoomed in and cut off two of the three objects he depicts. He made the preliminary sketch (known as *Nasturtiums and "La Danse" I*) quickly, with no alterations, while he heavily worked the final version (*Nasturtiums and "La Danse" II*), scraping away paint and applying new layers as he built up the image. The whirling figures of the draft version are more naturally pink-fleshed, rather than the ruddy orange of the final composition.

Matisse repeated this tighter viewpoint with cropped objects in an equally tall canvas that stood over six feet high (192 x 114 cm) that he called *Corner of the Artist's Studio*. The focus is a large green urn with a sprouting plant. Behind it is a patterned blue tapestry; before it sits a striking red and yellow striped canvas chair.

Matisse continued with the studio theme but included goldfish. He made three other paintings with goldfish that summer as the bowl moved inside to become part of a trio of objects in meditations on Matisse's artist studio and on the act of painting. The goldfish sit on a worktable beside a vase of flowers and a sensual, contorted sculpture of a reclining nude. Injecting something living into a still life was highly novel. By definition a still life includes inanimate objects. *Still* is the optimal word here: animals were usually dead. The French name *nature morte* is even more literal and specific in this regard.

While the three studio paintings with goldfish are versions of the same theme, each is quite distinctive. In *Studio with Goldfish*, the bright spring light of the garden outside is glimpsed through a gridded, opaque blue window and an open door, in contrast to the cool colors of the interior. There are hints of the exotic here, in the green robe draped over a screen and the goldfish themselves, done as submarine dashes of brilliant orange. Hanging on the studio wall in the picture is *Zorah in Yellow*. Today the color of the gown on *Zorah in Yellow* is less vivid than it was in 1912, as one of the pigments in the yellow has faded, rendering it over the years closer to a wheat color. But here, in the background of the studio canvas, it can be seen closer to its original bright shade of yellow.

The canvas's companion, *Goldfish with Sculpture*, is the same size but with brighter, more liquidy blues and greens, more abstract, more aquatic.

Matisse made a final goldfish painting of the garden studio, his controlled and sheltered reality between the real and painted worlds. In *Goldfish*, the focus on the trio of elements has been tightened and the colors given a smoldering intensity: vibrant oranges and blues, deep pinks, and a dazzling bouquet of blooms that demonstrates how effectively Matisse used colors to create moods.

During the highly productive summer of 1912, Matisse also returned to a major canvas that he had begun at least three years earlier, *The Conversation*. In the picture, based on his wife and himself, Amélie wears a long black dressing gown and sits majestically enthroned in a large chair. Before her stands the artist, stiff and erect in a posture accentuated by the vertical stripes of his pajamas. With her head tipped slightly back to look directly at his face, she seems to be demanding or asking something of him, or perhaps waiting for an explanation; he is as rigid as one of the stripes, with his hands in his pockets, not looking down at her, either unable to answer or completely self-absorbed. The title is specific—it is *the* conversation about something, not *a* conversation. The whole image is flat and backed by an electric, shadowless purplish-blue. Separating the couple in the center of the canvas is an open window looking out over the well-tended front court of their Issy villa, with trimmed greens and vibrant red flowers. The window's iron grillwork spells quite clearly NON, French for "no." While Matisse often painted people, this is a rare example depicting a relationship between them, and one of the few between a man and a woman. It was arguably the most significant work from the months immediately following Tangier.

As Matisse was finishing *The Conversation* in July, he received a visit from Sergei Shchukin, the Russian collector who was his most important client. For the last few years, Shchukin had been buying nearly all of his work.

Shchukin had a closer personal relationship with Matisse than with any other artist and frequently came directly to the studio to select pieces. For

Matisse, this was something of a mixed blessing. "He always picked the best," the artist liked to grumble.

This visit was no different. He selected five canvases on his summer visit, including the four finest done since his return from Morocco: *The Conversation*, *Nasturtiums and "La Danse" II*, *Corner of a Studio*, and *Les Poissons rouges*. The fifth was *The Moroccan Amido*. The painting of the young Moroccan groom was packed up and shipped to Moscow along with the others whose paint was barely dry.

14

In 1906, Sergei Shchukin visited Matisse's studio for the first time. Matisse was thirty-six, poverty-stricken, and considered something of a charlatan among the French art establishment after exhibiting his scandalous fauve paintings. He could hardly sell a canvas.

Shchukin didn't initially fully embrace the radical new fauve works. While drawn to Matisse's fiery colors, Shchukin selected during the studio visit a significantly staider still life from 1900, *Crockery on a Table*, of a porcelain tureen, cup, and a chocolate pot (a wedding present from Albert Marquet) arranged atop a table draped with a reddish cloth. The picture's tones are almost muddied, with browns and smoky reds dominating. Matisse had bought Cézanne's *Three Bathers* from Ambroise Vollard at the end of 1899, and the influence of that composition's shifting planes was already becoming visible and objects starting to lose their natural colors. *Crockery on a Table* was a somewhat surprising first pick as it was done in a significantly more muted palette than the artist had since become known for or that the Russian had seen in the recent Salons.

"I buy it [*sic*]," Shchukin told Matisse, "but I'll have to keep it at home for several days, and if I can bear it, and keep interested in it, I'll keep it." It was Shchukin's way to test a painting before fully committing to it. The idea went against the conventional wisdom of either liking a painting immediately when first seeing it, or not at all.

Matisse let Shchukin take the canvas, as well as two lithographs, and he also gave him a drawing of himself as a fisherman in Collioure (*Le Pêcheur*).

In Moscow, Shchukin hung the painting with other avant-garde works that he had been collecting since 1898 and left it for a month to see if it still kept his interest. It did. Decades later, Matisse recalled his relief. "I was lucky enough that he was able to bear this first ordeal easily, and that my still-life didn't fatigue him too much."

The purchase marked a key moment in Matisse's burgeoning career and gave him much-needed support—support that went beyond mere financial terms. Matisse gained a patron that encouraged him to paint as he wished, knowing he would have his backing, and that the works would be hung, not simply rolled up and locked away as an investment. Shchukin signed his letters to Matisse "your devoted" and meant it. "He was good because he always came back," Matisse's son, Pierre, who became a well-known gallery owner in New York, later said of the loyal Shchukin.

During his July 1912 visit to Matisse's Issy studio, Shchukin sat for a portrait, a charcoal study made for a planned oil. Slight but strong, the somber Shchukin performed a rigorous regime of daily gymnastics, kept a strict vegetarian diet, and insisted on sleeping with the window open even in winter. He had a large head, imposing mustache, and hair that had turned prematurely white by his forties.

In the Shchukin charcoal (see figure 11), Matisse whetted the paper and smudged the charcoal, creating prominent cheekbones and forehead, and giving the Russian a sly, foxy look, with intense, penetrating eyes, pursed lips, and carefully combed hair. The face appears almost masklike. "That drawing had an Asiatic character that Shchukin didn't like," Matisse later said. "He aspired to be European above all else. I brought out the Asian character in him and it got a little under his skin, I think. But, as Bonnard says, portraits always become good likenesses in the end." (For unknown reasons, the oil portrait was never done. Matisse hung onto the drawing his entire life.)

As a child, Shchukin stuttered so severely as to render him almost unable to speak. While his father sent his brothers to study at a German boarding school in Saint Petersburg, Sergei was kept at home to be educated with his sisters. He was nearly eighteen when finally allowed to go abroad. He spent the summer near Münster, Germany, being treated by a specialist for his stutter and then remained in Germany for three years to study commerce in a town known for its textiles industry.

Among his siblings, Shchukin had the best acumen for commerce, and back in Moscow he quickly ascended to running the family's wool and cotton business, eventually turning it into a textile empire. During a wide-scale revolt and uprising in Russia in 1905, he significantly increased the family fortune by buying as much fabric as possible on the cheap when prices collapsed, and then, having virtually cornered the market, selling them when the uprising was put down and prices rose. Matisse called him "shrewd, subtle, and serious."

The Shchukins were members of a commercial class growing wealthy at the turn of the twentieth century, part of a new generation of restless bankers, builders, and merchants who came not from aristocratic old money but families who had risen from poverty, even serfdom. "The Russian Fricks, Carnegies, Harrimans and Rockefellers of their times, they were the de facto rulers of Moscow," wrote Shchukin's first biographer, Beverly Whitney Kean. These families endowed charities, supported the theater and opera, joined exclusive clubs, and traveled widely. And they bought art. Collecting became a trend among the mercantile bourgeoisie. They weren't buying Old Masters as the aristocracy tended to favor, but more modern pieces that looked to the future.

For Shchukin, the passion for collecting came late. When he bought his first paintings, he was already over forty, head of the family company, and married with three sons and a daughter. He started off with fashionable paintings by artists little spoken of today (Carriere, Cottet, Simon, Guillaumin, Lehmann, Maglin) plus a lovely Vuillard interior to hang in his villa's private chapel. But his tastes soon shifted to more daring works. In 1899, he acquired his first Monet, *Lilac in the Sun*, a delirious 1872 study of light and color with two women lounging in the shade under the sprawling pink blooms of a lilac tree. It was the first Monet in Russia.

With both speed and scale, his collection grew. By 1904, Shchukin owned fourteen Monet paintings. He moved quickly onto works by Cézanne, Gauguin, Van Gogh, Picasso, Derain, and Matisse, binge-buying each artist in turn.

But Shchukin was far from spontaneous in his purchases. He deliberated on a work before committing to it, and expected an impact. "If a picture gives you a psychological shock, buy it. It's a good one," he once advised his daughter. Relying purely on his own intuition, the audacious collector ignored critics, friends, and the aristocratic class who rejected the deeply radical paintings he was compulsively acquiring.

In a decade and a half, Shchukin amassed the greatest collection of modern art in the world. His two-story home on Znamensky Lane in central Moscow essentially became the first permanent museum dedicated to modern Western art.

Shchukin was an unlikely man for such an achievement. "His courage surely surpassed that of any other collector of his time," said Alfred H. Barr Jr., the founding director of the Museum of Modern Art in New York, stressing the significant difference between Shchukin and the other major collectors of modern art at the time. Shchukin was not "a liberated expatriate living in Paris like the Steins, a wealthy museum director . . . an aristocratic dilettante . . . a radical politician or devoted founder of a private museum." Rather, Shchukin was "a very successful businessman who bought pictures out of the studios of Matisse and Picasso at the height of their controversial fame in order to hang them in his otherwise conventional bourgeois mansion in one of the most conservative cities in Europe."

The capital of French modern art was on the Moskva River, not the Seine. In one house alone there were hundreds of sublime works, including dozens from Matisse. "How many [of your canvases] are already there, and the most beautiful that no artist has seen in France?" Georgette Agutte remarked in a letter to Matisse in the fall of 1911, when he was exhibiting little at the Salons and selling almost everything to Moscow. "It's a shame for the development of taste in France."

Built in the late eighteenth century not far outside the walls of the old Kremlin, Shchukin's home had two stories, each about 5,400 square feet (500 square meters). A gift from his father, the Greek-revival palace, with Greek-style bas-reliefs, Louis XVI furniture, extravagant chandeliers and candelabras, and windows hung with elaborate silk drapes, was an unlikely place for breathtaking avant-garde works of art, from cubist landscapes by Picasso and Georges Braque to Matisse's *Red Room (Harmony in Red).*

In spring 1908, Shchukin began opening his mansion on Sunday mornings. Hanging such works much less allowing the public to see them was a bold act that invited mockery—or worse. (One displeased visitor scribbled over a Monet painting with pencil.) While the city's more conservative critics found it hard to digest the blaze of paintings that crowded the walls, they were a revelation for Moscow's artists and students.

From being involved in commissions with Matisse to offering local painters new artistic influences to study up close, it was important for Shchukin to be a part of the creative process. When he was home, Shchukin would act as guide, leading the curious, the mocking, and the repulsed from room to room, his hands dug into the pockets of his rumpled suit, patiently explaining the daring paintings. "The master of the house was polite, lighting this or that chandelier whenever necessary and explaining the different merits of his pictures," recalled an early visitor. "He resembled a crafty *maître-d'hôtel,* with white hair carefully combed over his brow and little eyes like mice popping from their holes."

The collection gained enough popularity to be included in Baedeker's 1914 guidebook for Russia: "No. 8 Bolsói Známenki Pereúlok is the *House of Sergius Ivánovitch Shtchukin*, with an admirable collection of modern French paintings, including examples by Monet, Sisley, Renoir, Degas, Cézanne, Gauguin, Matisse, and Picasso; adm. on written application to the owner." At the revolving front door, a liveried doorman welcomed visitors.

Just a few months before going to Morocco, Matisse had traveled to Russia with Shchukin to oversee the rehanging of his canvases on the walls of his patron's villa, to discuss new projects, and to see Shchukin's unparalleled collection of European art.

On November 1, 1911, the two men caught the Compagnie Internationale des Wagons-Lits' luxurious Nord Express service from Paris's Gare de l'Est to Saint Petersburg, where they spent a few days—their original plan to visit the Hermitage was thwarted when they found the great museum had already closed for the winter for repairs—before continuing on to Moscow.

Matisse had hoped to see the city covered under a blanket of white. But the snows would come late that year, and the days were mild and wet. Unsurprisingly, a disappointed Matisse sent a postcard to the Steins complaining of the awful, rainy weather. Moscow was, Matisse later said, "an Asian town, with brightly colored churches, fairly wide streets, low houses made of wood. The paving is dilapidated and people don't care what they're walking in. They say Moscow has a head of gold and feet in the mud."

Matisse found Shchukin's art collection unique because it held every painting Shchukin had ever acquired. (Conversely, the Steins had a high turnover, with new paintings frequently replacing old ones.) "I keep the first pictures I bought to show people where I started from and everything that I like today," Shchukin told Matisse. "My collection is the story of a collector."

It was a veritable museum of Matisse's career. Since Leo and Gertrude Stein stopped buying from him in 1907, the Russian had become Matisse's most important collector. By the time the two men arrived in Moscow together in the fall of 1911, in just five and a half years since their first meeting, Shchukin had bought nearly thirty of Matisse's paintings. These were framed with glass and tipped sharply at 45 degrees to avoid reflection. Matisse thought they should be without glass and hang together in a single room. He extended his trip for a week to await the arrival of two large commissioned pieces he had done for Shchukin, *The Pink Studio* and *The Painter's Family*. During his last week in Moscow, Matisse helped reinstall his works in what became known as the Matisse Room.

Stacked high on the colorful and ornamental walls of this salon, Matisse's paintings covered molded plasterwork, medallions, and cornices, the tops of mirrors, and thick, ropey plaster designs. The walls were pale green, the carpets on the wooden floorboards crimson, and the sofas pink. Frescoes of perched parrots and garlands of flowers embellished the vaulted pink ceiling with four west-facing windows suffusing the room with delicate light. The vibrant colors on the canvases matched the room's energy and tone.

The room became the favorite of Shchukin and the place where he would find respite from his problems.

15

In April 1908, while buying much of Matisse's output, the kindhearted Shchukin introduced the painter to another wealthy Moscow collector, Ivan Morozov, who lived just a ten-minute walk from Znamensky Lane. Shchukin took his fellow compatriot to visit Matisse is his Paris studio, at the time in the Couvent du Sacré-Coeur.

Although nearly two decades younger, Morozov shared many similarities with Shchukin, including hailing from a textile family. While the Shchukins were largely white-collar traders, the Morozovs had cotton mills in Tver, northwest of Moscow on the Volga River—that is, one made textiles and the other sold them. Both men, though, needed a certain artistic acumen to succeed, and had developed heightened senses of colors, patterns, and design.

It was this connection that helped deepen their link to Matisse. Among other artists, Matisse's visual sophistication from his upbringing among the textile industry was without equal. But he found counterparts in his two great Russian patrons. (Perhaps not uncoincidentally, Matisse's other great patrons during his career also came from the world of textiles, the American sisters Etta and Claribel Cone, who acquired, mostly from the 1920s onward, some six hundred pieces of his work. The Cone family had the largest denim mill in the world, supplying one-third of the globe's denim by 1910 and, from 1915, formed a partnership with Levi Strauss as their sole supplier. The Cone Collection now anchors the Baltimore Museum of Art's modern art collection.)

The Morozov family's business began with a relative who had been a serf and a weaver. Borrowing money from the owner of the factory where he worked, he paid off his twenty-five years of compulsory military service, and, using his wife's dowry, opened a small factory making lace. He repaid his loan quickly, and expanded manufacturing. Over the next generations the business grew, and under Ivan Morozov the company employed nearly fifteen thousand workers.

At the beginning of the twentieth century, Morozov was one of the richest men in Russia. Yet little is known about him. Deeply private, he left no personal papers, just a few photographs, and a single interview, given late in his life to Félix Fénéon, the critic and head of contemporary art at Galerie Bernheim-Jeune, where Matisse held a contract.

Morozov studied in Switzerland, obtaining a degree in chemistry at Zurich Polytechnic. As a teenager, he took weekly lessons from the noted Russian impressionist landscape painter Konstantin Korovin for two years, and while a student in Zurich spent his Sundays painting oil landscapes. But once he finished his studies, Morozov didn't pick up a brush again. He would have liked to have been an artist, but, aware of his own mediocre talent, eventually put his creative passion into collecting. As he told a friend, "I have to settle for delighting in the works of other people."

In Moscow, the reserved Morozov led a rather conservative, patriarchal life. His father had died when Morozov was young, and as his brothers withdrew into their own private pursuits, Ivan devoted himself almost exclusively to the family business.

Valentin Serov's 1910 portrait of Morozov shows a large, well-dressed middle-aged man with a goatee sitting somewhat awkwardly at a table. Leaning forward, wearing a sober dark-brown suit with a pearl stickpin holding his cravat in place, a gold cufflink and heavy pinky ring gleaming on loosely folded hands in front of him, he looks directly at the viewer in an inquisitive, penetrating gaze with his blue eyes "as if," wrote novelist and art critic Julian Barnes, "assessing our taste (and pocket)." That year Morozov bought three Matisse canvases, and Serov used the recently arrived *Fruit and Bronze*, with its bowls of pomegranates, vase, and swirling patterns of blues, reds, and oranges, as a backdrop for the portrait. Matisse's daughter Marguerite remembered Morozov as "bluff, genial and kindly—rather like an explosive child."

Although he married an ex-cabaret singer, Morozov remained largely aloof from Moscow's bohemian cultural scene and didn't socialize much with the art crowd. As playing a public role in the art world "repulsed him," he made little effort to do so, nor did he actively seek the attention of the press or critics. Because of this, Morozov (unlike Shchukin) was rarely attacked in public. Opposed to Sundays at Shchukin's home that attracted an eclectic range of visitors, Morozov allowed almost no one to see his collection. It was kept hidden, as sculptor and museum director Boris Ternovets put it, "with the jealous love of a miser."

Holding very different ideas on displaying paintings than Shchukin, Morozov had the rooms where he hung his collection stripped of all decoration so that nothing would impinge on their impact. In his neoclassic nineteenth-century mansion on Prechistenka Street, workers removed the ornamental moldings, covered the walls with a neutral gray fabric, and installed a glass skylight as any museum would require. While there is no precise record of how he displayed the works, it is thought that he arranged his impressionist paintings in the villa's large hall, placed works by Cézanne and Matisse nearby, and hung commissioned panels by Maurice Denis and Bonnard in the entry hall and stairwell. Upstairs were the postimpressionists, with choice pieces by Van Gogh, Gauguin, Marquet, Derain, and Orthon Friesz along with a couple of Picassos.

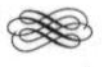

Morozov only began acquiring modern French works following his elder brother, Mikhail.

Mikhail Morozov had been the first in Russia to buy paintings by Manet or Van Gogh, or one of Gauguin's Tahiti canvases, and he acquired the only Edvard Munch held today in a public Russian museum. With taste running beyond established works, Mikhail bought Toulouse-Lautrec drawings, Degas pastels, a stunning Monet painting of a field of poppies, early Bonnards, works by Renoir, and an unusual Van Gogh seascape. He started collecting the same year as Shchukin, in 1898, and died five years later, not long after his thirty-third birthday, from a kidney disease. Until his early death, he was on par or even ahead of Shchukin as Russia's preeminent collector of modern art.

In 1903, Mikhail took Ivan with him to Paris. It was Ivan's first trip to the French capital and proved to be Mikhail's last. Until his brother's death later that year, Ivan Morozov had principally collected Russian painters—he was the first Russian to buy the still-unknown Marc Chagall—and essentially took over where Mikhail had left off. Morozov acquired Alfred Sisley's winter landscape *Frost in Louveciennes*, quickly followed by numerous works by well-known others. (Morozov never stopped buying art by Russians, though. By 1913 he owned 430 pieces by Russians. Shchukin, conversely, showed little interest in collecting Russian art.)

In October 1907, Morozov acquired his first Matisse from the Galerie Bernheim-Jeune, the recently completed *Bouquet (Vase with Two Handles)*, a still life of flowers in an urn-shaped white vase on a raspberry-red table. Long-stemmed blooms rise above the arrangement, their colors highlighted by the pale-blue background. It now hangs at the Hermitage in bright contrast beside Shchukin's first Matisse acquisition, the tobacco-hued *Crockery on the Table.*

While Moscow's new-money class might have been buying art, the city didn't have much of a market for acquiring pieces, nor were there any specialist auction houses. Le Mercier Gallery, Moscow's first private commercial gallery, wouldn't open until 1909.

That meant that, like Shchukin, Morozov bought mostly in Paris. Twice a year, to coincide with the spring and autumn Salons, he went to the French capital, going almost directly from Gare de l'Est to a cluster of galleries near the Opéra and Boulevard Hausmann. Morozov would ease his heavy frame into a low, comfortable chair, and assistants would parade pictures before him.

At the time, the narrow rue Laffitte was the commercial center of modern art. Along here at number 8 was the original location of the well-established Bernheim-Jeune (it moved near Place de la Madeleine in 1908). At number 6 was the small shop of Cézanne's dealer Ambroise Vollard, who showed Van Gogh, Gauguin, and Picasso. ("It was an incredible place," wrote Gertrude Stein of Vollard's. "It did not look like a picture gallery. Inside there were a couple of canvases turned to the wall, in one corner was a small pile of big and little canvases thrown pell mell on top of one another, in the center of the room stood a huge dark man glooming." That was Vollard.) Paul Durand-Ruel's gallery, which specialized in impressionists and handled the works by Degas, Renoir, Monet, Pissarro, and Sisley, was at number 16. And at number 46 was Clovis Sagot, an early promoter and patron of cubism. Not far away, at 28 rue Vignon, was Daniel-Henry Kahnweiler. Despite having a micro-size gallery—less than 175 square feet, or a mere four by four meters—Kahnweiler was the pioneering dealer of cubism and represented the four main cubists (Picasso, Braque, Juan Gris, and Fernand Léger). A bit farther to the north was Berthe Weill's gallery with fauvist and cubist works. Opened in 1901, Weill had been the first private gallery to show Matisse and was the first to sell one of his canvases, in 1902. And, since its move in 1908, Eugène Druet's gallery was found near Place de la Madeleine on rue Royale.

In Paris, Morozov (like Shchukin) stayed at Le Grand Hôtel. Filling an entire triangular block beside Palais Garnier, the opulent home to the Paris Opera, the hotel had eight hundred rooms for guests on four floors and another complete floor for their servants. Such was its grandeur that when Empress Eugénie, the wife of Napoleon III, inaugurated it in 1862, she said the hotel reminded her of the Royal Château de Fontainebleau. In the decades that followed, Le Grand's sumptuousness hadn't faded. From his hotel room, Morozov did little else but see (and buy) pictures.

In the first few years of these visits, Morozov left with just a few choice canvases, but his appetite quickly deepened, and his annual purchases multiplied. He bought a staggering fifty impressionists paintings—Monet, Renoir, Pissarro, Degas—before moving onto postimpressionists, acquiring eleven Gauguins and seven Van Goghs. But his real pride were his eighteen Cézanne paintings. He first encountered them at Vollard's gallery and snapped up four on the spot. He soon held the finest Cézanne collection in the world.

Nearly every single one of the European canvases Morozov acquired have the status of major works. Deliberate and thoughtful in selecting art, he never bought on impulse. He had a discerning eye, and rarely chose wrong. He was shrewd and got what he liked, preferring not to argue too much over the price. Vollard called him "the Russian who doesn't haggle." Though, in his own way, he did haggle, using his extraordinary patience. He was capable of waiting years to acquire a particular canvas.

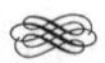

Even though the two Russians were both buying the same artists at the same time from the same handful of Parisian galleries and studios, there was little rivalry between them. To be sure, they were among the very few in the world who had such ample financial resources and so passionately bought cutting edge works of modern art, and there was plenty of room for them both. But the two men also had different buying styles. Shchukin thought Morozov acted too methodically and bought with the consistency of a museum buyer rather than a passionate collector.

While both had sharp eyes for fine works, Morozov suffered a certain lack of confidence and often sought second opinions. Indecision never plagued Shchukin, though. Matisse once explained the difference between the two men. "When Morozov would go to Ambroise Vollard's, he would say: 'I want to see a very good Cézanne.' As for Shchukin, he would ask to see all the Cézannes which were for sale and choose from among them himself."

Compared to Shchukin, Morozov was more timid and conservative in his choices. He had just three paintings by Picasso (one was the stunning 1910 *Portrait of Ambroise Vollard* made up of angles and gray and brown planes), whereas Shchukin acquired over fifty by the Spaniard, including many from his cubist phase, grasping early its implications—before cubism had a name—even if he compared their impact to "chewing shards of broken glass." Nor did Morozov's passion for Matisse reach the elevated heights of Shchukin. (Morozov eventually owned eleven choice Matisse canvases.) He was keen on Vuillard and Bonnard, while Shchukin bought only one of the former and none of the latter.

"Constantly cautious and restrained in his choices, fearful of conflict and of everything still struggling to establish itself," wrote the collector's future curator, Boris Ternovets, "Morozov preferred the calm search, in contrast to Shchukin's wandering spirit."

"Cautious and restrained" are highly relative terms here. Today these canvases are blockbuster exhibition hits, dorm-room wall prints, and reproduced across museum shop souvenirs on everything from notebooks to socks and umbrellas. But by the standards of the time, Morozov's collection held breathlessly daring works derided by the critics, the public, and state institutions, radical works that were smashing centuries of Western artistic traditions.

In these "unstable times," wrote a Russian critic in 1914, "only a madman, a speculator, or an 'amateur' art lover, whose aesthetic consciousness is loftier than the present day's, can collect the work of contemporaries." Shchukin and Morozov were far from amateur collectors, and they retained their passion for it throughout the years, never becoming jaded or seeing it as something transactional. They were not betting fortunes on the art, buying pieces as investments hoping to make money from them one day. Rather, they bought pieces that they liked or that made an impact on them. And they immediately hung the canvases on the walls of their homes where they lived. As collectors, they were viewed as highly eccentric, even downright mad. That made them, in the eyes of many, even crazier than the avant-garde painters themselves.

Matisse acknowledged their courage. "It took sheer nerve to paint in this manner, and it took sheer nerve to buy."

16

Shchukin believed that his collecting came with a steep price: art—and the pleasure he took from it—was a quid pro quo for the suffering he endured.

Tragedy struck Shchukin in November 1905, during a wave of social and political upheavals. His namesake and youngest of his three sons disappeared. Winter passed without any sign of the seventeen-year-old boy.

In April, Shchukin was in Paris for the 1906 Salon des Indépendants, where he saw *Bonheur de vivre*, Matisse's largest, most audacious work to date. He happened to be in the gallery when the dealer Ambroise Vollard moved through the crowd with a *vendu* (sold) notice as it had just been bought by Leo Stein. While few were impressed by the canvas, Shchukin was transfixed by its bold colors, distorted figures, and jarring shifts in scale, and told Vollard he wanted to meet the artist.

Before he could, though, a telegram reached him at Le Grand Hôtel. As spring weather had begun to warm in Moscow and the ice of the Moskva River that serpentined through the city thawed, the body of his son had appeared. Shchukin rushed home. Authorities ruled the boy's death a suicide.

Shchukin returned to Paris almost immediately. In early May, with the shock of seeing the throbbing colors of the Arcadian *Bonheur de vivre* still fresh, the grieving, fifty-two-year-old Russian climbed the 102 stairs to Matisse's fifth-floor studio on quai Saint-Michel to meet the artist.

Matisse was smarting from the voracious criticism of *Bonheur de vivre*, even by some of his staunchest supporters. Matisse's friend and master pointillist Paul Signac, who had bought the revolutionary *Luxe, calme et volupté* the previous year, and whose support had been so important to Matisse, wrote to another painter, "Matisse, whose attempts I have liked up to now, seems to me to have gone to the dogs. Upon a canvas of two and a half meters, he has surrounded some strange characters with a line as thick as your thumb. Then he has covered the whole thing with flat well-defined tints which—however pure—seem disgusting . . . ah! those rosy flesh tones!" Signac compared it to "the multi-colored shop-fronts of the merchants of paints, varnishes and household goods!" Considering Matisse's parents sold such items in a provincial town store, the slight would have been particularly cutting.

The meeting between Matisse and Shchukin that spring day launched the most important artist-collector relationship that either would ever have. Both found something they desperately needed.

On Christmas Eve the following year, tragedy returned to Shchukin's home. His wife, Lidya, a famed Moscow beauty and heir to a coal mining fortune a decade his junior, fell ill. Doctors found cancer riddling her body. A week later she was dead.

For a year, not a single new painting entered Trubetzkoy Palace. The greatest living collector of modern art abstained from buying anything new.

The bereaved Shchukin traveled to Egypt, as he had done the winter after his son's disappearance. With a caravan consisting of eighteen camels, fifteen Bedouins, two dragomans, a cook, and his manservant, he and his family set off for Saint Catherine's Monastery, built at the base of Mount Sinai in the mid-sixth century. It was to be a spiritual retreat, even though Shchukin was not generally the meditative type. "In a short time I have suffered a great deal and borne irreplaceable losses," he wrote in his diary. "I felt I didn't have the strength to begin a new life."

The caravan followed the ancient pilgrim route through the barren landscape to the isolated complex of Saint Catherine's, where Shchukin found an auspicious sign. "One afternoon, as he was exploring the priory, he came upon the cell of a young monk. Pinned to the wall of the tiny cubicle, like a small icon, was a reproduction of a work by Matisse, an unexpectedly vivid reminder of the outside world," wrote his first biographer, Beverly Kean. The young man was trying to paint in the fauve style using colors he had concocted himself and rather crude tools. The time that Shchukin spent with the young recluse helped him heal and take his mind off himself and his problems. It also made him decide to open his house and share his collection with the public. Once back in Paris, Shchukin sent off a large packet of paints and brushes to the monk and told the remarkable story to Matisse. Kean learned it from Matisse's daughter and frequent companion, Marguerite.

In early January 1908, not long after returning from Egypt, Shchukin received more bad news. A dozen years beforehand, he had bought the stake of his younger brother, Ivan, in the family company. Ivan purchased a handsome apartment in Paris on Avenue de Wagram, an elegant street that radiates north from Arc de Triomphe, and started collecting impressionist paintings. He soon sold these to his brother and moved onto significantly more expensive Old Masters, acquiring works by El Greco and Goya. A friend of Rodin and the Basque painter Ignacio Zuloaga, Ivan hosted many artistic notables during his weekly salon—Renoir, Degas, and Rodin were frequent guests to his "Tuesdays," as were the symbolist painters J. K. Huysmans and Odilon Redon, gallery owner Paul Durand-Ruel, and Anton Chekhov, plus well-known Russian dissidents, publishers, and journalists. But Ivan, the youngest of the Shchukin brothers and some fifteen years younger than Sergei, was a dandy and spendthrift, and quickly ran through his sizable fortune. Shchukin helped his brother out several times over the years, before finally cutting him off, suggesting that he sell some of his Old Masters.

When Ivan realized no more brotherly aid was forthcoming, he decided to put some of his canvases on the market. Most of his Old Masters, though, were found to be forgeries. Distraught and in debt, Ivan killed himself in the study of his home. Shchukin bought a tomb in Montmartre Cemetery and buried his brother. In a painful twist, not all of the suspect canvases turned out to be fake after all.

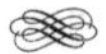

The mounting grief changed Shchukin. In a near frenzy, he bought bolder art, including sixteen of Gauguin's Tahitian paintings. Saturated South Seas colors throbbed off the crowded walls of his house. "The canvases hang side by side, touching, and at first you don't see where one ends, and the other begins," wrote the Russian critic Jakob Tugendhold of the Gauguins. "You have the impression that you are standing before a fresco or an iconostasis [the tall partition of religious paintings between the nave and sanctuary]. You see luxuriant, vibrant colours and you seem to hear the ring of solemn music in your ears, like a hymn to the joy of life." Among them was *La Femme du Roi*. After showing the painting to Leonid Pasternak (father of Boris, the Nobel Prize–winning author of *Doctor Zhivago*), Shchukin told his friend, "A madman painted it, and another madman bought it."

Shchukin also bought Picassos. When he was in Paris for the 1908 Salon d'Automne, Matisse took him to the Spaniard's Montmartre studio at the Bateau-Lavoir where he lived with Fernande Olivier and a massive dog named Fricka. Olivier, at least, was not impressed during the visit. In her journal that she later published, she erroneously wrote that he was "a very rich Russian Jew"—the Shchukins were Old Believers, Eastern Orthodox Christians who maintained certain religious practices from the seventeenth century—and went on to describe him in the crudest of terms: "He was short, with a large head, a pale, sallow complexion and features like a pig. He had a dreadful stutter and could only manage to explain himself slowly and with great difficulty, which was not only embarrassing but seemed to diminish his physical presence even further." As Olivier noted, "Picasso's painting was a revelation to the Russian."

Shchukin bought two canvases during the visit, including the early cubist piece *Woman with a Fan*. The Russian quickly became Picasso's most important collector, buying a staggering fifty more paintings by Picasso over the next six years, among them the monumental 1908 *Trois femmes* (*Three Women*) that capped Picasso's African period. Shchukin crowded these onto the walls of a single room in Moscow.

Matisse, though, remained the collector's most beloved artist. After finding the sign in Egypt, Shchukin continued to acquire as many of the Frenchman's brilliantly colored canvases as possible, buying much, even most, of Matisse's work from 1908 and 1909, and certainly all of the best of it.

In the spring of 1909, Shchukin commissioned large panels from Matisse to hang above the grand oak stairwell of his Moscow home. Shchukin had fallen for the austere and colorful *Bathers with a Turtle*, a painting of a trio of contorted nudes and a Mediterranean tortoise. The work had already been sold and Shchukin desired something in the same blue and green tones. "I see the painting all the time before my eyes," he wrote to Matisse from Moscow. "I can feel that freshness, that majesty of the ocean, that sense of sadness and melancholy."

The result was *Dance* and *Music* with primitive, ruddy-red figures that whirl and play on flat planes of vibrant blues and greens. "You are going to simplify painting," Gustave Moreau, his teacher at the Beaux-Arts in the 1890s, had told him. After years of patiently laying foundations, Matisse had finally realized that prediction in Shchukin's panels. The figures were deeply simplified yet remained highly expressive.

Dance is perhaps Matisse's best known and most widely reproduced work. Yet when exhibited at the Salon d'Automne of 1910 alongside *Music*, the two panels caused an outcry of hilarity. "The least that one can say is that all the madhouses possess similar pictures, but at least madness is an excuse," wrote one critic. Public opinion was virtually unanimous in condemning them as provocative, poisonous, deformed, naïve, and a failure.

Shchukin went every day to see the large, high-hanging panels and eventually lost heart and rejected them, using the excuse of the nude on *Music* because he had adopted two girls orphaned during the 1904–1905 Russo-Japanese War. It was the first time he had been swayed by public opinion. Shchukin asked Matisse for two smaller panels that could be hung in the bedroom for the same price.

The move shocked Matisse. For the past two years, he had worked on—or even thought about—little else. It was a particularly emotional time for the artist, as his father had just died. He had been in Munich looking at an important show of Islamic art when he received word of the death. He rushed home to Bohain for the funeral and had scarcely returned to Paris when he was given the unexpected news about the panels. Matisse's gallery offered Shchukin replacements from another painter, further infuriating the artist.

On the last day of the autumn Salon, Shchukin departed Paris for the long rail journey back to Moscow. By the time the train reached Poland two days later, he had changed his mind. From the station in Warsaw, Shchukin telegrammed Matisse: "Considered while traveling decided take your panels please send Dance and Music express delivery greetings."

The following day from Moscow, the Russian wrote a longer note to Matisse. "While traveling (two days and two nights) I pondered a great deal and came to feel ashamed of my weakness and lack of courage. One should not quit the field of battle without first attempting combat," Shchukin told the painter. "For this reason I have decided to exhibit your panels. People will make a clamor and laugh, but since I am convinced that you are on the right path, time will perhaps be on my side, and in the end I shall emerge victorious."

Once he had seen them loaded onto a train carriage headed to Moscow in early November 1910, Matisse boarded a southbound train for Spain. He arrived in Madrid twenty-six hours later. That night he couldn't sleep. Insomnia set in. Within a few weeks, undone by chronic sleeplessness and shattered nerves, he had a breakdown. "All artists have this particular makeup, that's what makes them artists, but with me it's a bit excessive," he wrote to his wife from Spain, aware of the precarious state of his own mind. "Perhaps that's what gives their quality to my pictures."

"Your panels have arrived and have been hung," Shchukin wrote in the meantime, neglecting to mention that a dab of red paint had been placed over the offending genitalia on *Music*. "The effect is not bad. Unfortunately, in the evening, by electric light, the blue changes greatly. It becomes almost murky, almost black. But overall I find the panels interesting and hope to come to love them some day."

His enthusiasm was tepid, but—importantly—he remained faithful. "I have complete confidence in you," he added. "The public is against you, but the future is yours."

When the young Russian artist Boris Ternovets, who would later be the director of the museum that held the panels, saw them hanging at Shchukin's house just after they had been installed, he was particularly stunned by *Dance*. "It is impossible to express in words the perfection, the convergence, the sheer accomplishment of this composition. The extended limbs, all of them extremely contorted, do not shock the eye in any way, so masterly is this painting's relentless inner tension. If you stand in half-darkness and close your eyes to slits, the impression you receive from these paintings is fantastic and fairylike; every detail is in motion, with an irresistible, wild energy." Ternovets captured the rare contemporaneous impression of seeing the mural for the first time above the stairwell of Shchukin's home, and, as a particularly astute critic, a near singular voice in grasping their greatness at the time. "This is the best thing that Matisse has ever done and perhaps the best thing done in the twentieth century to date. It is not a painting, because it has no form; nor is it a picture. It is monumental decorative art of a completely different sort, a thousand times more powerful and moving than anything that came before."

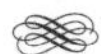

Misfortune continued to stalk Matisse's main collector. In January 1910, on the third anniversary of his wife's death, Shchukin's twenty-one-year-old son Grigori shot himself in the heart with a revolver at home. The boy, with a benign tumor at the base of his skull, deaf from birth, and racked by debilitating migraines that only his mother had known how to soothe, was certainly deeply distraught over her death.

It was Shchukin's second son to commit suicide, and some detractors went so far as to say that it was his degenerate taste in art—namely, the works by Matisse, Picasso, and others that he hung on the walls of the family home—that led the youngster to take his life. Shchukin, at the time in Paris recovering from a serious eye injury sustained on a third trip to Egypt, caught a train to Moscow to bury another son.

"A profoundly different Shchukin is borne from these tragedies," according to Shchukin's grandson, André-Marc Delocque-Fourcaud. His collection absorbed an increasing amount of his time, and in it he found solace. "Collecting becomes a sort of cure. His drawing room becomes his orangerie, where he says he can find a little rest, breathing all the beauty on the walls." He escaped into the colors of Western European modernists, especially those of Matisse. If the act of painting was a way for Matisse to forget, at least briefly, his deep anxiety, then contemplating the canvases was a way for Shchukin, at least briefly, to forget his losses and the Shakespearean level of family tragedies that beset him.

To all of the art-filled spaces in the house, Shchukin preferred the second-floor Matisse Room. It was, he said, an "aromatic hothouse, sometimes poisonous, but always filled with beautiful orchids."

17

Summer began to wane. Nights cooled, and then the days, too, as autumn blustered into Issy-les-Moulineaux. Plums, grapes, and the first apples were being sold from wooden boxes, the last of the melons. Flocks of mallards, teal, and pintails flew south in V-shaped formations over the Matisses' villa. Leaves in the broad canopy of trees within their walled garden began to change colors and drop as the Salon d'Automne approached.

The Salon was one of the two most important annual independent art exhibitions that had been established in response to the conservative and rather rigid official Academy-sponsored ones. The Salon des Indépendants, the exhibition of the Société des Artistes Indépendants held in springtime, was launched in 1884 and accepted the work of any artist wishing to participate. There was no jury (nor medals) but rather worked with committees. (Matisse was elected to the hanging committee in 1906.) It was important to artists and grew substantially over the years. The 1905 show included 4,269 works by 669 artists.

In 1903, an autumn rival opened in the basement of the Petit Palais. The Salon d'Automne was immediately popular and soon moved into the vast Grand Palais exhibition hall, which had been built between the Champs-Élysées and the Seine for the 1900 Exposition Universelle. The third edition, in the new location, had 1,625 works by 397 artists, and retrospectives of Renoir, Manet, and Ingres. Unlike its spring counterpart, the autumn Salon had a jury of liberal, artistic peers. Not everyone was fully impressed by the jurors, though, as an entry in Marcel Sembat's journal about the 1913 edition makes clear:

> This group convenes, raises umbrellas to vote, or runs through the corridors to judge the paintings. Matisse opens his eyes wide when he meets us: "I know not one!" Escaped schoolchildren: out of the Beaux-Arts! Flashy and suspicious rich kids [*rastaquouères*]!
>
> Their paintings? Filthy duds [*navets*]! And they judge! It is true that they have more taste when it comes to judging than talent when it comes to creating.
>
> And the boys' race to review! The paintings carried away at a trot, parading on wooden horses in front of the tired and sleepy faces of the jury!

Matisse routinely showed to both Salons. In 1904, he submitted fourteen paintings plus two clay sculptures cast in bronze to the Salon d'Automne, works done that summer while staying with Signac and his family in Saint-Tropez. At the Salon des Indépendants the following spring, he exhibited eight pieces, including the dazzling *Luxe, calme et volupté*, which Signac, perhaps rightly sensing some of his own pointillistic influence, bought. And to the notorious 1905 Salon d'Automne, where fauvism was launched, he sent eight oil paintings and two watercolors, all done within the preceding few months. While the 1907 Salon des Indépendants received only the powerful *Blue Nude* (*Memory of Biskra*) from Matisse, the number for the 1908 Salon d'Automne jumped to a staggering thirty works—eleven paintings, six drawings, and thirteen sculptures. (It was a busy year: he also published "Notes of a Painter.")

But in recent Salons, his submissions had significantly dropped off, and he had shown little to the last few editions. At the previous Salon d'Automne of 1911, he exhibited just two sketches.

Matisse had returned from Morocco too late for the 1912 spring Salon des Indépendants, held that year at Quai d'Orsay and again dominated by cubism. Anyhow, he was not yet ready to show his Tangier paintings. Perhaps adding to his hesitancy was the exhibition in New York organized by Alfred Stieglitz that had just closed, which had been first to be dedicated predominantly to Matisse's sculpture.

While known primarily as a painter, Matisse turned to sculpting in clay from time to time over his career, often when he was having difficulty with a canvas. Throughout his life he created around seventy sculptures, largely small, freestanding figures that he did in clay and then had cast in bronze. They were radical innovations in portraying the human figure and certainly completely different to his flattened, colorful paintings. "I did sculpture because what interested me in painting was to bring some order to my brain," he later told Pierre Courthion. "It was a change of means. I took to clay as a break from painting at the time I'd done absolutely everything I could in panting. Which means it was still about organizing. It was to put my sensations in order and look for a message that really suited me. When I found it in sculpture, I used it for painting. To come into possession of my own brain that was always the goal, a sort of hierarchy of all my sensations, so that I could reach a conclusion." But by that point in his career, his sculpture was having scant success. The exhibition in New York had been a complete failure. Critics attacked it. Not a single piece sold.

Now, for the 1912 Salon d'Automne at the Grand Palais opening on October 1, he again decided not to exhibit anything: not the portraits of Amido or Zorah, the Villa Brooks landscapes, or any of the remarkable new canvases painted in Issy, including the four goldfish paintings, the large works of his studio interior, or *The Conversation*. It was the second Salon in the row that he was going completely unrepresented, and further indication of Matisse's influence being swept aside.

While Shchukin had accepted the standing portrait of Amido on his visit that July, Matisse had been unable to fulfill Morozov's commissions for a pair of landscapes. Morozov had been waiting for these since early 1911. In the summer of that year, Matisse had written, "I have been thinking about your landscapes since I have been in Collioure and fear that I will not be able to do them this summer." He had promised to do so that winter, when he went to Tangier. He didn't, even though he told Morozov the following July that they were nearly done and he would see them displayed at the Salon d'Automne. That didn't happen. Matisse was presumably referring to ones done in Villa Brooks that, ultimately, he didn't feel were right.

Matisse procrastinated in writing to Morozov again with the news that he failed to complete the landscapes, waiting until he could offer some sort of new arrangement. On September 29, 1912, Matisse at last penned a brief note to Morozov from Issy-les-Moulineaux:

> Dear Sir.
>
> I am embarrassed to write to you that I have not been able to do your two landscapes; consequently they will not be at the Salon as I had written you, but I leave tomorrow for Morocco where I count on painting them.
>
> In presenting my excuses, I ask that you pay my respects to Madame and that you consider me your devoted
>
> Henri Matisse

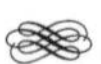

Matisse had decided to return to North Africa. He was leaving the following day for Marseille to catch a steamer to Morocco.

Tangier! He couldn't get it out of his mind. The light, the colors, and the softness of the landscape, the Islamic decorative arts that patterned the city, and Zorah, who, in her yellow robe, had spent the spring and summer staring down at Matisse from the wall of his studio. (He had finally sold *Zorah in Yellow* at the end of September to an Englishman.)

Tangier, though, had become highly unstable, and even dangerous to visit again.

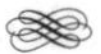

On April 17, 1912, just days after Matisse's departure from Tangier, Moroccan askars (soldiers) in the Fez garrison mutinied. Feeling betrayed by their sultan and displeased with their French officers, the askars rampaged across the city. "The insurgents marched through the streets carrying the severed heads of Frenchmen on pikes," Walter Harris reported in *The Times*, and displayed the mutilated bodies before the sultan's palace. It took the French two days of heavy artillery shelling to put down the uprising. By the time the French managed to get Fez back under control, some six hundred Moroccan Muslims had been killed, around sixty French, and in the mellah, which lay in ruins from shelling as the French had wrongly assumed that the Jewish community was supporting the uprising, over forty Moroccan Jews. The French used the riots as a pretext to tighten their rule.

In 1832, Eugène Delacroix had gone to North Africa as part of an official mission to expand French influence in the region, just two years after France had conquered part of Algeria. When Pierre Loti traveled to Morocco in 1889, France had taken control of Algeria as well as Tunisia, which became a French protectorate in 1881. By the time Matisse had left Morocco in 1912, North Africa's slow journey to colonial submission by France was virtually complete.

"The Treaty of Fez gave the French government authority but very little power," wrote historian C. R. Pennell. "The cup it had seized was very nearly empty. To take possession of Morocco, it would have to conquer it." Hubert Lyautey was appointed resident-general, a position he would hold for over a dozen years, earning him the moniker "The Maker of Morocco" and "French Empire Builder." With some seventy thousand troops under his command, Lyautey set about consolidating the territory, and bringing remaining pockets under French control. Once he had pacified Taza, a key pass where the Rif Mountains and the Middle Atlas range meet, the French controlled virtually all of North Africa west from the Libyan border with Tunisia to the Atlantic, at least along the wide coastal belt. In Morocco, areas dominated by Berbers would largely remain essentially unconquered for decades, including the Rif Mountains to the east of Tangier.

During the past summer, the French forced Sultan Abdelhafid to abdicate to his more pliable younger brother. He traveled to Rabat, where a ship was waiting to whisk him to France for a visit. On the quay before stepping aboard a French cruiser that would take him to Gibraltar, where he would transfer to a more comfortable P&O steamer for Marseille, he finally handed over signed documents. He had bargained until the last moment and secured an seventy additional 40,000 pounds.

Politically, things were changing fast in Morocco. In just over a month's time, France and Spain would sign a treaty establishing a Spanish zone of control in Morocco, granting it rule over a northern strip of the country, with Tétouan as its capital, and two swaths of land in the deep Saharan along the Atlantic coast.

Tangier was bestowed with exceptional international status in order to keep the Mediterranean open and guarantee safe passage of ships through the Strait. This wouldn't be fully implemented for a few years, and in the meantime, Tangier remained nominally under the control of the *naib*, a representative appointed by the new sultan, although in reality his powers were largely ceremonial.

Matisse planned on stopping just briefly in Morocco en route to Algeria and Tunisia. Both places had more established winter spots for the French and offered the type of sublime light that interested him. He certainly would have been enticed by André Gide's description of Tunisia in *The Immoralist* (1902): "The quality of the light here is not strength but abundance. The shade is still full of it. The air itself is like a luminous fluid in which everything is steeped; one bathes, one swims in it."

Along with the good light, North Africa would allow him to further assimilate the lessons and deeper understanding of Islamic art, and continue his unrelenting search for a way forward. He could do it again away from the distracting pull of cubism that continued to dominate and drive the Paris art world, and from futurism and orphism (an offshoot of cubism that focused on abstraction and bright colors) that were gaining traction.

Matisse set off for Tangier the day before the Salon d'Automne opened in the Grand Palais. Undoubtedly without regret, he would also miss the opening of a large cubist exhibition as well as the publication of the first major monograph on the movement. Matisse was isolating himself further from the Parisian avant-garde.

Leaving the drab northern light behind, he was returning to Morocco to pick up where he had left off with Zorah's portrait. Matisse's inspiring *hivernage* in Tangier had powered him through a prolific and successful six months at the easel in Issy. He had been reflecting and drawing on the stay since he had left Morocco six months before. Matisse was impatient to get back, and departed once summer had finished.

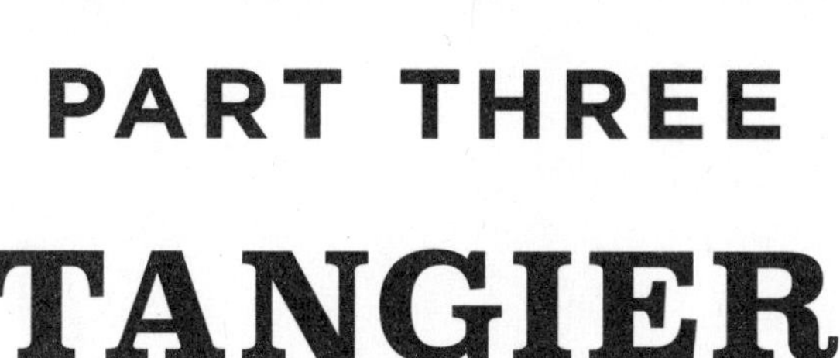

PART THREE

TANGIER

18

On October 6, 1912, Matisse sailed from Marseille to Tangier on the SS *Ophir*, catching one of Royal Rotterdam Lloyd's mailboats on her return run to Rotterdam from the Dutch East Indies.

Launched in 1904, the sturdy *Ophir* with modest tonnage would have a less illustrious career than her slightly newer and larger sister ship, the SS *Rindjani*, which Matisse had traveled out to Tangier the previous winter, or the even newer SS *Tambora*, which he had traveled on back to France in April. In the spring of 1918, the *Ophir* would be seized by the US government while in port in Pearl Harbor and turned over to the US Navy. On a transatlantic trip to Marseille, it caught fire and burned for three days before being grounded in shallows off Gibraltar on Armistice Day, November 11. Refloated and towed back to the United States, it sat unsold until being scrapped in 1922.

But when Matisse sailed on her to Tangier that early autumn, she was comfortable. Passengers took their generous meals in the dining room, wrote letters in the salon, played deck games, and spent hours on lounges watching the Mediterranean, with the long views of the sea broken by sightings of the Balearic Islands off the port side and the Spanish coast off the starboard.

Matisse was making the trip to Tangier alone this time. Amélie had stayed behind in Issy-les-Moulineaux. He was only planning on a short stay, just long enough to complete Morozov's two landscapes and another "souvenir" for Shchukin to accompany the portrait of Amido, and to finish a pair of canvases from the previous winter that he didn't consider done. He wouldn't be gone long. While the kids were away, staying with family in Ajaccio, Corsica, there was some work being done in the garden that Amélie would supervise.

Considering the important role that she played in his productivity and emotional stability during the previous winter in Morocco, it was a risky decision to go on his own. He had compared her leaving him in Tangier that past spring to a child being left behind by his mother.

As the steamer's pale-gray hull plowed toward the Moroccan coast, Matisse watched the horizon with trepidation in regards to the weather he might find upon arrival. His memories of how unhappy he had been in the first weeks of his previous stay remained vivid.

He was again arriving in Morocco under significant pressure to work well. Just before leaving, he renewed his contract with Galerie Bernheim-Jeune. He had signed his first one in 1909. Prices in the new contract were stipulated as the same as they had been for three years with no increase, and there was a new clause added that related to hard-to-sell pieces. It was clear that the gallery was losing confidence in Matisse's commercial prospects. It was yet more stress on Matisse to make strident gains during his stay.

The hundred-hour-long journey was thankfully uneventful, and the *Ophir* entered the calm Bay of Tangier on schedule on October 8. This time, Matisse was prepared for the hectic arrival of shouting boatmen and porters who ferried passengers and their luggage to the pier. The temperature was a pleasant 75°F (24°C) in the shade with just a slight breeze and no rain in the forecast when he stepped ashore.

It was the dry season, and the smell of the port was pungent. Landing two years before at a similar time, a British diplomat fresh out of Cambridge had marveled at the olfactory assault heading from the harbor up through the old city on a hired mule: "My nostrils were assailed by a stench so powerful and nauseating as almost to be possessed of beauty."

Matisse paid his pier dues, passed through the thick-walled customs building, and, with his luggage on a mule, walked up the steep ramp embedded with pebbles for traction to the Bab al-Masra gate and entered the noisy, cosmopolitan old city. At the green-roofed Grand Mosque—built over the Portuguese cathedral, itself atop an earlier mosque constructed over a fifth-century church on the site of a Roman temple dedicated to the cult of Hercules—he turned and made his way up the crowded, narrow street that crossed the breadth of the medina, out through the Bab al-Fahs gate, and up to the Hôtel Villa de France, where the manager, Mademoiselle Davin, welcomed him back. Matisse climbed the stairs to the third floor and followed the porter to *chambre* 35, the same corner room he had stayed the previous winter.

Pushing open the tall slatted wooden shutters, Matisse took in the changes. Rather than inundated by rain as in his previous arrival, the north of Morocco was parched by merciless sun. The deep greens that overwhelmed him had vanished, and in the hills around the city he would find an unfamiliar and unexpected landscape. "All yellow, the earth tawny colored, the grass burned up by the summer sun," he later recalled.

There was drought. People in the countryside were in despair. The dry spell would continue without respite throughout autumn. "Everyone is desperate here because the planting is going to fail because of the drought. Me, inside, I rejoice," the driven, self-absorbed, and brutally honest Matisse would write to his daughter six weeks later on November 21, "because it is the perfect weather for my work."

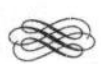

Matisse opened his luggage. Along with his clothes, collars, and vests, writing paper and pens, books (including a Maurice Leblanc adventure of the gentleman thief and master of disguise Arsène Lupin and a philosophical work by Henri Bergson), some neatly folded fabrics from his "working library," and carefully packed painting materials, he had brought a pair of unfinished canvases from the previous winter in Tangier.

One of the paintings was *Acanthus*, which he had labored over for far longer than any other work during his stay and caused him so much grief. During the past months in his Issy-les-Moulineaux studio, he had looked at the purple and pink landscape and told those who saw it, "It's not like that; it's better than that. You'll see next year, when I rework it."

Now back in Tangier, Matisse made arrangements to paint again in Villa Brooks. He returned to the gardens with the canvas and set up his easel in the same spot he had the previous stay. The scene was different. It seemed, he later recalled, "smaller." The verdant vegetation had withered.

This didn't completely matter, as he was not trying to capture an impression of a single moment, or even its natural, literal colors.

But when he saw *Acanthus* before its subject again, Matisse changed his opinion about its status. "Everything I thought lacking in my canvas is there—and it isn't in the landscape at all!"

He put away the painting, packed up his materials, and went back to the hotel. He wouldn't return with his easel again to Villa Brooks.

In his room at the Villa de France, Matisse *did* work on the other painting he had brought with him back to Tangier, though. He placed *Landscape Viewed from a Window* on his easel in front of the room's side window. It was nearly done. Looking north out over the kasbah, he washed the white of the distant citadel with pink to mellow its contrast against the piney greens and lush blues.

Such blues! While Tangier is known as *la ville blanche* (the white city), pulsating blues are everywhere: the sky, the sea, certain walls in the kasbah, patio doors in courtyards, patterns on hand-painted tiles, women's gowns hanging in the market. Blue is the city's signature color, and became the signature color of Matisse's Tangier work just as red was a hallmark of his early fauve paintings done in Collioure. It was the color in Morocco that he managed to wring the most sensations and force.

"So what could be called the 'Morocco of Matisse' is an inexhaustible source of Mediterranean colors dominated by a subtle, graceful, extreme, and changing blue," wrote Ben Jelloun, the first Moroccan to win the Prix Goncourt, France's top literary award. "It's a blue of dreams, the one that invades the sky just after the storm, a blue washed away from the suspicion of doubt. It is the reflection of the sea in the sky, a limpid screen on which the signs of such a long wait will be imprinted, a modest veil resting on a gaze coming from afar. Matisse blue is a performance of light, winter in Tangier." It would be *that* blue that completely overwhelms *Landscape Viewed from a Window* and, ultimately, most mark Matisse's Tangier canvases.

And it is the blue that, a dozen years later, Joan Miró, another painter bewitched by the color, would generously dab in a patch on an empty primed canvas and write, in studied cursive between school primer-like pencil lines, *ceci est la couleur de mes rêves*—"this is the color of my dreams." Blue was the color of Matisse's Moroccan dreams.

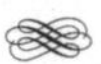

In deciding that *Acanthus* needed nothing else and completing *Landscape Viewed from a Window*, Matisse had closed the work from his previous stay. He was ready to move on to something new.

As the heat shimmered up from the parched landscape, and golden dust hung in the languid air, he clamped a clean canvas onto the easel, shifted the angle of the view slightly to catch more of the sea, and made a remarkably different version of the window view from his corner room.

Matisse outlined the scene in *Open Window at Tangier* with grayish-brown paint, and then quickly brushed in bands of color: patches of deep, orange-infused mustard and purple-tinted iris blue fill the sky; the trees and medina rooftops blend together in large brushstrokes of oranges and greens and yellows. St. Andrew's Church, which had been a key focal point of the previous window view, gets reduced to an unrecognizable roof line of emerald green. Today that green is generally taken as foliage, as looking now over the same view from *chambre* 35 all but the church tower is shrouded in trees. But photographs from 1912—as well as Matisse's wiry sketches—show that the greenery had not yet enveloped the building and the church stands quite bare on its plot with cypress saplings just beginning to grow along the fence.

Rather than the sharp contrasts of blues, greens, and white of the other window view, this one shifted to a harmony of oranges, yellows, and greens with some blues. The dusty, golden light is there, the heat, the sea pale blue under the unrelenting sun. Matisse worked quickly, with hurried, energetic brushstrokes that left drops of paint splattered on the canvas.

As in the earlier view, vases sit in the foreground, drawing the viewer back into the room. There are four vases, though Matisse only filled one of the pots in with color. The blossoms are all quickly brushed with thinned paint, three in a darkened blue and one in red with hints of candied crimson. The frame of the curtain and windows have disappeared, turning the picture itself into a window.

The canvas was more abstract than anything Matisse had done up to that point. He was building in a new direction; his style was evolving. *Open Window at Tangier* is an intimation of what was to come.

What Matisse was keen to do was to paint Zorah again. As soon as he had landed in Tangier, he began asking around for her. Mademoiselle Davin was of no help in locating her, nor was Amido. No one had seen her. The girl had disappeared.

19

Matisse settled quickly into a routine. He sketched in the morning and painted in the afternoon. After finishing, he liked to take a horse for a ride through the peninsula's pine-forested hills toward the squat Cape Spartel lighthouse. If the tide was low, he could also ride along the beach. Occasionally he went to see a film at Tangier's only cinema, the Tivoli Theatre, which had showings at 9:00 P.M. on Tuesdays, Thursdays, and Saturdays, and 5:00 P.M. matinees on Thursdays, Saturdays, and Sundays. If Matisse walked down to the Petit Socco in the medina, he might find Walter Harris holding court on a café terrace (or maybe playing the café's piano inside). At night, he read, slicing opening the pages of his novel as he followed the capers of Arsène Lapin, and retired to bed early. "Don't imagine there's anything madly exciting going on here, apart from work," Matisse wrote to Amélie in one of his frequent updates. He told his children staying with family in Corsica: "Here, it's always the same. Apart from my canvases, one meal follows another, one night after the next . . ."

Tangier had no museums or galleries. The Gran Teatro Cervantes was still under construction and would open within a year and draw the likes of the great Italian tenor Enrico Caruso. The French community was only just growing (the Lycée Renault would also soon open). Horse racing down on the beach took place in spring and summer. As a Christian, Matisse couldn't go inside the mosques, marabouts, or shrines, and as an outsider—a British diplomat posted to Tangier that year found it "cliquey and socially oppressive"—the city's great houses, with mosaics and exquisite Moorish design work, were largely closed to him.

The English guidebook *Mediterranean Winter Resorts* published the following winter noted the lack of entertainment options in its "Amusements" entry:

> Visitors do not, of course, expect to find—and would probably be disgusted if they did—in Tangier the entertainments and amusements of an ordinary European watering-place—bands, theatres, promenades, cafés, etc. The chief charm of a winter residence at Tangier is, next to its delicious climate, the opportunity it gives of seeing Moorish manners and customs, and Oriental life in all its varied and most interesting aspects. Even the discomforts of Tangier as a residence—roughly-paved alleys for streets, no roads, no means of conveyance except mules and donkeys, no street lamps, and no drains—are readily forgiven by the artist and the lover of the picturesque, as showing that no attempt has been made to modernise the town. This paragraph, then, somewhat resembles the chapter of the conscientious historian of Iceland on the snakes of that island—"There are no snakes in Iceland."

Matisse had not come to Tangier for a winter season of social calls, evenings at the casino, and dancing by the bandstand. He had come to work. So this suited him: the steady rhythm of meals, sketching, and painting sessions that made up his days, studied, uninterrupted concentration on his art away from cubism, critics, Salons, and snipping Picassoites.

In Tangier, Matisse was free to push ahead with his work with little distraction from the art world.

While the ordinary-looking Matisse would not have drawn scrutiny heading to the dining room after the dinner bell sounded at the Hôtel Villa de France, his fellow guests would have found his Tangier canvases utterly shocking. Even though he had toned down the fierce colors of his fauvist period, he was still creating wildly unconventional paintings rejected by not just general society or even the more tolerant art establishment, but even many of his fellow avant-garde artists. There was nothing typical in them at all. Upon seeing the jarringly colored works, most other artists considered Matisse quite literally mad. Even Gertrude Stein was baffled.

Indeed, many of the clients in the hotel would have been startled to find the creator of such reactionary paintings to be the neatly dressed, mild-manner bespectacled gentleman sipping mineral water in the dining room or studiously admiring the flowers in the garden.

The outward bourgeois respectability of Matisse compared to the paintings he produced—that is, the man versus his art—was an unexpected and contradictory juxtaposition. As the American painter and journalist Clara MacChesney wrote in *The New York Times Magazine* after visiting him that following summer at his home and studio in Issy-les-Moulineaux: "M. Matisse himself was a great surprise, for I found not a long-haired, slovenly dressed, eccentric man, as I had imagined, but a fresh, healthy, robust blond gentleman, who looked even more German than French, and whose simple and unaffected cordiality put me directly at ease." Matisse was aware of the misleading preconceived notions that his paintings gave off about him. "Oh, do tell the American people that I am a normal man," Matisse pleaded with MacChesney, "that I am a devoted husband and father, that I have three fine children, that I go to the theatre, ride horseback, have a comfortable home, a fine garden that I love, flowers, etc., just like any man." The style of his paintings, he stressed, were not a reflection of his personality.

Marcel Sembat captured such preconceptions the following year in the most extended essay on the artist up to that point. Matisse aroused reactions that ranged from scandal-inducing to pity to envy, Sembat wrote, and nearly everything that he heard said about his friend was wrong. "Stripped of the legend, the real Henri Matisse, the man who comes to the gate in gardener's gear when you ring the bell in Clamart, the flesh-and-blood Matisse, is no monster or raving madman, no hoodlum or phony, and no skilled manipulator of snobs and scandals either," Sembat wrote. "Just the opposite. A fair-haired gentleman of slow, deliberate speech, he has a serious and reflective air."

His fellow guests at the Hôtel Villa de France, as well, might have even complained to the management about the chemical odors of turpentine and white spirits that emanated from *chambre* 35 and lingered in the hallway. Most were neither artists nor bohemians, but largely of a professional (or clergy) class, and not expecting to be staying in an establishment where a corner room on the third floor doubled as a painting studio for some of the most progressive works being painted by an artist anywhere. The manageress, though, would have not been too sympathetic to any complaints, as she helped in securing models for Matisse and had even given him a place on the hotel grounds the previous winter to paint Zorah in secret.

The gated grounds of the Hôtel Villa de France helped Matisse sustain his concentration and certain level of calm.

Tangier was still a city of unpaved streets and open sewers, and leaving the hotel meant an assault on his senses and his nerves. In the markets, Matisse encountered beggars with open sores, pools of blood from recently butchered animals being dismembered, and bones, filth, and excrement ground into the dirt. The physical act of walking around Tangier was not easy. As a British guidebook from the time put it, "There are no streets—as we understand the word—in the town. In fact, [famous French tightrope walker and acrobat Charles] Blondin is said to have remarked that walking on a tight-rope was easier work." Donkeys and mules carrying loads were hurried through the streets, forcing Matisse to duck suddenly into cubbyholes to let them squeeze pass.

Every trip he took to a café or the French *poste* in the Petit Socco, to the money-changer stalls on rue des Siaghins, or even to sketch in the kasbah, meant fending off attention from "touts and alleged guides, who know a dozen words of as many languages," according to one traveler the previous year. "You are badgered to buy picture post cards; vile imitation Moorish articles are hawked—scarves, shawls, fake-jewelry, amber beads, daggers, pistols, powder-horns, ornate but useless Moorish arms." Tourists were routinely fleeced in their shopping. This was something to be expected, even warranted, according to the then-acting American consul. "Perhaps the Moor and Jew are justified in looking upon the visitor to Morocco as legitimate plucking. I know that they consider all foreigners as scum of an unhallowed earth, without brains and without respect for their gods, with nothing more than money to make up for the lack of all these things. So, mayhap, we should be looked upon as fish entering the net."

With his portable easel and paint set, and a close eye on the uneven streets he trod, Matisse headed to the kasbah. He entered the gate and followed a series of narrow, cobbled alleys past the domed marabout he had painted the previous winter, the Kasbah Mosque, and the sultan's palace, Dar al-Makhzen.

The stout, meandering palace was built in the early 1700s by Pasha Ahmed Ben Ali al-Rifi, whose father had been commander of the Sharifian army that drove the British from Tangier in 1684 and was responsible for rebuilding the city's fortifications that the occupiers had destroyed before departing. After being forced to abdicate that previous summer of 1912, Sultan Abdelhafid went to France and then returned to Tangier, having negotiated the right to reside in the city. With his retinue of 168 people, he took over the seventeenth-century Dar al-Makhzen until a new palace could be built for him, and was living there by the time Matisse returned to Tangier. (The sultan would never inhabit the new palace, though. With the onset of World War I, the French exiled him to Spain and canceled his stipend for his German sympathies. Italian authorities acquired the property in 1927. Today it is home to, among other things, the Italian club and its popular Casa d'Italia restaurant.)

Adjoining the palace was the men's and women's prisons. Visitors could get permission to see the male prisoners engaged in basketmaking, although the sight of the half-starved men huddled in the cells was far from pleasant. Built in the 1700s, the prison operated until the 1970s. When Matisse was in Tangier, it was a popular tourist attraction recommended in the guidebooks.

Situated diagonally from the palace on the broad square stood a local court, where in the morning a *cadi* could be seen through the marble columns of the façade sitting on a rush mat administering justice.

But, as with the previous winter, Matisse had no interest in such picturesque scenes and kept walking.

Just beyond these government buildings was the Bab al-Assa gate, the southern portal of the kasbah, where a steep footpath descended down into the dense medina. From a platform at the top of the steps, Matisse had made numerous sketches and painted *View of the Bay of Tangier* the previous winter. This time he set up his easel inside the arch to capture the gate itself. It is another window view but an eastern one this time, with the curving horseshoe arch—a marker for the Islamic world—framing the traditional old city.

In *The Kasbah Gate* (or *Entrance to the Kasbah*), the blue keyhole entryway itself dominates the picture, with a series of echoing curves showing the ancient wall's thickness (see figure 12). A bright, rose-red path invitingly leads the viewer's eye through it and into the medina of flat roofs, sun-whitened walls, flowers, and hashed, green trellis topped with abundant blooming roses.

The city's blue shadows dominate the picture. With the sunlight parching the city, Tangier is inert with midday drowsiness. The overall mood is calm. A shadowy figure—a *bowaab*, or watchman, who was responsible for opening the tall wooden gate doors in the morning, closing them in the evening, and keeping an eye on comings and goings between—crouches quietly inside the arch. Rendered only by an outline of sketchy brushstrokes, the man dissolves into the wall.

Assa literally means "stick," and Bab al-Assa can be translated as the Gate of Whipping (or Beatings, Lashes, or even Blows), named for the sultan's soldiers striking prisoners as they passed through it en route to the prison. When Matisse was there, howls and shouts could still be heard as guards left "broad white stripes like the bars of a prison" on the backs of passing criminals. Matisse's painting of the gate belies its name and reputation, and exudes nothing but calming peace.

Done on the same size canvas as *Landscape Viewed from a Window*, the stunning, lushly abstract work was as mysterious and evocative as anything he had painted.

20

Matisse wanted to paint figures, not landscapes or urbanscapes. Specifically, he wanted to paint Zorah, who could not be found.

While walking through the kasbah a week or so after arriving back in Tangier, he came upon an unveiled woman named Fatma lounging in a doorway, "stretched out like a panther," he told his wife in one of his daily updates. With Amido's aid, he arranged for her to sit for him.

Tangier's Muslim population was an ethnic mix of Berbers, Arabs, Moors that had been expelled from Spain, and sub-Saharan Africans originally brought as slaves or descendants of those captured in battles and serving in the sultan's private army. Matisse called Fatma a *mulâtresse* (mulatto), perhaps from the union with a southern slave, but he also referred to her in letters as a *négresse* and a *mauresque*, or Moorish.

Matisse painted *Fatma, the Mulatto Woman* as a companion piece to *The Moroccan Amido* for Sergei Shchukin on a narrow, mirror-sized canvas nearly five feet high and two feet wide (146 x 61 cm). To Georgette Agutte, on October 30, he wrote of the window landscape painting, work on *The Kasbah Gate*, and his portrait of Fatma, seemingly done, as with Zorah the previous year, in a hidden room at the Hôtel Villa de France arranged by the manager. He had started a new portrait of a "Moorish" woman, he told her, but was struggling with it. "When I thought I had finished, I brought the painting home, and haven't had the courage to turn it around for fear of disappointment," he wrote to Camoin. "It is a decorative canvas that I am required to do, and I think that will be it, but I would have wanted more." For a week he left it facing the wall.

Eventually Matisse did turn the canvas around and resume work on it. "I have just finished my afternoon session with the Negress, which was the fourth, and it's going well so far," he wrote to his wife a dozen days later. "I haven't yet started a canvas in the mornings, I make drawings that tire me less to save myself for the afternoon session because my canvas of the Negress interests me so much and I would like to give myself entirely to it. Work with her is not very convenient, and if Hamido [Amido] were not always there, I would really have a problem because she does not speak a word of French. She is always tired, she always wants money. I have already advanced her four sessions, and this afternoon she wanted 10 francs more. I gave her only 5, because she threatened not to come again, which would have been a problem because the canvas is going so well." The woman even stood him up, costing him a work session. There were ten good days of weather predicted, he told his wife. "I will take advantage of it to finish my Negress as I may return [home] after that."

He managed to finish the portrait of Fatma. With more paint, more colors, and more texture than the earlier one of Amido, it is sumptuous. Wearing a brilliant pale turquoise kaftan patterned with white flowers, she stands full length in three-quarter profile with one hand resting on a table and the other tucked at the hip into a wide waistband sash that appears either embroidered or studded with colorful beads. Her head is cropped just above the forehead at the top of the canvas, as is most of her slippered left foot at the bottom. Cocking her head, she looks away in a haughty, disinterested, even defiant gesture. A gauzy veil—its transparency conjured by painting a turquoise glaze over her copper-colored skin—is pushed back away from her face, revealing a brow captured with a straight line and dark dashes for eyes.

Fatma's face itself is sketchily drawn in comparison to the splendid details of her magnificent gown, which is the focus, even real subject, of the picture. Against a teal background of turquoise cooled with a touch of black, the gown radiates a dazzling glow that Matisse achieved by layering washes and glazes over the primed canvas. He scumbled the gown with white and added white flowers for decoration. Matisse heavily worked the pale gold and blue decoration running down the center of the chest, and dashed the sash around her waist with blue, red, and black lines.

Ultimately, there is something enigmatic about her portrait. Fatima's body faces the observer, but she turns her head and feet to the side and appears like a figure from ancient Egypt, a Persian miniature, or a fifteenth-century Russian icon.

While painting Fatma, Matisse received a new commission from Agutte and her husband, Marcel Sembat. They had bought the small *View of the Bay of Tangier* from Galerie Bernheim-Jeune, and after seeing *Zorah in Yellow* hanging in Matisse's studio that summer, desperately wanted, she told him in an October 28 letter, "*une petite marocaine*." "Is it indiscreet to ask you to do something for us? a very small canvas, I think, No. 6, does not fit into the recordings of Bernheim? or so No. 5, but we desperately want a little Moroccan girl, like the naturally posing woman in yellow, it's an order, I would never dare tell you that, but I can write it, if you could tell us make this little canvas for 1000 f—eh, is it possible?" she wrote in a single, rushed sentence. "That would be very, very nice. I said, I won't speak of it again. It's up to you to do as you wish."

Matisse agreed. While Agutte's letter crossed in the mail with his letter complaining about Fatma, who would have to do as a model for lack of options. "We are very happy that you work for us," Agutte responded when he agreed, "with such joy we will see this little Moroccan lady when you return!" Thrilled with the prospect, she was keen to know more details, as the underlining in her letter emphasizes. "Write, <u>send me the sketch</u>

with the color tones of our little painting." Matisse sent a sketch that indicated the color scheme.

Keeping with the scale of the commission, Matisse used a small canvas not much larger than a sheet of letter paper (13¾ x 10½ in; 35.5 x 27.5 cm). Wearing a vibrant, glimmering red kaftan with a blouse heavily embroidered in golds, turquoise, browns, and black, Fatma sits cross-legged in a brilliant blue niche studded with large red dots. While she has a somewhat impatient expression, the informal pose lacks any tension or awkwardness.

If, in the previous standing portrait, Fatma's features are barely filled in, here they border on caricature, with a broad nose, saucer eyes of black smudges, and thick lips. Unlike the preceding canvas where Fatima is specifically named, in this one she is generic. Matisse titled it *La Petit mulâtresse* (*The Small Mulatto Woman*; see figure 13).

"Her condition [as the likely daughter of a slave] did not allow her to wear such beautiful clothes," wrote Ben Jelloun of Fatma. "That's probably why you paid particular attention to the background: a deep blue with red stars as if the sky was populated that night with so many dreams and angels. Light is everywhere." The red spots hold the painting together. "If we remove them, the canvas falls. If the number is reduced, the young woman will feel abandoned. It's like in a sentence or rather in a poem: if you remove a word or two from a verse, the whole poem gets lost. . . . The eighteen red spots (dots, crushed roses, large nailheads, or traces of something we know nothing about) are what make this portrait come alive."

Matisse finished the painting by the end of November, and immediately sent it off to his friends in France. "The painting is installed in our room, near the mirror, symmetrical with [the painting of] Marguerite, and it looks wonderful," Sembat wrote on Chambre des Députés stationery, referring to the 1906 portrait of Matisse's daughter, *Marguerite Reading*. "We are simply delighted, and we thank you for offering us this beautiful painting at a friendly price, at a price affordable for us, even though we know very well that Bernheim would have easily paid you double for it. I want to tell you that we are not unaware of this sacrifice and that we are grateful for it." A few weeks later, Agutte wrote to Matisse, telling him how good the portrait looked in their room next to the fireplace. Rodin was coming to lunch that week and she would take him upstairs to see the painting, she promised, and would report back truthfully with the august sculptor's opinion.

Despite its small size, the canvas exudes unusually potent force. From across the large gallery at the riverside Musée de Grenoble where it hangs today, the vibrant colors draw immediate attention to it. Surrounded in a plain, thick gold frame, Fatma floats in undefined space, with just enough shading in the blue to give it a hint of dimensional depth, like a doll presented in a deep-blue box that has been decorated with the red dots to mimic the color of the splendid robe.

For its original owners, Fatma's stature was far from doll-size. "It is in an old Louis XIII frame in very faded old gold that my wife found for her," Sembat told Matisse. Dating from the seventeenth century, these frames were characterized by the carved and gilded decorative floral patterns that ran along them. It was a fitting mount. "She imposes herself completely as a sovereign." A sovereign, indeed, but a deposed one, hanging far from her Moroccan home on a bedroom wall outside Paris.

To France, the picture carried traits of the artistic culture from which she came. Fatma's portrait shows the strong influence of Islamic art that was becoming increasingly manifest on Matisse's easel. With the rich ornamentation of her clothes, her position sitting as if on a shelf, the halo of red dots around her that accentuate the decorative character of the painting, and even the small size of the canvas, it has been compared to a vase, a trinket, and decorative porcelain tile, even a Persian miniature.

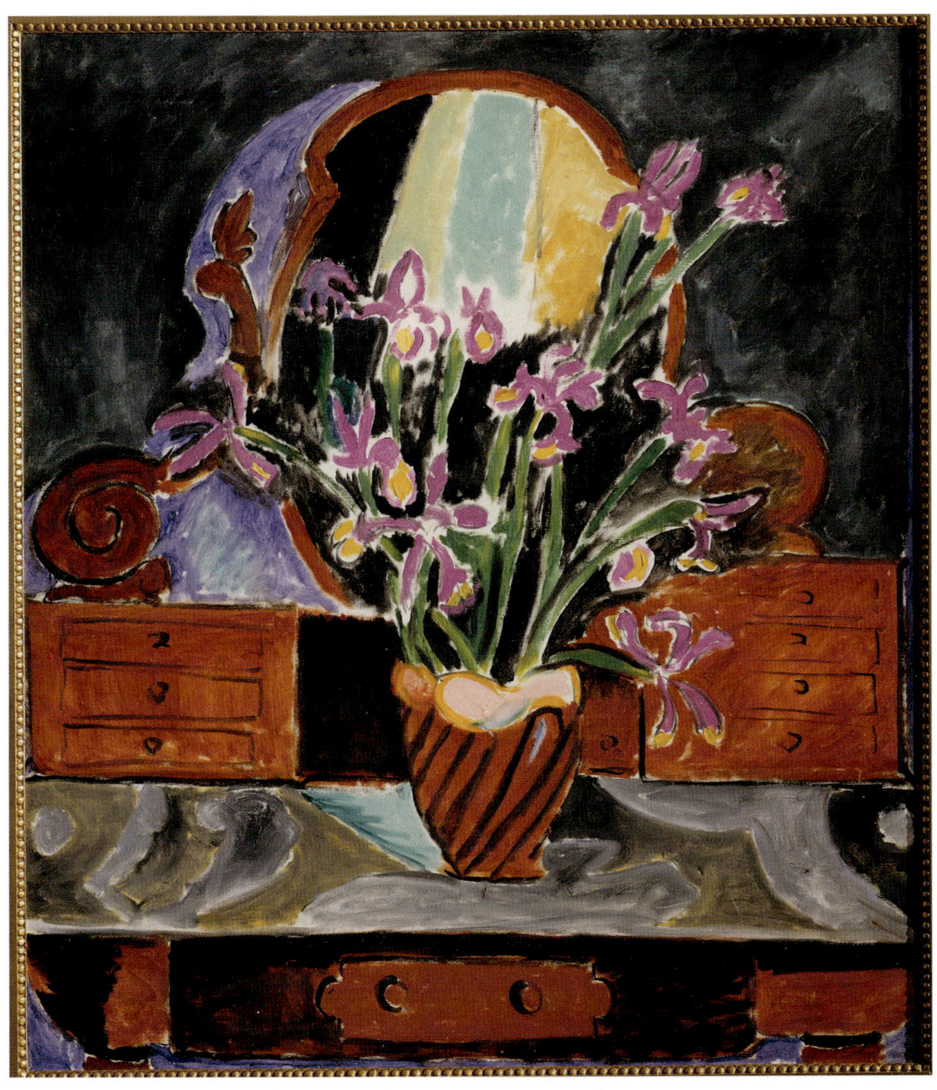

Figure 1. Henri Matisse, *Vase with Irises*, 1912.

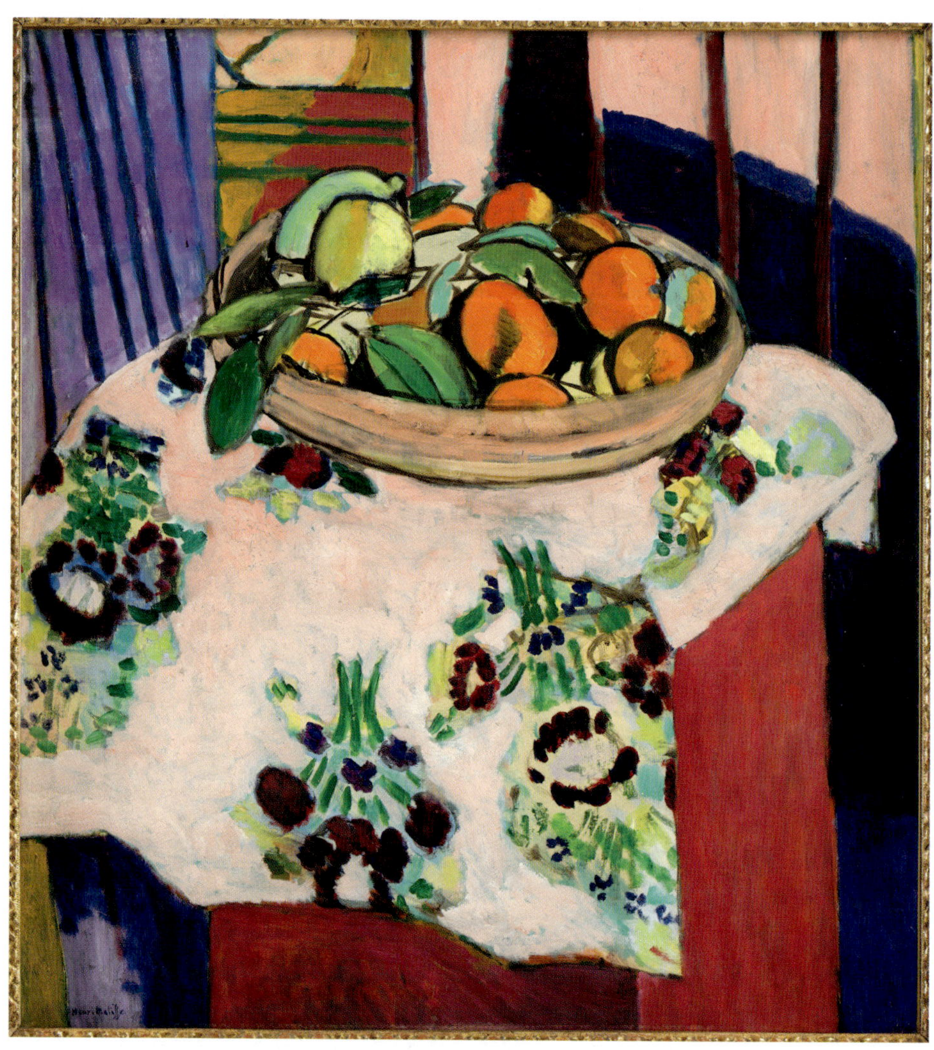

Figure 2. Henri Matisse, *Basket with Oranges*, 1912

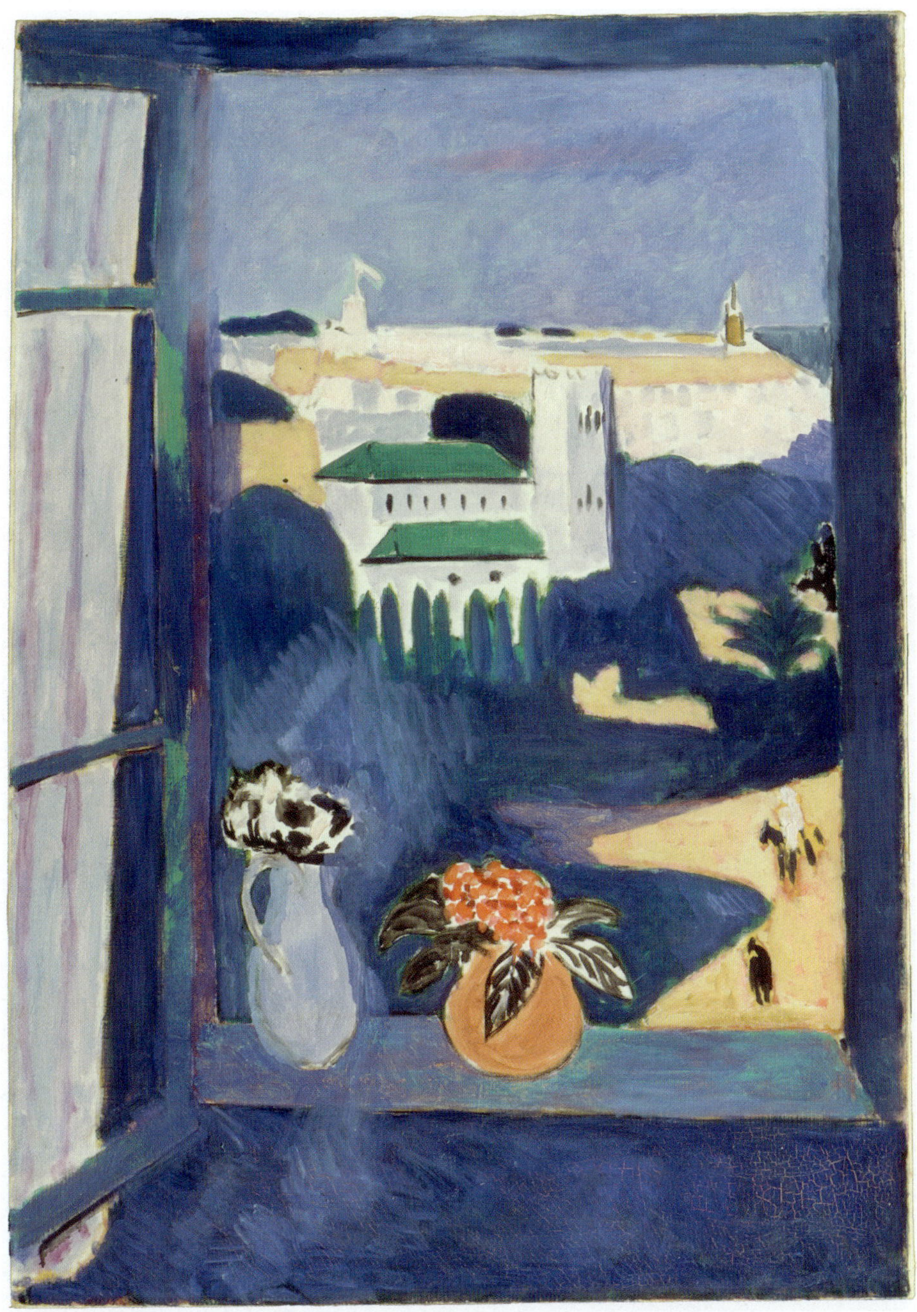

Figure 3. Henri Matisse, *Landscape Viewed from a Window*, 1912

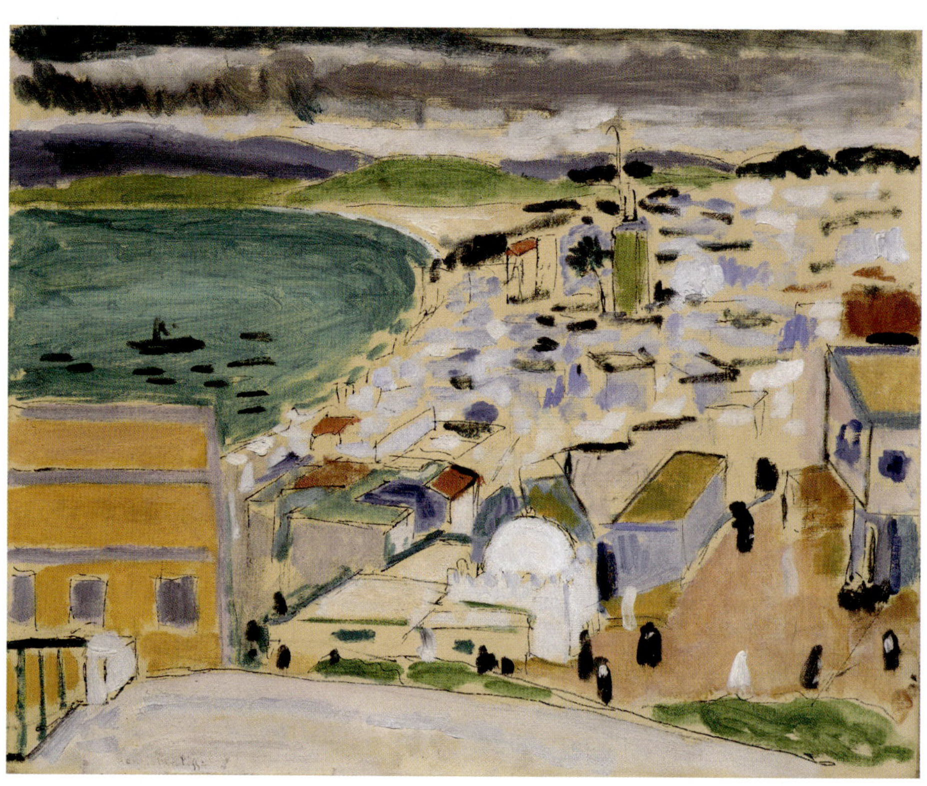

Figure 4. Henri Matisse, *View of the Bay of Tangier*, 1912

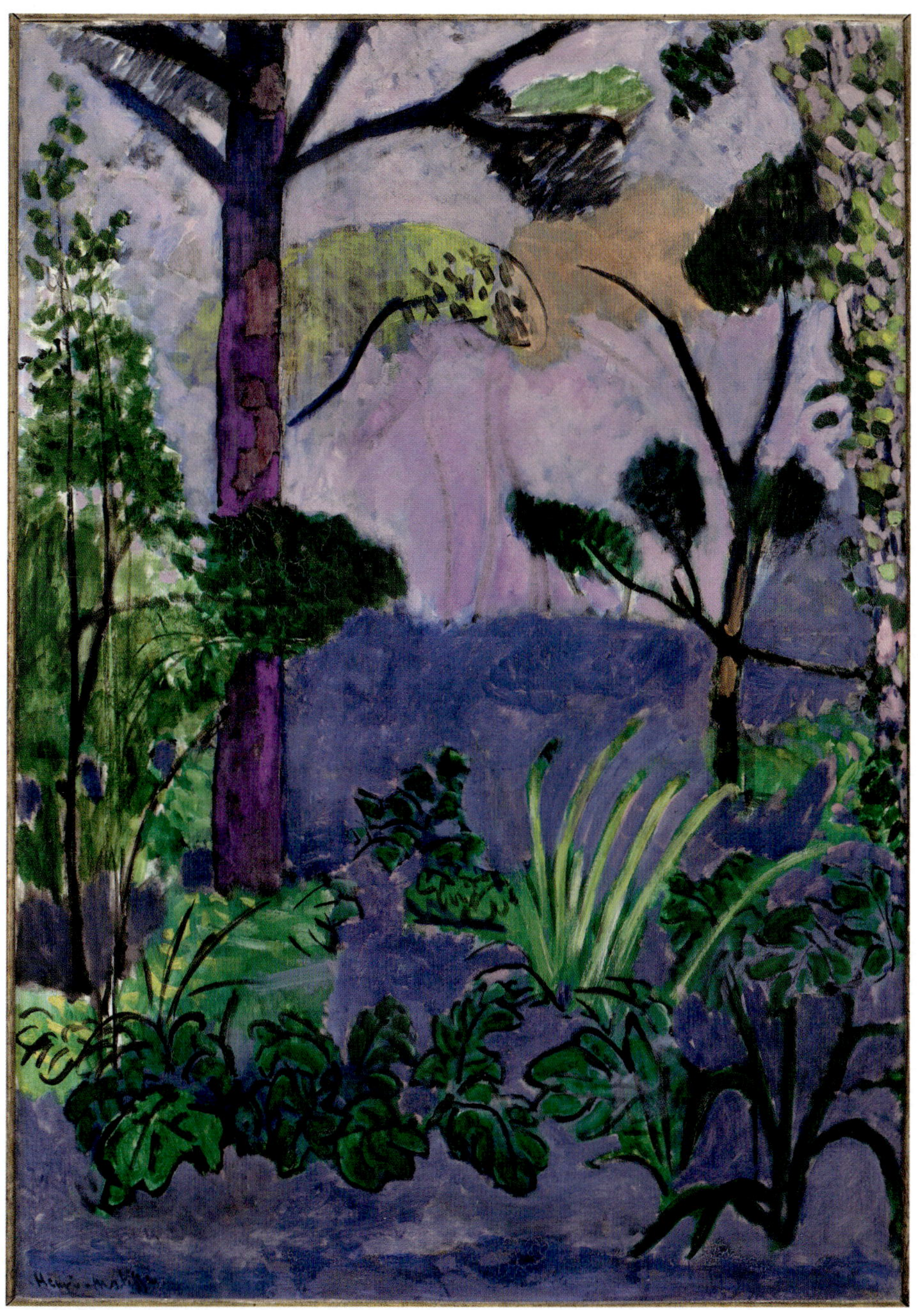

Figure 5. Henri Matisse, *Moroccan Landscape (Acanthus)*, 1912

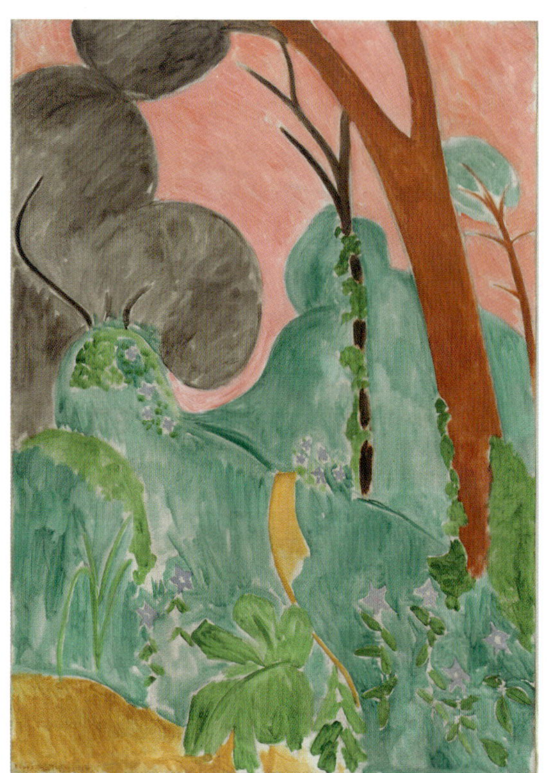

Figure 6. Henri Matisse, *Periwinkles (Moroccan Garden)*, 1912

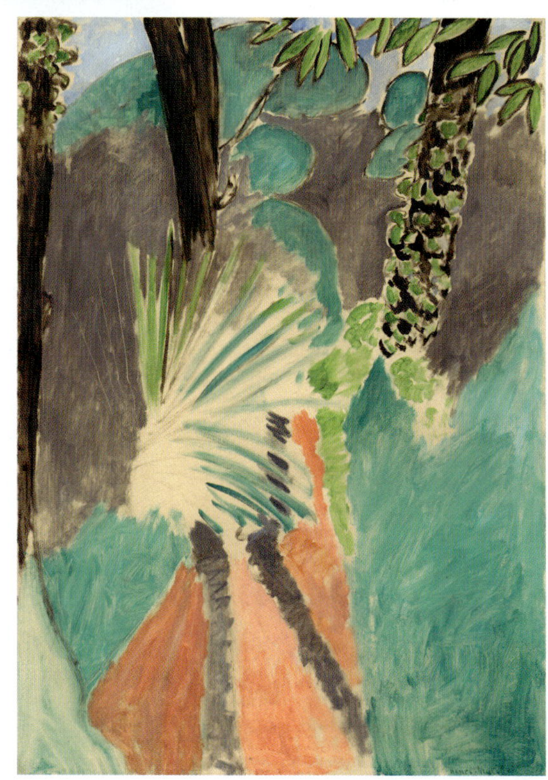

Figure 7. Henri Matisse, *Palm Leaf, Tangier*, 1912

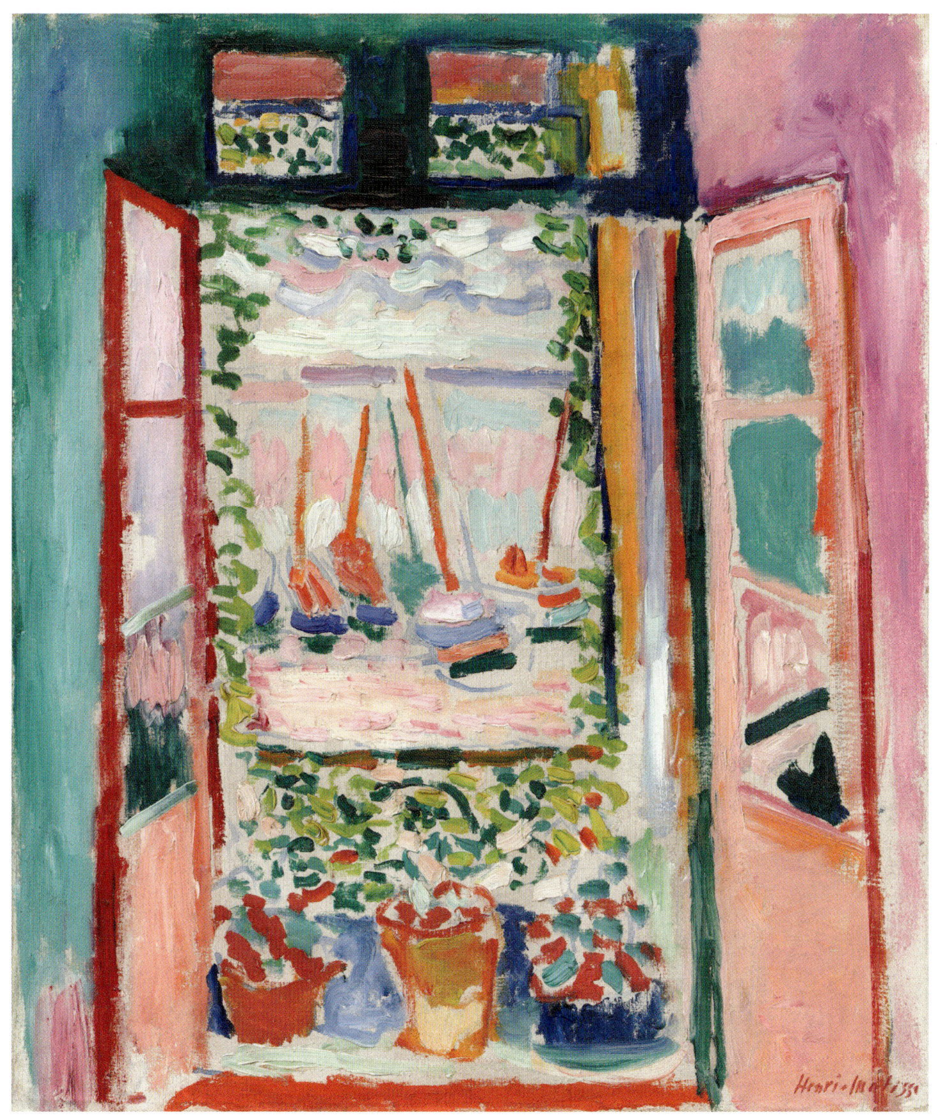

Figure 8. Henri Matisse, *Open Window, Collioure*, 1905

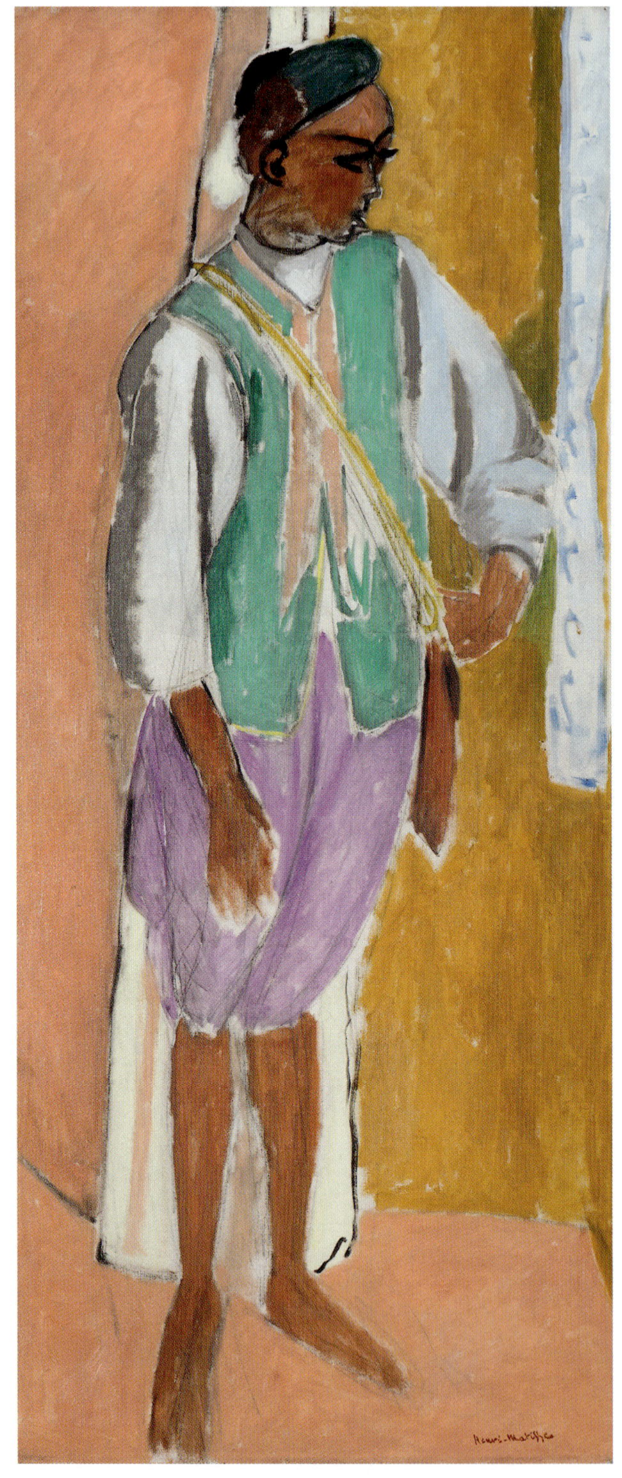

Figure 9. Henri Matisse, *Moroccan Amido*, 1912

21

"J'ai toujours beaucoup aimé l'Orient, vers lequel je suis sans cesse attiré," Matisse once declared. ("I have always loved the Orient, to which I am constantly drawn.") Another time, he said: *"La révélation m'est donc venue de l'Orient."* ("The revelation therefore came to me from the Orient.")

But in these much-quoted phrases, Matisse didn't so much mean that place to the east and south of Europe that the now-outdated term referred to as the region's art and artistic traditions.

Matisse's passionate interest in Islamic art began at the turn of the twentieth century when, as a budding, thirty-year-old painter, he visited the Paris Exposition Universelle of 1900, with its Turkish and Persian pavilions and Coptic art exhibition, and then the important 1903 exhibition of Islamic art at the Musée des Arts Décoratifs. Organized by the Louvre's legendary curator Gaston Migeon, who was the first to introduce Islamic art into France's national collections, the Arts Décoratifs' exhibition was unprecedented in terms of scientific rigor. The catalogue lists 952 items that were displayed in the Marsan Pavilion, at the northern end of the Tuileries Palace. The broad selection ranged from fifteenth-century Indian miniatures and sixteenth-century Persian silk prayer rugs to Syrian wooden boxes encrusted with ivory and decorated copper basins from Mosul made in the thirteenth century. Two years later, the Louvre would inaugurate a room with Muslim art with, an impressed Matisse said after visiting, "the most beautiful ceramics that I have seen."

A passionate regard was developing, a new way for Matisse to look at space, patterning, and the repetition of motifs that expanded and animated the canvas. The arabesque—a form of artistic decoration based on intertwined and flowing lines—was of particular interest, and Matisse loved the interdependence of the shapes it created. Carpets that he saw at these and later exhibitions as well as while in North Africa would play a key role in his art.

Matisse's connection with these objects that he sees and admires, and that begin to impact his artistic thought, according to Rémi Labrusse, an expert of Matisse and Islamic art, "is not stylistic but aesthetic: he is not concerned with imitating one of the styles or techniques of Islam; rather, he gathers from them a global proposition of a relationship to artistic forms, and his admiration for the works is all the more fruitful because it is not defined as an influence but as a dialogue: a dialogue with a tradition as a whole."

In the spring of 1906, an intrigued Matisse traveled to Algeria for two weeks. It was his first time outside of Europe. After spending a day in the capital Algiers, he caught the sluggish night train to Constantine, an ancient city dramatically perched above a gorge ("Nice place!" he wrote on a postcard to Derain. "But the heat!"), and then headed south to Biskra. A gateway to the Sahara and home to Bedouins and Arabs, Biskra was a vibrant oasis with 150,000 date palms, orchards, and cassia trees as well as Roman ruins. After making it a colonial garrison town in 1844, the French extensively planted palms and fruit trees, erected a church and townhall, opened a casino in a Moorish-style building, and built fine hotels for visitors who came to the winter resort that became known as the "Nice of Algeria."

In *The Immoralist*, Gide described Biskra as "a place full of light and shade; tranquil; it seemed beyond the touch of time; full of silence; full of rustlings—the soft noise of running water that feeds the palms and slips from tree to tree, the quiet call of the pigeons. . . ." For someone as enraptured with light as Matisse, the oasis sounded like an ideal destination for him to work. That didn't happen. While there, he managed to paint only a single, small canvas, *Street in Biskra, Algeria*. Done with thick smears of paint, it was similar to his recent fauve landscapes from Collioure. On one side of the street runs a series of colonial houses with palms, and, on the other, a long, shaded terra-cotta wall where a lone figure hunches. Akin to the near-phantom one in *The Kasbah Gate* that he would paint a half-dozen years later, the figure is merely outlined and marked with identifying dashes of red for a fez hat and browns for the face.

Matisse felt his stay was too short to accomplish much and saw that he couldn't just simply apply his then-current fauve palette and style to Biskra's street scenes. Besides, he told Henri Manguin, "the light is blinding." And although this was certainly true, art historian and curator Roger Benjamin has pointed out, if any French painter should have been prepared to deal with Biskra's strong desert light, it would have been Matisse.

While Matisse considered the trip a failure, the experience was a revelation, and after returning home he began working out his dialogue with Islamic art on the canvas. For aid, in his luggage he carried back from Algeria bowls, jugs, and some boldly patterned carpets woven on Biskra's rudimentary looms that would appear in his paintings.

In Collioure that summer of 1906, he painted *The Red Carpets* (also called *Oriental Rugs*; see figure 14). The titular carpets weren't just a touch of local color for the painting, they were its main motif. Covering a long table, one of the carpets is a meadow of red with a pointillistic confetti of fallen purple and yellow petals, while another carpet, in bright blue with purple buds, can be glimpsed peeking out from under it. A third carpet, draped to show volume in its folds, is deep turquoise with an abstract red floral pattern. Tilting toward the viewer, the fruit bowls, gourd, and other objects that break the flatness of the picture appear to be about to slide off the carpet. The still life loses its sense of depth and takes on something new with its combination of contradictory flat and three-dimensional elements.

It was Matisse's first explicit translation to the canvas of Islamic art's decorative elements. "It expresses the artist's leanings not only towards the colors but also the geometrical forms of Islamic design," wrote Labrusse of the painting. "With an almost aggressive lack of picturesqueness, it gives a concrete embodiment of the idea that the meaning of a visual composition does not rely on its narrative quality but on its ability to transmit a stream of vital energy through the spectator's eye."

Matisse had tapped into something new and saw how powerfully expressive such patterning could be—and how rich it was with possibilities.

It was a pivotal painting for the artist and can be called his first decorative still life. His friends Agutte and Sembat bought *The Red Carpets* from the Galerie Bernheim-Jeune.

Returning to Collioure for the winter of 1906–1907, Matisse took a bolder step with his Algerian experience. At the end of January, he was working—in a shift, from imagination and memory rather than a model—on a reclining nude sculpture in clay of a woman with one arm raised over her head and a bent knee. "One day I was working on her, full of enthusiasm, when the tray she was on slipped off the turntable; it flipped over—squashing my shaped clay underneath, of course," Matisse later explained. "The sound of it falling and the shout I gave brought my wife rushing up from the room below; she found me still apoplectic, calmed me with a few words, and immediately took me out for a walk in the country."

The accident and setback loosened something in him. "The next morning I picked up my work and managed to set things straight, at least straight enough to go on working on it. But before that, full of the confidence that it had brought me, I took a big canvas and painted *Memory of Biskra*."

That first morning, before even picking up the fallen clay sculpture, Matisse had captured the essence of the picture on canvas. By the end of

February, the painting was finished. Done in energetic, vigorous brushstrokes, the blue-shadowed figure reclines on a luxuriant bed with flowers and is backed by a colorful spray of palms rendered in greens, yellows, pinks, and even reds. The curves of the body are echoed in the shapes of the luxurious foliage that surround the buxom woman.

Under its original title *Tableau no. III*, the large painting (36¼ x 55¼ in; 92.1 x 140.4 cm) was the only work that he showed at the 1907 Salon des Indépendants in spring. Later known as *The Blue Woman* and then, finally, for the first solo exhibition of the artist at the MoMA in 1931, *Blue Nude* (*Memory of Biskra*; see figure 15), the startling canvas would be highly influential to the likes of Modigliani for its sculptural qualities and seemingly influence Picasso in his work on *Les Demoiselles d'Avignon*. But critics were aghast at the primitive, even grotesque reclining figure, with its muscular, misshapen body, exaggerated limbs, and lumpy buttocks. For the third Salon in a row, Matisse offered a canvas that was the most notorious work on show, drew the severest fire from the public and critics, and was again bought by Gertrude and Leo Stein. The Steins hung it at rue de Fleurus and delighted in how it shocked their guests.

Some of the deeply hostile reactions came from early supporters, like the influential critic Louis Vauxcelles, who had been championing fauvism. "I admit to not understanding. An ugly nude woman is stretched out upon grass of an opaque blue under the palm trees. . . . This is an artistic effect tending toward the abstract that escapes me completely."

Vauxcelles's comments seemed rather tame compared to the reaction that the canvas would draw in the United States. When it showed at the 1913 Armory Show, it was signaled out as the epitome of ugliness and burned in effigy.

It is not hard to imagine the unsettling shock of seeing the canvas hanging on the wall of the Parisian home of the Steins well over a century ago. Seen today in a museum setting, *Blue Nude* feels uncompromising and unconventional, even radical. Among the over 1,200 works of Matisse held by the Baltimore Museum of Art, the largest collection of Matisse in any public institution in the world (over five hundred are from the Cone Collection), it is the premier one, and hangs with dominant, flaunting pride of place in a broad, central gallery. Just to the side sits in perfect juxtaposition a 1930 bronze casting of the original *Reclining Nude I* sculpture (see figure 16).

The Baltimore Museum of Art also has in its collection a third version of the same reclining nude done on a glazed ceramic tile. When Matisse was in Paris for the spring Salon to show *Blue Nude*, he made his first ceramic decorative tiles. For about a year he worked with a ceramicist in Paris named André Metthey, who was close to, and often worked with, Georgette Agutte. In all, Matisse made about forty vases, dishes, and tiles with Metthey.

Among the tiles was one of the identical motifs as *Blue Nude* titled *Reclining Nude*. With the same contorted pose and raised arm over the head, the figure is thickly outlined in indigo blue and backed by a loose and almost uncontrolled pattern of pale turquoise and orange blots that cover the tile. Imperfect, rather more amebic in shape than round, these blots seem to have spread after being applied, leaving the very center of a number with a nipple of dark green, like the center of a blossoming flower. The horizontal figure does not fit on the small, nearly square tile (3 13⁄16 x 4¾ in; 9.7 x 12.1 cm), and her feet get trimmed off somewhere around the ankles as do the ends of the fingers of her resting hand along the bottom of the tile.

Matisse was trying a variety of means to express the motif, including on the form that was one of the most associated with Islamic art.

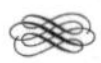

While these were important steps in Matisse's thorough exploration of new, non-European possibilities of art and lengthy journey of absorbing the lessons of Islamic art, the most significant experience came when he visited a large exhibition in Munich in October 1910. Matisse spent a week in Munich with his friends and fellow painters Albert Marquet and Hans Purrmann. Joining them was Matthew Stewart Prichard, a Paris-based British expert in Byzantine art who Matisse had met through Michael and Sarah Stein.

The exhibition *Meisterwerke muhammedanischer Kunst* (*Masterpieces of Muhammadan Art*) was (and is still) the largest ever assembled exhibition of Islamic art. It included nearly 3,600 objects from across the Islamic world: ceramics, mosaics, ornate calligraphy, tiles, miniatures, over two hundred carpets, and more than seven hundred textiles. (Coincidentally, there was a section with pieces from the extensive collection of Sergei Shchukin's older brother, Petr.)

Pure, bold colors, patterns, and curving, arabesque lines dominated the art and ceramics of the show done by numerous skilled hands. From growing up among weavers and fine silks, Matisse understood that there was no real distinction between artist and artisans, who were generally anonymous. In Islamic art, the distinctions were collapsed.

The exhibition's main focus was textiles, of which Matisse was both deeply informed and keenly interested. "I will have the pleasure of desiring, as billionaires cannot, these beautiful carpets that they own and which therefore no longer interest them," he wrote to Agutte from Munich.

In early November 1910, just weeks after attending the Munich show, an inspired Matisse headed for southern Spain to see the Moorish art and architecture of Sevilla, Córdoba, and Granada, the trio of cities in Andalucía where numerous centuries of past Islamic rule remained most manifest. After the small-sized works on display in Germany, he was keen to see larger-scale decorations on two of the greatest works of Islamic architecture in the world, the Alhambra in Granada and the Great Mosque of Córdoba.

"What do you say about my idea of staying and working one more month in Sevilla, Granada, or Tangier?" he wrote to Amélie from Sevilla on December 2. He knew that his wife was unhappy that his trip was lasting longer than originally planned. The beginning of his journey had been tough, with insomnia and a breakdown. But now, recovered, he was hoping to get to work. "You know, if it upsets you, I won't think about it anymore. It's because I see, being rested, a good amount of work to do. Everything I see inspires me a lot, whereas in Paris, with the gray sky, I am quite paralyzed."

He didn't continue south to Morocco, though, or remain much longer in southern Spain, and returned home to France.

Back in his studio and, that summer, in Collioure, the lessons came together in four substantial canvases—both in size as well as importance—that were deeply influenced by the Munich exhibition and his travels in Moorish Spain: *The Painter's Family*, commissioned by Shchukin while Matisse was in Granada; *Interior with Aubergines*; *The Pink Studio*, which Shchukin bought; and *The Red Studio*, which the Russian ultimately rejected. These large interiors show him now overtly using the lessons of Islamic art that had been percolating in the artist over the past dozen years.

"Islamic pattern offers the illusion of a completely full world, where everything from far to near is pressed with equal urgency against the eye," wrote Robert Hughes, noting Matisse's admiration of this and his transposition of it onto canvases like the celebrated modernist milestone *The Red Studio*, painted just before he went to Morocco. In that large, highly original work that acts as an artistic autobiography with identifiable past works displayed around the studio, Matisse seems to have discarded the third dimension and embraced the type of flat representation he had seen in Germany.

Matisse was primed for his arrival in Morocco. His appreciation and understanding of Islamic art had been progressively building, and in Tangier he plunged into the life that nourished the art that inspired him.

It came at the right time, as Ben Jelloun has perceptively noted. Had he gone to Tangier a few years earlier, he would have perhaps been overwhelmed and left soon—too soon—as he had done in Algeria in 1906. But by 1912 Matisse was ready to fully immerse himself.

While in the museums and exhibitions, and even in the rich legacy of Moorish art and architecture in Andalucía, he had seen fine examples, in Tangier Matisse fully found the functional version of that decorative art seamlessly integrated into the everyday, from mosques and marabouts to jewelry and carpets. "It is a rich language, linked with Saharan, Africa, Arabo-Berber and particularly Islamic influences and traditions," wrote Moroccan art historian Mohamed Sijelmassi. "This art has always remained aloof from conventional reality. It is essentially geometrically patterned, but its geometry is not merely a surface shell; it is deeply embedded, leaving room for many mental suppositions and interpretations; it offers a limitless world of optical imaginings." Such art required no historical or literary background, no previous knowledge of art, to be understood or to be enjoyed.

In Tangier it flooded his senses. He may have gone in good part for the soft and mellow light, but he found far more. *"Le Maroc est encore plus riche que la lumière,"* Ben Jelloun wrote. "Morocco is even richer than light." Matisse was transfixed, and his art was being transfigured.

22

Dependability and consistency were everything to Matisse, with the weather as much as models. Although Matisse knew he was fortunate to have Fatma pose for him, he tired of her exhausting demands and threats, and stopped working with her after the second painting even though female models were nearly impossible to find. Unpredictability was his enemy.

The days were perfect to paint, though. *"Ici toutes les journées sont radieuses,"* he wrote to his daughter, Marguerite. "Here all the days are radiant." After finishing the two portraits of Fatma, he turned to a male model, a Berber from the Rif Mountains, "a magnificent mountaineer type," he said in the letter, "savage as a jackal."

In Arabic, "Rif" means the edge of a cultivated area. With a backbone of limestone peaks, Africa's northernmost range forms a protective, almost impenetrable arc along the country's Mediterranean coast. Hamlets, grassy grazing hills, and intense cultivation form a mosaic around patches of dense forest that change with the elevation: scrub, holm, and cork oaks; Mediterranean pine trees; wild olives; and orchards of plums, figs, and almonds turn, as the hills climb, into Aleppo pines, tall maritime pines, thuya, fir, and, eventually, magnificent stands of towering cedars.

The Rif Mountains stretch eastward from Cape Spartel, near Tangier, with their dramatic rise beginning beyond Tétouan. Matisse visited Tétouan the previous winter, traveling by mule at the end of March on his only known excursion from Tangier. It couldn't have been an easy ride. The previous summer, his old friend Albert Marquet had made the journey and wrote to Matisse upon arriving after twelve hours on a horse, "My butt is marmalade." From Tétouan, Matisse glimpsed the largely unexplored range. Isolated and mostly inaccessible, the Rif was known as *bled es siba*, "land of lawlessness," with the strongest tribal structure in Morocco and famously severe blood feuds. The Rif was essentially unconquered when Matisse visited Morocco, and remained so for decades to come, becoming a symbol of a place that could not be subjugated.

Matisse would have seen plenty of people from the Rif in the Grand Socco beside his hotel in Tangier. Many of the women selling foodstuff came from that area. "They crouch on their haunches, and beneath enormous, canopy-like straw hats. They are packed tight, shoulder to shoulder, and on the ground between their outspread feet are fowls and groups of eggs and bunches of wild dates," a Scottish visitor had written the previous year, while their male counterparts wandered the market. "Here are a score of warriors from the Riff Mountains, their dark brown *djellabahas* or cloaks studded down the sleeves and round the hem with rosettes of bright-coloured wool. Ancient flintlocks are slung across their shoulders—useless weapons, surely, or the authorities would not permit them in the town."

Matisse managed to convince one of these men to pose for two very large canvases. "Convince" is perhaps not the best word. "The very fact of posing for you is a concession made to his rigor. A Riffian does not pose," insists Ben Jelloun. "Man of the mountain, rebellious and tough, he does not compromise with the principles, his principles. He is a force of nature who looks down on the city. The Riffian is a proud man, very proud. He dies for his honor. He kills for his honor. He has a sense of family. He never negotiates." This man, then, would *allow* the artist to capture him in detached repose.

Enveloped in an emerald djellaba, the traditional calf-length robe with deep sleeves and a peaked cowl, the man is regal, grandiose, and self-possessed. In *The Standing Riffian*, Matisse filled in the robe with quick, scrubbing brushstrokes and embellished it with decorative rosettes using bare canvas and dabs of red and green (see figure 17). Wrapped around his head is a turban-like *rezza* in green and ocher. The face is painted in ochers and oranges, with a green and yellow beard. His left eye wanders to the side in an unsettling blur. While Matisse included the strap of a leather pouch that held rifle cartridges, he omitted the flintlock that the man likely also carried with him into the city. The background is ambiguous, half blue and half green, and gives no sense of place—only the magnificent robe itself does that.

The portrait's colors are striking. But it is the man's authority and immense presence that makes the strongest impression. Dominating the canvas, he seems to be moving toward the viewer with a gesture that's not so much threatening as powerful and unpredictable. "The firm torso, a bandolier over his right shoulder, his wide forehead and clear gaze," wrote the noted Algerian author Abdelkader Djemaï in a book-length essay on Matisse's Moroccan paintings, "this mountain-dweller expresses, despite his silence and his uncertain arms, a peaceful force that could suddenly turn like milk or the wind."

It is in that unreadable gaze where Ben Jelloun thinks Matisse best captured his fellow countryman. "In reality, this face is closed; impenetrable, inflexible. The man from the Rif is there. He does not hide, but does not give in." His face will never offer Matisse what is truly in his heart, and Matisse will never be able to portray the interior life of the man on the canvas. The inaccessibility is at the self-possessed man's own accord. It is as if he is wearing a mask for the sitting. Fittingly, there is a distinct feeling of distance, or distancing, in the portrait.

While *The Standing Riffian* shows the man at half-length in generous, even heroic proportions, in a second portrait Matisse cast him on an even mightier scale. In *The Seated Riffian*, the man sits on a spartan box stool with his thin legs spread and feet planted widely apart, his bright yellow babouche slippers accentuating the vibrant vermilion red of the floor (see figure 18). The hood of his brilliant green djellaba falls over an unusually broad shoulder. His face is half in green shadow; his head, a patchwork of sage green and mustard yellow planes, stares straight out from a background of vertical bands of brilliant yellows and greens and a patch of blue (perhaps a window) at the rear. A blush of pink plays across his lips. The canvas lacks any blacks or grays or even neutral tones. It's a bold and gorgeous work, deeply expressive in its coloring and its visible, energetic brushwork: long brushstrokes painted with real energy and conviction.

Matisse brought the man close to the viewer—uncomfortably close. He used a significantly larger canvas for this portrait of him. It measures over six and a half feet high and five feet wide (200 x 160 cm), yet the Riffian still doesn't fit. The top of his turbaned head gets cropped off and his left babouche nudges the bottom of the frame, emphasizing his stature. He is literally larger than life. Were he to stand, the man would reach well over ten feet (nearly three meters) tall.

As with the standing version, the impact of *The Seated Riffian* comes from the subject's presence and sheer size that is even more exaggerated. The angle of the floor is raked, and with the tenseness of his pose, it seems that at any moment the man will fall or spring forward out of the picture. The canvas hangs quite high in the main gallery of the Barnes Foundation in Philadelphia, with the visitor's eye level not far above the man's foot at his shin, emphasizing the towering presence. It is unlike any of Matisse's other portraits and is certainly the most imposing one of his entire oeuvre.

While initially intending only a short stay in Tangier, Matisse straightaway began making significant progress. The weather was good, the light stable. After only a few weeks, he began hinting in his letters to Amélie that he might remain a while longer in Tangier. "You see that without seeming excited, I taste what surrounds me here. If it didn't interest me so much, I wouldn't be able to stay. I would get bored," he wrote toward the end of October, trying to justify to her, or to himself, the idea. "It's because I feel calm and peaceful that work goes so smoothly," he assured her. "I'm not like I was a year ago, fortunately, because I wouldn't stay a week."

Amélie, though, was unhappy in Issy. Her letters turned gloomy and then worrying. Matisse told her to go out, to get the train to Paris, to not fall into depressive apathy. She stopped writing to him.

Matisse urged Camoin to visit her with Marquet. Camoin wrote back at the end of October that she was less than enthused at him being away. "Marquet and I spent Thursday afternoon with your wife; as you can imagine, we did not find her very happy to be alone, but we urged her to be patient."

Amélie went to spend the day with Agutte, who reported to Matisse on November 12 that she had been happy to have come "because she is terribly bored, make her come if you stay, because it is very sad for her, her house without a husband, without children, it is abominable, it's enough to cause terrible spite [*spleen*], I told her that she was a good soul, that in her place I would have left to find you a long time ago without even permission, and finally I preached insubordination to her," Agutte wrote in a breathless sentence, underlining *l'insubordunation*. She advised Amélie to go to Ajaccio, Corsica, where her two sons were staying. "But that didn't suit her, it's you she misses and with her garden finished and the workers gone, she should have embarked straight away, and you would have been delighted to see her come unexpectedly like that—I'm sure of it!" But Amélie was, Agutte added, too shy, and reminded Matisse of his fortune to be married to "a quite kind, a good, devoted creature. You are lucky to have such a charming wife."

A cold snap at the end of October in Tangier gave Matisse migraines, and by early November he was fatigued and tired. But he was not ready to return to France. He had decided to stay on in Tangier. At the French post office behind the Grand Mosque, he sent Amélie a letter, and then, for good measure, a cable, asking her to join him immediately. He needed her with him in Morocco. He missed her as she did him.

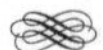

The dutiful and supportive Amélie arrived in Tangier on Sunday, November 24, on the Deutsche Ost-Afrika Linie's SS *Adolf Woermann* from Marseille, having come directly upon receiving her husband's urgent messages. It was a pleasant, fair day, with the temperature 62°F (17°C) in the shade, when Matisse went to meet her ship. Tangier's port was busy. Along with Amélie's German ship, three French steamers, two Spanish, and a Dutch one also called in that same day.

Amélie did not come alone. She had traveled with the painter Charles Camoin, a dear friend of Matisse from the École des Beaux-Arts and one of the original fauves.

Camoin took a photograph of Amélie and Matisse (see figure 19) in their room at the Hôtel Villa de France. Pinned to the wall behind them is *Landscape Viewed from a Window*, unframed, unstretched, and with its edges curling. *The Standing Riffian* is also tacked up, and a sleeve with rosettes can be glimpsed on the wall behind Matisse. In the room, a patterned piece of material is thrown over a sturdy leather traveling trunk while another covers part of a low settee.

Looking handsome but severe, Amélie wears black traveling gear and an oversize black hat with a large bow. ("She always placed a large black hat-pin well in the middle of the hat and the middle of the top of her head and then with a large firm gesture, down it came," according to Gertrude Stein.) In a gloved hand Amélie holds a thin walking stick like a switch, its tip resting on the floor in the manner of a stern headmaster, and from the other dangles a considerable handbag. Matisse, wearing a dark suit and riding spurs, stands beside her, appearing somewhat cowed. Unlike his wife, he has removed his black hat inside—showing a high forehead and thinning hair combed in a side part—that he clutches in a hand. The shy and timid Amélie offers the camera a pinched, perhaps stoical expression.

Staying in the hotel room beside the Matisses and spending the days and evenings together for the next three months, Camoin saw up close the comforting influence her presence had on Matisse, and what a key she was to his work. Matisse himself had few illusions about the importance she played in allowing his art to hit its mark.

23

By the time Amélie and Camoin arrived in Tangier, Amido had managed to locate Zorah. The French-speaking bellboy at the Hôtel Villa Valentina, who Matisse had painted on the previous trip and had acted as translator during his sessions with Fatma, tracked Zorah down in a *maison hospitalière*, where she was working in a government-regulated brothel. The young outcast had become an official prostitute.

The girl would pose again for the painter, but not at the Hôtel Villa de France as during the previous winter, even in a discreet room arranged through the manageress. "Therefore, by police order, she could not go out to work," Matisse later explained. "So I had to go and paint on the terrace of this *maison* every morning."

On a sheet of paper Matisse made a pen-and-ink drawing of Zorah in profile, and on another page did a trio of smaller sketches, three versions of her face that resemble Delacroix's note-taking in Tangier. He then began a full-length portrait.

Matisse set up his easel on the flat roof terrace of the brothel and painted Zorah between jobs. When the *patronne* called, she would go back downstairs to attend to a client and then return. There is little to indicate her circumstances or those of the painting sessions.

Zorah Standing (see figure 20) has the same dimensions as the standing portraits of Amido and Fatma, but done in a full-fronted pose rather than turned slightly to the side. Nearly life-size, Zorah wears a magnificent bluish-green kaftan with black-and-white embroidered hems and billowing, open sleeves whose insides he thickly dabbed with a loaded brush of white paint. The floor is burnt orange and the wall a bright, pastelly raspberry color, which is echoed in the shade of the thin sash around her waist. As with the other Moroccan portraits, she fills the canvas: her head grazes the top edge, her slippered feet the bottom one. The girl's brilliant yellow babouches appear to be sliding off, lending her feet a strangely elongated look.

Matisse worked Zorah's face very lightly with paint, and left the primed canvas bare around the eyes, giving her something of a bandit's mask of white. While the Riffian man wears a turban of green and brown, Zorah has a patchwork headscarf of blue, red, and yellow. With clasped hands, a small mouth pinched shut, and large, almond eyes, she looks at the painter with an expression of awkwardness, even discomfort. Lacking the ease of Amido or the haughty, slightly mocking pose of Fatma in their standing portraits, Zorah's pose is silent and dignified. Her energy gathers in the planes of strident colors while the intense expression on her face reveals a glimpse of her personality.

There is a relationship being depicted on the canvas between sitter and painter, between a young Moroccan girl and a bearded, rather severe Frenchman bearing down on her from behind an easel with his bright blue eyes and thick-lensed glasses. While landscapes and urbanscapes can transcend a specific time, portraits record a single moment of a specific encounter, in this case on the roof of a Tangier brothel that had become her home.

Even to the most astute observer—that being unveiled meant she was likely a prostitute—the painting offers few clues to her circumstances. Snippets of context only came decades later. "Over there, the girls are given a small room (2 by 2 m) with a mattress, a hole in the wall, a jug of water, one single very beautiful dress, which they throw out when it gets dirty," Matisse said in 1949 when he was working on the Vence Chapel in the South of France. He was spending significant time with Brother Louis-Bertrand Rayssiguier, a Dominican novice and architect who helped with the project (and also posed for Matisse). In his notebook, Rayssiguier recorded their conversation following an afternoon session posing at Matisse's home above Nice:

> "I won't tell you who Zorah was . . ."
>
> "Why should I care!"
>
> In fact, he tells me when he returned to Morocco the following year, he asked his guide where Zorah was living. They finally found her in a brothel with two other women, a Jewess and another Moroccan. He got her to pose. She looked like a little saint. Her madame would call her down from time to time in the middle of a sitting. She would come back up the stairs a short while later, blushing and nibbling on a biscuit.

The *petits beurres* were offered to her, it seems, in lieu of extra money. Matisse was forbidden to pay her beyond the set government rate.

It is something of a paradox that Matisse depicted Zorah, an actual prostitute being painted between clients in a brothel, in an almost holy image that embodied the medieval myth of the Madonna and the whore: Saint Mary of Egypt, Abraham's niece Saint Mary the Harlot, Saint Mary Magdalene.

But if the unusually oblong canvas of Zorah standing before an almost-violent red background resembles any holy figure at all, it is a lithe saint on a Russian Orthodox icon. The semblance was not coincidental. When Matisse was in Russia in the autumn of 1911, just prior to his first Tangier stay, he took an immediate and intense interest in religious icon paintings, whose colors and spiritual force deeply moved him.

While Russia was experiencing an exceptionally creative flowering, Matisse was less interested in the contemporary riches of the country's artistic silver age than by ones done many centuries before. On his second day in the country, Shchukin took him to visit a well-known collector of icons in Saint Petersburg. Matisse was immediately besotted. They continued on to Moscow, the religious center of the country. On the day he arrived, Matisse looked at the collections of Shchukin and Morozov—together the greatest gathering of modern Western art in the world—and then in the evening went to see icons in the unapparelled personal collection of Ilya Ostroukhov. "You should have seen his delight at the icons. Literally the whole evening he wouldn't leave them alone, relishing and delighting in each one," Ostroukhov wrote the next day to the daughter of the founder of the Tretyakov Gallery. "Today Shchukin phoned me to say that Matisse literally couldn't sleep the whole night because of the acuity of his impression." Ostroukhov was a trustee of the Tretyakov Gallery, which was founded in the 1850s and became the foremost museum of Russian fine art in the world. When they visited the gallery, Ostroukhov reported that Matisse "grew excited in the icon hall, where we spent about 1 ½ hours opening all the glass doors of the cupboards."

A stupefied Matisse told Shchukin, "I spent ten years searching for something your artists discovered in the fourteenth century."

During his two and a half weeks in Moscow, Matisse, often with Ostroukhov as his excellent guide, sought icons out in churches around the city, and saw icon figure paintings on walls, stacked high on iconostasis, and as life-size frescoes with their vivid colors soaked into the plaster. Inside the fortified expanse of the old Kremlin, just minutes from Shchukin's house, was a trio of cathedrals whose walls held some of the finest examples in Russia. The limestone Cathedral of the Assumption, built in the fifteenth century on the site of three previous churches, had a lofty iconostasis of vermilion with rows of images of saints adorned with precious stones. Across the small Cathedral Square stood the Cathedral of the Archangel and, with its nine gilded onion domes topped by gold crosses, the Cathedral of the Annunciation, which held many superb icons including some done by the two greatest medieval icon painters, Theopones the Greek and Andrei Rublev. They covered the walls and ran up the iconostasis in six rows, one on top of each other, with gold and red dominating striking images darkened by years of candle smoke and incense.

"The individual character of a saint is revealed in the detailed and bold line drawing of the face as well as the flat, but clearly suggestive shape of the figure," according to art historian Alison Hilton. "It is a matter of two separable techniques: the fundamental pattern of shapes and colors which strike the eye immediately ('icon-like' describes a painting whose elements are upright and formal, and sharply outlined against a solid-color background) and, on top of this painted surface, not merely a subordinate filling in of details in black or gold, but a drawing fine in its own right."

The enthusiasm of an enchanted Matisse could not have been greater. "They are really great art. I am in love with their moving simplicity which, to me, is closer and dearer than Fra Angelico," Matisse told a Moscow newspaper during his visit, referring to the fifteenth-century Dominican friar and painter known for brilliantly colored figures bathed in light. "In these icons the soul of the artist who painted them opens out like a mystical flower. And from them we ought to learn how to understand art."

For the last few years, Matisse had kept a low profile in Paris in the face of nonstop criticism. In Moscow, pleased with the attention, he gave numerous interviews and was heavily quoted in the press, who delighted in his ideas:

> "The main task of the artist is to pursue the harmony of colours. It's not at all a matter of force, of brilliance, but of their harmonious combination. *Tout est dans la mesure.* Some do attain a sense of conviction. I would say," he added with a smile, "*il faut peindre les choses délicates avec la force.*"

Matisse's last line can be translated as "you have to paint delicate things with strength."

While *Zorah Standing* lacks an icon's familiar and widely recognized narrative or established set of symbols—the way of holding the hands, say, or certain props—the image shares their playing-card flatness, oblong shape, and lack of fixed vanishing point, as well as strong and pure colors. Backed by a rich red wall, Zorah stands erect staring straight out at the viewer with overly large eyes like a transfixed saint.

"The Byzantine principle of religious art is symbolized by the long, sorrowful figures of patriarchs and martyrs marshalled along church walls," wrote Hilton. Matisse would have seen examples of these oversized figures. "Distortion kept icons, too, from mere reality, and brought the best of them toward a higher reality." The icons were painted to convey an element of the supernatural, and these martyrs and saints on church walls are imbued with special powers.

Matisse had done *Fatma, the Mulatto Woman* for Shchukin as a pendant to the portrait of Amido, but, not surprisingly, when the Russian eventually saw *Zorah Standing*, he chose it instead, reacting to a certain familiarity in the painting. While Matisse did not seemingly seek to portray an obvious spiritual element in Zorah's portrait, the distorted rendering elevates her above realism and conveys a sense of wonder. The image exudes a quiet power that Shchukin, as an Eastern Orthodox Christian, could fully understand.

24

Toward the end of November, Matisse began an even more magnificent portrait of the girl, *Sur la terrase*, known in English as *Zorah on the Terrace* (see figure 22). Imbued with fairytale beauty, it has no real narrative nor much context, yet it is charged with wonder, mystery, and a sense of overwhelming silence.

Wearing a blue kaftan patterned in white and gold and cinched with a thin red belt, Zorah kneels on a deep blue carpet. Luminous open shade washes over the roof terrace. A triangle of pale, yellowish-pink light cuts across the side to soften the cold bluish-greens of the wall, and, running along the top, a streak of blue sky. Beside her sits a large glass goblet with three goldfish—smokey flashes of ruddy-orange—and a pair of golden-yellow babouches that look as if she had just slipped them off to pray. Trimmed in light purple, patterned with crescents of midnight blue, and lined with red insoles, the shoes are not outlined in color but the opposite: Matisse traced their shape with the wooden tip of a brush through the wet paint down to the bare canvas. The fishbowl and slippers are untethered, and the girl seems to physically hover over the carpet beside them.

In a fluidly done preparatory sketch in diluted oil (*Zorah Seated*), Matisse depicted Zorah kneeling in a slightly askew position, with her knees to the side. The sketch was done in the same format as *The Kasbah Gate* and *Landscape Viewed from a Window*, and she fills most of the space. But when he began the painting itself, he switched to a wider, almost square-shaped canvas and shifted Zorah's position so that her body and knees were forward and she faced him directly. With the additional space, he added the slippers and bowl of goldfish.

The girl's hands clasped in front of her are a blur, moving like the goldfish inside the bowl, as if unsuccessfully trying to hold herself tight. Her enigmatic expression gives little away, and certainly nothing of the situation. The only clue in her mood might be in the eyebrows that arc significantly higher above her eyes than in the previous painting, lending her a look of apprehension, or wariness, or even weariness. Maybe it is the expression of wanting desperately to please the painter in a completely foreign situation. ("You are used to having someone pose for you," Ben Jelloun wrote in his lengthy essay. "For Zorah, everything was new. She must have told this story to her friends. No one must have believed her.") Perhaps Matisse was impatiently trying to get her to resume the same precise pose after returning from a client in the brothel downstairs.

Matisse worked this canvas more than the other Tangier portraits, and colors surface through the upper layers of paint. This is particularly noticeable in the deep orange that shows through the blue of the carpet that he applied in a thick wash. He painted Zorah's lips at the end over a dark mouth tinged with blue, in an imperfect, almost clumsy smudge, a tight oval rosebud of thick, ruddy red paint pressed against her brownish face.

Here Zorah seems smaller and younger than in the standing portrait and significantly more so than the one of her in a yellow robe done the preceding winter: more doll-like, more innocent.

She is too young to have developed the mask that the Riffian sitter wears. The Riffian in his two portraits never feels vulnerable. But Zorah does. She appears completely unguarded: exposed but not weak. Kneeling barefoot before the artist, she seems to be offering herself—in submission, in supplication. It feels more intimate than any of his Tangier paintings.

Decades later, Matisse described the brothel's terrace to Pierre Courthion. "That's where I painted Zorah in a blue silk dress adorned with large golden interlacing, on her right a ball-shaped aquarium in which a few goldfish swim and on her left lemon-yellow sandals with a blue design. All in the luminous shade exalting the colors. Only the sky and a corner of the terrace wall are touched by the sun," he told the Swiss critic. "She looked like a little saint."

Despite painting Zorah in such a submissive posture, he was going against one of the key tenets of Orientalism: the sexually available Arab woman. Zorah is innocent, even asexual. There is a sensuality in her portrait, but it isn't a sexual sensuality, and it does not seem that Matisse ever viewed her as such. He was intrigued by her bearing and presence, by a sense of innocent wonder.

Zorah is the previous, virginal incarnation of the numerous odalisques he would later paint in Nice throughout the 1920s. "As for odalisques, I had seen them in Morocco," Matisse would say somewhat defensively toward the end of his life, perhaps referring to what he saw in the brothel of Zorah, "so I was able to put them in my pictures back in France without playing make-believe."

Yet with those later odalisques he was playing make-believe, and, to the viewer, a thinly veiled one at that. Nice in the 1920s was home to a burgeoning cinema industry and many of his models were film extras, including the most important during his early years in Nice, Henriette Darricarrère. He had the women pose in stage sets erected in his apartment-cum-studio like scenes from the *Arabian Nights*. With a bed and thin mattress, colorful tapestries, mirrors, and various knickknacks, they appear captive: objects reduced to patterns like the textile wall hangings behind them. They exist in a sumptuous interior harem cloyingly resplendent with bright colors, decorative patterns, and bulging, sinuous forms. The mirrors, cushions, and embroidery could have been lifted from the room in Delacroix's *Women of Algiers*. (The same could be said of the women, as Robert

Hughes put it, "displaying themselves like late refugees from Delacroix.") It was an imaginary Orient. It was of a very different place that he captured while in Tangier.

Reclining, sitting, or even standing, wearing exotic, often diaphanous costumes in various stages of undress, with bangles dangling from a pale arm lifted to accentuate the curve of their bare breasts (or simply better to show them off), the odalisques' postures are drowsy with sex, and their gazes inviting. Unlike the somewhat blurred image of Zorah, those done later in Nice are easier to focus on, to stare at. Acknowledging the viewer—the voyeur—the women appear to be either waiting for sex or resting afterwards in rooms that vibrate with lust. The term *odalisques* had clear associations with the Orient, and with the idea of sexual availability. (*Oda* comes from the Turkish for "chamber" or "room," and *-lık* a suffix that expresses function.) It was certainly a connotation that Matisse was aware of. Among the numerous odalisques in the collection of the Musée de l'Orangerie in Paris, there is one from the early 1920s of a woman standing against a blue-patterned wall with one arm behind her back and the other behind her neck. She is naked except for a heavy amber necklace and a diaphanous wrap around her waist. Matisse titled it *Odalisque bleue ou l'Esclave blanche—Blue Odalisque or The White Slave.*

While the odalisque paintings are festive mosaics of colors and patterns, splendid as intricate jewel boxes, Matisse doesn't appear that interested in the women as people, as individuals, on the canvas. Odalisques were his principal subject from 1917 to 1930, and the models are largely interchangeable. They appear calm and authoritative, passive, bored even—professionals doing a job. Their weary expressions drip with ennui, or perhaps tiredness from the arduous task of holding a pose. With very few exceptions, they are not even sexy. (*Odalisque with Green Sash* from 1926 at the Baltimore Museum of Art, with one hand cupped under a bare breast and her pants sliding down her wide hips like a modern perfume advert, is arguably the sexiest.) The women feel like part of the pattern, part of the decoration.

"Matisse has almost done away with the female figure altogether," wrote noted British art critic Charles Darwent, "reducing her to a transparent wash, a kind of painterly Cheshire Cat."

On a fundamental level, people started to paint to remember. Delacroix traveled to Morocco before the invention of the camera and captured what he saw in his notebooks. These illustrations are, literally, souvenirs, a word whose origins mean "to remember."

Do Matisse's pictures even resemble Zorah? We don't know what Zorah actually looked like. Even if there was a photograph, it would not hang beside the paintings of her for comparison. Besides, a close likeness, in the end, doesn't matter, and is certainly not the merit of the picture's quality. A good painted portrait does more than simply represent the sitter on a canvas. It captures an internal likeness that a photograph never can, that elusive and hard-to-pin-down element that makes the subject unique.

Matisse was carefully observing the girl as he worked, looking for what made her exceptional. What he captured was also a portrait of Zorah looking *at him*: Matisse (or the viewer) is caught in *her* gaze. In all three portraits of her, the girl stares straight ahead at the artist as if he—as if we—were invading her private space.

Matisse clearly cared for Zorah, and he portrays that intangible, indefinable *something* about the girl in his paintings. An essence of Zorah seeps into the portraits that viewers not only remember but return to again and again. Bewitched by her serenity and enigmatic expressions, especially in this third portrait of her kneeling on the terrace, they lean in to see if any fragments of her story can be gleaned by looking closer. She is immortalized without a biography. What happened to her? some wonder.

Sometimes that gets asked aloud. "You have made her so close to me that I would like, to feel even more intimate with her, to know her life better," wrote Djemaï, addressing the artist directly in his book on Matisse's time in Morocco that he titled *Zorah sur la terrasse*. "I'm not fond of mystery—her portrait is enough for that—but I would have liked, for example, to know if she had been in love with a man as young as her, if she had married and had children and grandchildren. Is she a girl from the city or the countryside, driven out by exodus and misery? Had she also contracted consumption or a venereal disease? At what age and in what year did she die? Did she ever come to France, did she ever leave Tangier?"

After Matisse's painting of her kneeling on the terrace, there is nothing else known of Zorah. When Marquet was staying at Hôtel Villa de France the following winter, Matisse sent a postcard asking if he had seen her. There is no recorded response.

25

On the last day of 1912, Matisse turned forty-three. He began 1913 in Tangier with the promise of a new studio, even if it had cost him a week's work and did not start auspiciously.

On December 14, he had written to Agutte letting her know that they were sending off *The Small Mulatto Woman*. Since Amélie's arrival at the end of November, the weather had been good, with only a few days of rain and an eastern mistral wind, he wrote. He was confident that it wouldn't last—though he would leave Tangier, he said, if it persisted. And while weather and light were a continual preoccupation, leaving Tangier, at least immediately, was unlikely. He had finally managed to find the kind of well-lit space he had been hoping to get. "For a week, I haven't worked—I've been preoccupied with renting a photographer's studio which is 5 m long by 3 wide, all glass," he told Agutte. It was located among the warren of zigzagging lanes in the residential quarter of the medina. "It had to be repaired a bit; I got it for around thirty francs, but it is very clear and completely white. Unfortunately in a very dirty house but as it is on the terrace, there is air."

He was already testing the space, he told Agutte, though it wasn't off smoothly. "I started a bouquet of flowers yesterday to try out my workshop." A floral still life was his anchor, a place to begin, to take a first reading of a new situation. "This morning when I opened the door to my workshop I found the flowerpot which has this round shape without a foot." He added a sketch of the pot, which is similar to the central brown one in *Landscape*

Viewed from a Window. "I found it tipped over from the box on which it was placed, and the bouquet upside down crushed on the ground. I cannot therefore continue this painting. I am unpleasantly surprised by this and to take my mind off things I am going for a walk this afternoon with my wife." A good walk was often a remedy for many of Matisse's problems.

January's weather began as unstable and cloudy, and on the 8th, rain arrived, battering the city, keeping Matisse from even making it to the new studio. "The year is off to a bad start here," he wrote to Henry Manguin on January 11, "the storm for four days has given us the jitters." The rains eased for two days but returned for another four-day-long wet spell. Certainly, he was panicking that the inclement weather would persist as it had done the previous winter.

As when enduring those rains the year before, he did a floral still life sitting atop a piece of hotel furniture in his room. It was likely then that he painted the surprisingly large *Bouquet of Flowers on a Veranda*, also called *Arums* (*Calla Lilies*)—it is about five feet by three feet (146 x 97 cm)—of a flowing vase of lilies (see figure 23). Many of the flowers are simply outlined in gray paint and not filled in with color. Rather, it is the white primed canvas that lends the bouquet its brightness and a sense of airy etherealness.

This canvas was a preparation for the denser, more complete *Arums, Iris, and Mimosas* (*Blue Vase with Flowers on a Blue Tablecloth*; see figure 21). In a delightful contrast between fleshy, vibrantly alive flowers and printed ones, a vase of saturated blooms rests on a dark blue cloth patterned with lighter blue petals. Drawing the eye along its suggestive, almost erotic curves, a long, arrow-shaped calla lily leaf dangles provocatively in the center among blue irises and clusters of yellow mimosas. The colors of the flowers are brought out in contrasts: the white, fluted lilies against green; the blue irises against pink; the yellow mimosas against azure blue. The wallpaper in the background has a similar floral pattern as the tablecloth but in a reverse of blues. Perhaps purposefully, Matisse included the same curtain in *Basket with Oranges* done during the rainy spell the previous winter.

Through the rain-splattered windows, the low clouds clung to the hills beyond the bay, their grays melding sea and sky, obscuring Spain to the north, and turning the light steely and cold. The weather threatened to derail his work. He had been on form, producing an unfaltering string of master works since arriving. Even *Arums, Iris, and Mimosas*, done by force of weather rather than choice, ranks among the most sensational floral compositions he painted over his long career.

At least this time there was someone else besides Amélie to listen to Matisse's weather complaints. He and Camoin, who had arrived with Amélie and was staying in the room next door, ate together, swam off the beach, took long walks in the Marshan, and looked for motifs to sketch in the kasbah, went to the cinema at the Tivoli Theatre, and played dominos and billiards in the evening. While Matisse showed him how to ride a horse, Camoin taught Matisse chess. "You play chess to get fooled," Matisse wrote to Marquet in Paris on a postcard trying to entice him to join them in Tangier. "Camoin trembles to see you again. He introduced me to chess; it's really a game to lose your mind. I will stick to the basics."

For Camoin, the trip to Tangier would change the tenor that his paintings had taken during a troubled personal period.

The Marseille-born Camoin became friends with Matisse along with Marquet, Jean Puy, Agutte, and others in the Beaux-Arts studio of Moreau, which he joined not long before the master's death. For a teacher, Camoin had another in Cézanne, who he got to know in 1902 during his military service in Aix-en-Provence. In 1903, Camoin exhibited at the Salon des Indépendants and at the inaugural Salon d'Automne. Berthe Weill—the first to sell Matisse or Picasso—gave Camoin his first individual exhibition in 1904. At the historic 1905 Salon d'Automne, he showed his colorful summer landscapes with the other soon-to-be-labeled fauves.

But recently he had been having a hard time. He had separated from Émile Charmy the year before. Charmy had moved to Paris in 1903 and painted alongside him as well as Matisse and Marquet, experimenting with fauve colors and, quite exceptionally for a woman at the time, the female nude done in tactile impasto and bold colors. (Georgette Agutte was another woman in their circle doing female nudes.) Charmy also exhibited in the 1905 Salon d'Automne, where her work caught the eye of Weill. She and Camoin eventually became lovers and shared a studio. In 1911, Camoin left their studio on Place de Clichy for one that was a ten-minute walk away on rue Lepic in Montmartre. His paintings darkened and became, in his mind, mediocre.

A decade older, Matisse generally played the wiser half of their relationship, offering support and reassurance. Throughout periods of his life, such care was necessary for Camoin, as he acknowledged in his diary in 1947: "I need friendship, affection, unfortunately I need to be encouraged. I lose confidence in myself too quickly, perhaps because of a lack of precision in my conception of art and of what I can and must do."

At Matisse's prompting, Camoin had spent the summer of 1912 in Collioure with Marquet to get some distance from Charmy and their separation, and now he urged him to come to Morocco. For the first time since the early fauve years, the two would be painting together.

Camoin's stay in Tangier did not start off favorably. Not long after arriving, he was hospitalized with diphtheria, and nearly died. The Matisses nursed him back to health and encouraged him to work.

Being with Matisse and being in Tangier—the light, the colors, the new motifs—made Camoin want to paint. "In recent years, Camoin had evolved towards a brutal and jarring style of painting: the joy and lightness of the Fauvist years had followed a period dominated by dark canvases with strong shapes, surrounded by a thick black line," wrote Claudine Grammont in the catalog of a 2022 Camoin retrospective at the Musée de Montmartre. "In Morocco, Camoin recovers his grace." The canvases are airier and seemingly freer than even the ones from Collioure the previous summer that had begun to brighten. "He reconnects with colors of light, soft greens, pastel pinks, and airy blues applied in light and transparent glazes which let the shapes breathe." Green and lilac dominate his Tangier palette. One of his finest paintings he did during his stay is *Minaret in Tangier.* Radiant and full of swirling light, the canvas was bought by Agutte and Sembat. "Of this city crushed by the sun, the painter offers a warm and luminous vision," according to a book by the Musée de Grenoble, where the painting hangs. "He remembers what's essential: the emotion he felt in this place and reviving it through color."

But if for Matisse the gardens at Villa Brooks the previous winter had been where his revelation of Tangier's light had taken place, for Camoin it was the lengthy curl of beach fronting the city. "The beach embodies the quality of Moroccan light, a fluid and moving substance, a mist in which space appears as a single flow," noted Grammont, a past director of the Musée Matisse in Nice. "A place of clarity, it is a corner of paradise: like the Matisse garden, it is the setting for a sweet reverie, for swimming—he and Matisse took a midnight swim well in December—and represents a certain happiness of Moroccan living."

"I am very happy and delighted with the winter I spent here with you in one of the most attractive countries I have seen," Camoin would write a few months later to Matisse after they parted in Tangier, "not to mention the precious impulse at work that I could not fail to find with you." And despite the illness, over the next four months in Morocco he made fifteen paintings and no less than seventy-nine sheets of charcoal and ink drawings. "*Période rare de santé et d'heureux travail,*" Camoin later remembered it: a rare period of health and happy work. He seemed to have forgotten the bout of diphtheria, or else considered that what followed the illness that nearly killed him simply trumped everything else.

Besides his wife and Camoin, the person that Matisse saw the most in Morocco was the Canadian painter James Wilson Morrice, an acquaintance from Paris. The previous winter, Morrice arrived within a couple of weeks of Matisse and after unexpectedly encountering him in Tangier, moved into the same hotel. Matisse and Morrice even traveled back to Marseille together on the same ship. That second winter, Morrice arrived in December and immediately joined the Matisses and Camoin at the Villa de France. Over the two winters, Matisse and Morrice spent some fifteen weeks together in Tangier.

Just four years older than Matisse, Morrice was the son of a wealthy textile merchant in Montreal. He had left Canada at twenty-five and, except for trips back to see his family, spent the rest of his life abroad, mostly in France and North Africa. He died in Tunis in 1924, not yet sixty years old. "He was travelling always over hill and dale," Matisse later said of him, "a little like a migrating bird but without any very fixed landing place."

Morrice held a significant position among artists in Paris, and was a feature in the annual Salons, both as a committee member (with Matisse) and exhibiting artist. He was not only respected by art critics but also sought out by writers. Somerset Maugham, Aleister Crowley, and Arnold Bennett all used elements of Morrice for characters in their novels. Critics have pointed to Morrice as the model for Warren, the often-inebriated artist "with a pate as shining as a billiard-ball, and a pointed beard," in Maugham's *The Magician* (1908).

> "Hasn't he had too much to drink?" asked Arthur frigidly.
>
> "Much," answered Susie promptly, "but he's always in that condition, and the further he gets from sobriety the more charming he is. He's the only man in this room of whom you'll never hear a word of evil. The strange thing is that he's very

> nearly a great painter. He has the most fascinating sense of colour in the world, and the more intoxicated he is, the more delicate and beautiful is his painting. Sometimes, after more than the usual number of *apéritifs*, he will sit down in a café to do a sketch, with his hand so shaky that he can hardly hold a brush; he has to wait for a favourable moment, and then he makes a jab at the panel. And the immoral thing is that each of these little jabs is lovely. He's the most delightful interpreter of Paris I know, and when you've seen his sketches—he's done hundreds, of unimaginable grace and feeling and distinction—you can never see Paris in the same way again."

The influential art critic Louis Vauxcelles considered Morrice the greatest North American painter since Whistler and published a lengthy and laudatory piece on him in a Canadian magazine. "His knowledge of painting is profound, and, while able, is disdainful of cleverness, and, above all, there is the result without the apparent effect: because the artist, although very sure of his pencil and brushes, occupies himself principally with the sentimental spirit of the subject rather than with the precise character and contour," Vauxcelles wrote in 1909. He added, "*Harmoniste*, I call him, of a rare taste, refined and subtle. With few tones, but carefully considered, he obtains the most profound and appealing effect."

In his jacket pocket Morrice discreetly carried small pochades and a little paint set. Sitting in a café terrace on the Petit Socco or in the new part of the city observing Tangier's animated street life, the Canadian would place the set on his lap and discreetly capture the unfolding scene in a few brushstrokes on the panel, often of wood taken from cigar boxes. He did one of Matisse in a café wearing a white hat with its brim tipped down in a rakish angle. The grains of the wood come through the light brushwork.

"Apart from our working sessions," Matisse recalled, "we were always together." They also painted many of the same scenes in Tangier, with

Morrice working on smaller-scale canvases in colors that, around Matisse, seem to brighten from his muted, Whistler-influenced palette.

Morrice was a keen advocate of Mediterranean travel for an artist: "A painter should go South; it cleans your palette for you." Like many other painters, he was drawn to the region's distinctive light. His more expansive compatriot John Lyman, another Canadian who crossed paths with Matisse in Paris—he attended Académie Matisse—and traveled widely in Morocco and Tunisia, put it this way: "You only understand it little by little. It surprises you at first, because you had imagined an Orient full of bright colours—and it's not that at all. The light of North Africa is all nuanced, made up of a thousand delicate, pearly reflections that the eye only becomes sensitive to after a certain time."

A deeply private man who left virtually no personal papers, only two brief references to his time with Matisse have been found among Morrice's things, both in his painting notebooks from the early 1920s.

Matisse was just slightly more forthcoming on Morrice, his *bon camarade* whose favorite word was "gusto" and who enlivened his Tangier stays. "You know the artist with the delicate eye who delighted in interpreting landscapes of closely related values in soft and muted hues. . . . As a man, he was a true gentleman, a good companion, with great wit and humour," Matisse said for a posthumous exhibition in Paris two years after the Canadian's death. "He had, as everyone knows, an unfortunate passion for whiskey." Matisse was famously abstemious, and in Morocco would sip soda water while Morrice tended glass after glass of whisky. Morrice became known for this predilection, and local kids followed him around Tangier chanting, "Whisky! Whisky!"

The two bouts of rain were, thankfully, short-lived, and on January 18 fine weather and stable light returned.

Back in October, not long after he arrived and Tangier was still in drought, Matisse had written in a long letter to Georgette Agutte that he was already considering leaving, despite the good light. "I don't know where I will go when I leave this beautiful country which I found very changed because this season gives the idea of the European countryside after winter, the greenery is sickly, not russet or red like at home, but dull and dead, many trees already have no more leaves and the valleys, the hillsides are earthy in color [as] the grass appears dead. It takes a good period of rain to revive the life that gives Tangier its charm."

And while the wet tempests may have interrupted work, once they had passed, greens burst forth in a revived landscape that began, finally, to turn more familiar to Matisse and gave it back that "charm" he had said was lacking. "I had to endure the torrential rains again before rediscovering the springtime Morocco that had so enchanted me the year before," he later recalled.

Matisse scrapped any plans of continuing on to Algeria and Tunisia, and stayed in Tangier, remaining productive throughout the rest of January and into February.

Modern painting was undergoing a radical change. Looking around in new ways, artists were moving away from three-dimensional representations and finding both simpler and more complex ways to depict the world. cubists were fragmenting it into geometric shapes. Picasso and Braque were experimenting with paper collage, offering the illusion of everyday to canvases with cuttings from popular newspapers like *Le Journal* and *Le Matin*.

Matisse's paintings were also changing that winter. They were getting progressively flatter and if not more symbolic then at least less literal. A half dozen significant canvases behind him, and a host of sketches, he was ready for a truly grand painting he had been planning for months. And now, with the new studio space and the return of good light, he could finally begin work on it.

26

Leaving the kasbah through the southern Bab al-Assa gate, steps drop steeply down into the medina, roughly cutting between two neighborhoods: Amrah, the most populous quarter in the medina, and Jnan Kaptan, once home to the legendary fourteenth-century traveler Ibn Battuta, the "Prince of Travelers" who reached Guangzhou, Samarkand, and Timbuktu during twenty-eight years of globetrotting. (His modest tomb is here.)

Matisse was walking along the steps one afternoon not long after arriving in Tangier on his second stay when he heard violin music coming from a café. Somewhat uncharacteristically—Matisse was arrogant but shy—he went inside, took the violin and horsehair bow from the musician, and began to play. As a boy, he had studied the instrument for a time and then picked it up again later. "Curiosity pushed me to see the musician and to astonish him, I took his instrument and charmed the whole café. They were five or six," he reported to his wife, still in France. "I played very well," he added with a note of pride. "My sensitivity was overexcited by my work session that I had just finished, it was midday, and I made some pretty sounds for them."

It was a traditional "Moorish" or "Arab" café—in contrast to the "modern table-and-chair café," as Paul Bowles distinguished in the 1950s. "In the back of practically every such establishment there is an open space covered with reed matting, generally raised above the level of the floor; entry into this part of the room demands the removal of one's shoes. Here the men sit with their legs tucked under them and, more often than not, in spite of the unofficial prohibition, pull out their kif [hash] pipes and smoke them as they have always done," wrote the American novelist, an outsider particularly equipped to illuminate the city's unfamiliar cultural mores. Bowles first visited Tangier in 1931 at the suggestion of Gertrude Stein (who naturally recommended the Hôtel Villa de France to him) and lived in the city from 1947 until his death in 1999. "The cafés are like men's clubs," he wrote. "A man frequents the same one year in and year out. Often he brings his food and eats there; sometimes he stretches out on the matting and sleeps there. His café is his mail address, and rather than use his home, where there are always womenfolk about, he will use the café for keeping his social appointments. . . . It is here that the endless stories and complicated jokes which so delight the Moslem mind are told, and where the average man is at his happiest and least inhibited."

While those habitués might regard strangers who entered with a wary eye, it was, Bowles noted elsewhere, "in the café that the foreign visitor, too, can feel the pulse of the country. Nowhere else can he manage to observe a group of individuals repeatedly and at length in their daily contacts with one another, or succeed in existing at their tempo, achieving in occasional unguarded moments a state of empathy with their very different sense of the passage of time. And to experience time from the vantage point of these people is essential to understanding their attitudes and behavior."

Bowles could have been writing about Matisse's experience. Made to feel welcome by its regulars, Matisse took to occasionally stopping by after a working session at around 5:00 P.M. "It's a quiet café where serious people go," he wrote to Amélie at the end of October. The men played cards or games, listened to music, or lounged, some with a long, reed-thin kif pipe known as a *sebsi*. Some even slept. Glasses of sweet mint tea sat on the floor among slipped-off babouches. "Inside it's painted in oil paint with white arcades against a blue background, up to the height of the picture rail," he explained to his wife. The musicians sat on a raised wooden platform known as a *soudda*. Above, from the ceiling, hung a dozen cages of small songbirds, and, out the small window, a glimpse of the Bay of Tangier. At the heart of the café was a water boiler for tea sitting atop a bed of coals, a tin box of Chinese green tea leaves, and a cone of sugar to break off into pieces to sweeten the hot tea. "*C'est très intime*," Matisse wrote.

Soon after first visiting, Matisse had the idea for a large work based on the café, and sharing nearly everything with his wife, immediately sketched out the idea for her in a letter.

Once Camoin arrived in Tangier with Amélie at the end of November, he joined Matisse on his afternoon visits. (Not Amélie, though. This type of café was the exclusive domain of men.) They slipped off their shoes and sat on the floor. The two Frenchmen eventually began sketching in the café, catching the customers and their surroundings in quick pencil and pen-and-ink drawings.

Both had learned to draw with Delacroix-like rapidity two decades before as students in Paris. They sketched together in the Petit Casino on the Passage de l'Operá in the afternoons, capturing quick, bare descriptions that could illuminate characters in just a few lines. On the street, they drew horses and waiting hansom cab drivers, and, to practice their speed, stood in doorways along the lengthy rue de Richelieu to sketch passersby—Camoin tapped a walking stick on the pavement making them turn just long enough to record in a lightning sketch—and even passing cyclists.

Matisse was ready to begin working his café sketches into a large painting, now made possible with his rented atelier in the medina. In January, Amélie sent a postcard from Tangier to their son Jean. "[Your father] is currently doing a café interior which is off to a good start."

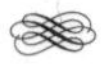

Café marocain—called *Moroccan Café* but also *Arab Coffeehouse* and *Moorish Café* in English (see figure 24)—was the largest painting Matisse did in Tangier. It measures five foot nine inches by six foot eleven inches (176 x 210 cm).

Unlike the other Moroccan canvases, he painted it with tempera, a water-soluble paint that creates a flat, opaque, matte surface. It eliminates the sheen of oil paint as well as its thickness and contours. This helped to flatten the walls, floor, and even the sitting men, who appear to almost float on a plane of pale turquoise. He worked and reworked it with the quick-drying paint. A line of horseshoe arches run along the back; done in black, they are the most intense color on the canvas, against the traditional laws of color composition where colors should become weaker. Perspective in the picture has been abolished for decoration.

It feels like a move east, a shift in Matisse's inner geography. The canvas has been called "the most Oriental of his Oriental paintings," which is not to say Orientalist.

Pushed to the verge of abstraction, it is the surface of memory spread out like a tableau of Persian miniatures illustrating a scene from the *Arabian Nights* writ large. It has a dreamy symbolism about it, yet no clear meaning. In his private journal that summer after seeing Matisse's Morocco works and writing extensively on this particular canvas, Marcel Sembat wrote, "The landscape of the thousand and one nights, but of the artist's thousand and one nights." Matisse gathered the experience and presented it in his singular vision.

The meditative, greenish-blue work consists of half a dozen turbaned figures with anonymous faces in the café. In the foreground and the focus of the work, a pair of men sit and stare at a glass bowl with a pair of goldfish. (It is the same thick-stemmed, goblet-shaped glass bowl as on the terrace beside Zorah.) Beside it sits a small, oblong vase of red flowers with leaves that are merely outlined with the same brown paint as the goldfish bowl. One of the men in the foreground sits upright, his arms lost within his robe and his turban a halo of gray, the other stretches out on his side beside him with his attention intently focused on the goldfish. The quartet in the background are as anonymous as a chorus; the most distinctive of them plays a violin.

The aquamarine canvas shimmers with heat and drowsy contemplation, with stillness, with calm. Even the goldfish appear not to be moving but merely hovering in the water. Time itself feels suspended.

Radiant, ethereal blue overwhelms the six figures and ultimately the viewer as a drive toward luminescence with the brush peaked. Standing before the massive canvas at the Hermitage Museum in Saint Petersburg is to be engulfed with a sensation of nirvanic torpor and transported, through its wash of flat turquoise that emanates light from within, to a place which lies on the other side of reality.

Across the bottom is a row of slippers that Matisse later painted over in a sequence of thickly brushed ovals, though they can clearly be seen with the naked eye when looking at the hanging canvas. The white robes of the men have turned gray over time, and only the orangish-ocher color of the faces and arms break up the turquoise that dominates the picture. Matisse painted a pale-ocher frame around the canvas itself in the same color as the men's skin and decorated it with pink discs. Besides acting as a boundary, the decorative frame helps draw the viewer's attention to the figures and also accentuates its link to Persian miniatures.

Matisse had stripped away most of the café's features captured in his sketchbooks. But while the slippers, tea glasses, instruments, flute-like hash pipes, and even the birdcages have disappeared, their essence remains. "A host of birds sang sweetly in cages hanging from the ceiling," Sembat wrote in *Cahiers d'aujourd'hui* after seeing the painting in spring. "Matisse declined to paint the cages, but a touch of the sweetness of the song passed into his painting." The painting stirs with the emotion of a whispered song. (As Matisse himself like to put it, "Retain only what cannot be seen.")

"Why did he eliminate the slippers, the pipe, the features on the faces, the varied colors of the burnooses?" Sembat wrote. "Because for Matisse, to perfect is to simplify. Because consciously or not, deliberately or despite himself, whenever he has strived to hardest he has moved towards simplicity. A psychologist would see it immediately: by instinct Matisse goes from the concrete to the abstract, the general." When Sembat called the painter's attention to this, Matisse responded, "The thing is, I move the way my feelings point, *toward ecstasy*. Then too, it's how I find peace of mind." Matisse desired no details, not even the expressions on the men's faces as they contemplated the fish, to disrupt the picture's blissful mood.

With *Moroccan Café*, Matisse's Morocco work reached its climax and conclusion. The artistic thrust of his second stay in Morocco peaked with this painting and its soothing grace. Sembat once said that it was a craving for peace that was a driving force behind Matisse's paintings. The culmination of two winters of gradual abstraction and years of study and synthesizing of the lessons of Islamic art, *Moroccan Café* fulfilled Matisse's well-known 1908 statement: "What I dream of is an art of balance, of purity and serenity, devoid of troubling or depressing subject matter. . . . a soothing, calming influence on the mind."

Matisse had been building toward this painting in Tangier, and with it, wrote his biographer, Hilary Spurling, "Matisse had reached a pitch of abstract purity and intensity unprecedented at that point in the West."

He had driven himself as far as he could in Tangier. It was time to go home.

In the office of the shipping agent, he booked two tickets to Marseille.

In mid-February, Matisse and his wife departed for France. Since October, he had completed a dozen, mostly large-size canvases along with many drawings. The second Tangier stay had been as prolific as the first but even more successful. In the luggage were some of the greatest paintings he would ever make. Apart from two versions of the Riffian and two highly different window views from his hotel room, he didn't repeat himself. Each work feels stunningly new and original. Nearly all of the twelve paintings are considered masterpieces. It was arguably the richest and most productive four-month spell of painting of his life that he had just experienced.

Camoin remained in Tangier with Morrice until March. "Since you left," he wrote to Matisse not long after his departure, "the weather has suddenly turned to rain, and Morrice suddenly turned to whisky. It starts with a few glasses of rum in the morning at breakfast! So you can imagine the stammering I hear at noon and in the evening!"

It was not an easy sea journey for the Matisses. "We made a picturesque crossing," he wrote sarcastically to Camoin, "a magnificent storm. We learned in Marseilles that there had been, the night of our arrival, three victims."

They didn't immediately continue to their home in Issy-les-Moulineaux, though. First, they traveled up the Côte d'Azur past Nice to the port town of Menton, near the Italian border, where his widowed mother was spending the winter. After visiting her, they caught a ship for Corsica. Their two boys were staying in Ajaccio.

It was here in Corsica, fifteen years before, that Matisse, a northerner from a dull, gray, smoke-stained industrial town, had his baptism in Mediterranean light. He had stayed six months. This time his visit to the island was brief. "In Menton we found good weather," he wrote to Camoin in Tangier after arriving in Corsica, "and in Ajaccio cold and miserable weather."

It was time to return to Paris. He was ready to face his critics and doubters.

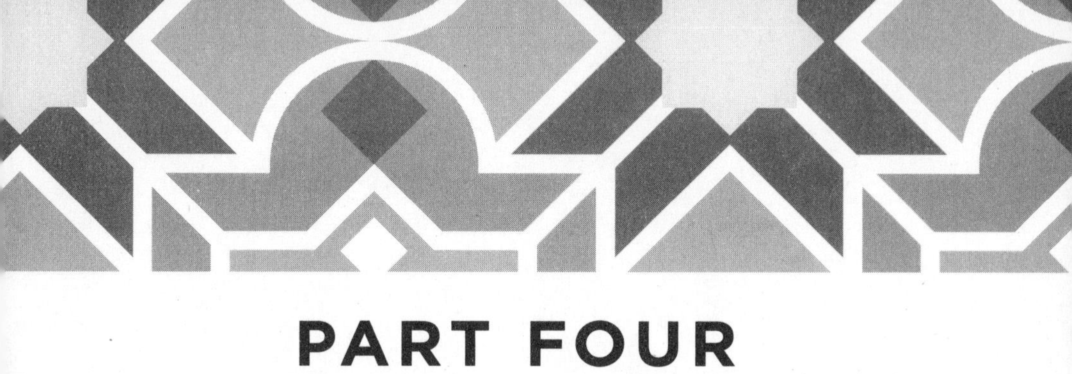

PART FOUR

ISSY-LES-MOULINEAUX, PARIS, AND NICE

27

Galerie Bernheim-Jeune sat just off Place de la Madeleine, the grand rectangular square that's home to the imposing, Grecian temple-like Church of the Madeleine and not far from Place de la Concorde, the Champs-Élysées, and Tuileries Garden. Opened in 1863, the venerable gallery held early exhibitions of many notable avant-garde, including Van Gogh (his first, in 1901), Cézanne, Bonnard, Vuillard, and Seurat. Matisse exhibited here in 1910. This was something of a retrospective as it included no new works (nearly everything was done before 1905) and only nine were for sale—of the sixty-five works, twenty-five were borrowed from the Stein clan—yet it still managed to provoke a storm of fury and open questions of the artist's sanity.

Since that exhibition, Matisse had shown little publicly. Picasso, Braque, and their fellow cubists were at the forefront, forging ahead with new styles and new ideas. To many of the art-world cognoscenti, Matisse was not so much unfashionable as becoming virtually obsolete.

But now he was back and ready to fight for the crown that had slipped since the heydays of their famous fauve exhibitions of 1905 and 1906. It would be on his terms—that is, in his own gallery rather than at the spring 1913 Salon des Indépendants, where he chose not to submit anything. When Félix Fénéon, the critic, collector, and avowed anarchist who ran Bernheim-Jeune's contemporary art department and was Matisse's main contact at the gallery from 1907 until 1920, offered him an exhibition of Moroccan work, Matisse immediately accepted.

Exposition Henri-Matisse: Tableaux du Maroc et Sculpture focused on new pieces in a direct counterattack against disparaging critics. The exhibition ran for just six days, from April 14 to 19, and apart from thirteen earlier sculptures plus six drawings, it consisted of new canvases from Tangier. The thin catalog with its orangish-brown cover lists eleven Moroccan paintings, while photographs taken inside the exhibition also show that it included *Periwinkles (Moroccan Garden)*, *View of the Bay of Tangier*, and a sheet with three pen-and-ink studies of Zorah's face.

Just three paintings were for sale. The catalog listed five as "App. à M.S.S." (reserved for Monsieur Sergei Shchukin): *The Standing Riffian*, *Zorah Standing*, and *Fatma, the Mulatto Woman*, and two large still lifes, *Arums, Iris, and Mimosas* and *Arums (Calla Lilies)*. Three works were "App. à M.I.M." (reserved for Monsieur Ivan Morozov): *Landscape Viewed from a Window*, *Zorah on the Terrace*, and *The Kasbah Gate*.

Unable to complete Morozov's long-overdue commission for a pair of landscapes, Matisse decided to offer him instead this trio of paintings. "They have been a great success," he wrote to Morozov on the day the exhibition closed, "and I think surely that you will be satisfied although you have waited a long time." In the letter, Matisse offered elaborate instructions on how to remove any fingerprints that might be on the gray frames that were made for the exhibition.

The pleased Morozov replied straight away. "I have just received your three paintings, and I hasten to inform you that Madame Morozov and I think they are splendid, and we thank you very much for this fine achievement." Enclosed was a check for 24,000 French francs, paying off the commission. Shchukin also wrote to Matisse. "Mr Morozov is ravished by your Moroccan pictures. I've seen them, and I understand his admiration. All three are magnificent. Now he is thinking of ordering from you three large panels from one of his living rooms."

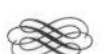

With the art world enthralled by cubism, the short exhibition generated only a handful of reviews. The few pieces, though, were largely laudatory. "Every painting and drawing by Henri Matisse possesses a virtue which cannot always be identified, but which is a true force. And it is the strength of the artist not to oppose it, to let it act," wrote the poet and influential critic Guillaume Apollinaire. "With all good faith and a pure concern for knowing and realizing himself, this painter never ceased to follow his instinct. It leaves him the task of choosing between emotions, judging and limiting fantasy, and that of scrutinizing deeply the light, nothing but light." Apollinaire thought that while Matisse had "stripped" his art in order to simplify, it "had not failed to become more sumptuous."

Of *The Kasbah Gate*, Louis Vauxcelles—who had famously coined the terms fauve and cubism—wrote: "My most grave objection to all this is that the essential theme of a picture is light, whereas three quarters of the pictures by Matisse are only exercises in color. Matisse is an eye." As Oxford professor Alastair Wright has pointed out, this was likely a nod to Cézanne's famous description of Monet ("Only an eye, but my God, what an eye") and even to Ingres's of Gustave Courbet ("This fellow is an eye").

"Look at it!" Sembat wrote in *Cahiers d'aujourd'hui* of the exhibition. "Friend or foe, you recognize a Matisse painting from the very first glance. It resembles nothing else, it bears his personal stamp. It is his and his alone! It is original." Matisse, Sembat added, "is profoundly original," but naturally so. "Matisse is original without trying to be."

Camoin, who had been with Matisse in Tangier and knew the works intimately, agreed. From Marseille, where he had just arrived from Tangier, he sent Matisse a letter, telling his friend how much he regretted not being in Paris to see the exhibition. "I think that you worked a lot there and that all your efforts are well contained in the interior of the Moroccan Café and the Riffins . . . finally, you must be happy!"

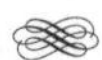

Moroccan Café was the boldest, largest, and most striking work in the exhibition, and it failed to sell.

In March, before the exhibition opened, Matisse tried to tempt Fénéon and the Bernheim-Jeune with *Moroccan Café* and *The Seated Riffian*. "We are turning them down because their size makes them too complicated to manage," Fénéon replied. In April, Matisse wrote to Shchukin about *Moroccan Café* and then offered the painting (and the still-unsold Riffian picture) to Morozov in a mid-April letter. Shchukin said he would have a look in July. Matisse, in the meantime, wrote again to Morozov in May, this time including a copy of Sembat's laudatory article ("the best thing that has been written about me"). Morozov declined.

It took Madame Matisse's involvement to finally sell *Moroccan Café*. She personally showed it to Shchukin during a summertime visit to Issy when her husband was absent. The Russian decided to buy it, paying Matisse 10,000 francs for the painting.

Moroccan Café would head to Moscow along with the other key Moroccan canvases. The only paintings from Morocco that would remain in France were *View of the Bay of Tangier* and *The Small Mulatto Woman* from Georgette Agutte and Marcel Sembat and today at Musée de Grenoble, and *Basket with Oranges*, which would become a part of Picasso's personal collection and end up in the Musée Picasso in Paris.

In Moscow, Shchukin hung *Moroccan Café* not with the rest of his Matisse collection, but in his private dressing room.

"The longer you look at it, this picture of a Moorish Café," Sembat had written in his article, "the more there rises up in you a sense of dreamy contemplation."

Shchukin took Sembat's advice quite literally. "It is the picture which I love now more than all the others," he wrote to Matisse, "and I look at it every day for at least an hour." The canvas became a calming presence for the troubled man beset by family tragedy.

Matisse would have been pleased. His paintings, he believed, were "meant to be felt and submitted to" rather than merely looked at on a wall. In this, it held something of the power of the finest icon paintings.

28

Once the exhibition at the Bernheim-Jeune closed, Matisse settled down to work. In Issy-les-Moulineaux, he resumed the routine established in Tangier of daily horseback rides, simple dinners, and early nights. He hired a horse and stabled it in an outbuilding on the property so that he could change into his gear and ride immediately after finishing a painting session.

That summer, he renewed his friendship with Picasso. Both sent Gertrude Stein postcards at the end of August 1913 with news that they had been riding together in the forests around Issy. It was a not-so-subtle notice to Stein that Matisse was back in the avant-garde fold.

Just as Collioure had given Matisse the distance to make the breakthrough with fauvism, in Tangier he found his own way in the face of cubism and the shadow of Picasso. He had built toward the sumptuous austerity of *Moroccan Café*, and now, shifting direction slightly, forged ahead with his driving artistic exploration. In the warm studio that summer—the doors opened to the garden, flies buzzing about, dogs lounging at the feet of the artist clad in the summer cotton work pajamas—Matisse worked on two of the most significant paintings of his career.

They didn't come easily, though. Work remained, as always, a continual struggle. In mid-September he wrote to Camoin, "I've wanted to write to you for a long time, but I'm preoccupied with my work and I can't manage to write your letter. When I have a moment, the ideas do not come to me, you know this malady. Right now, I'm tired and I need to clear my mind of all worries." While he had worked on little that summer, he said, he had pushed ahead with *Bathers by a River*, *Portrait of Madame Matisse*, and the bas-relief sculpture *Back II*. He lamented not being able to start yet on a large painting of a Tangier beach as he had planned. (He would never paint it.) But he believed he was moving forward, even if slowly. "I think I have taken a step all the same, and it's always hard."

The monumental *Bathers by a River* (see figure 25) had originally been conceived to accompany *Dance* and *Music* in Shchukin's Moscow home but abandoned early. With new inspiration from a scene he witnessed in Tangier, he returned to the massive canvas measuring about eight feet by twelve feet (260 x 392 cm). In a quartet of vertical bands, four faceless figures stand among foliage and a river. Originally a waterfall and then a blue river, Matisse transformed the river of the title into a thick black band with a white snake rising up into it: the serpent's appearance in Eden. It feels both ancient and modern, both peacefully pastoral and raked with tension. Matisse wasn't completely satisfied with it that summer, though, and returned to it again a few years later to finish. When the Art Institute of Chicago acquired it in 1953, Matisse said that he considered it among the five most pivotal paintings of his career.

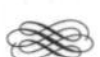

Matisse spent much of the summer and early fall of 1913 working on a more intimate picture, *Portrait of the Artist's Wife*. Amélie sits somewhat awkwardly on an uncomfortable-looking garden chair wearing a fashionable bluish-gray suit, an orangish scarf casually pulled around her shoulders, and a delicate ostrich-feather toque. It had required nearly a hundred sittings in their Issy garden and made Amélie cry when she saw her face ultimately reduced to a chalky gray mask with vacant, black eyes, thin, arching eyebrows, and a pinched expression that revealed nothing of the sitter. Along with the earlier *Woman with a Hat* and *Madame Matisse (The Green Stripe)*, it was one of the most significant portraits he had done of her. It was also the last. The picture ruptured their painter-model relationship. She would never sit for him again.

Shchukin saw the unfinished picture on the easel. While he had originally commissioned *Bathers by a River*, he bought the *Portrait of the Artist's Wife* instead once Matisse had completed it in late October. The portrait had an uncanny similarity to another in Shchukin's collection, Cézanne's *Lady in Blue*, purchased from Vollard's gallery in early 1909. (Matisse saw it when he stayed with Shchukin in Moscow.) In a strained, almost frozen pose, the sitter in Cézanne's picture has a distinct sadness about her, yet remains dignified in her fine blue dress and matching hat. In both pictures, the women's faces are tipped down, drawing the viewer's eye to the front of their modish suits, for Cézanne a triangle of blue, for Matisse a rectangle of turquoise framed by sharp lapels.

For the 1913 Salon d'Automne, Matisse submitted only this portrait of his wife, and only at the last moment. He had exhibited so little in the recent Salons and remained beset with hesitancy.

Eight years before at the same annual Salon, Matisse had shown *Woman with a Hat*, and it had been reviled and ridiculed. Since then, cubism had prepared viewers for this updated portrait of Amélie.

"Henri Matisse's portrait of a woman is the best thing in the Salon," Apollinaire began his review of the Salon, and hailed the painting alongside the *Woman with a Hat* "as the artist's masterpiece." Apollinaire's praise could not have been greater. "The portrait he is exhibiting here, full of voluptuousness and charm, marks, in a sense, a new period in Matisse's art, and perhaps in contemporary art as a whole: until now, voluptuousness had almost completely disappeared from contemporary art, and was to be found almost nowhere except in the magnificent sensual paintings of the aged Renoir." ("Voluptuous" is a strange choice for an adjective, because Amélie appears anything but that in the portrait.) In another review of the Salon, Apollinaire ended with this kicker: "If there is a masterpiece on view at the Salon d'Automne, it is this and nothing else."

A young André Breton—who would launch surrealism a decade later—was equally moved and later recalled the deep impression the canvas made on him, as would his fellow surrealist Louis Aragon. Even Picasso was struck when he saw the painting on the easel during a visit to Issy-les-Moulineaux. Seemingly in response, Picasso made his late-cubist masterpiece *Woman in a Chemise in an Armchair* of a woman seated in a velvety purple armchair holding a newspaper in a raised hand.

"I saw the Salon d'Automne and didn't find much new there," Matisse reported to Camoin in Marseille. "The cubists have been scattered so that they pass fairly unnoticed." That was wishful thinking. Cubism was still the most visible modern art style on view and dominated the Salon.

But *Portrait of the Artist's Wife* shot Matisse back to the forefront of the avant-garde conversation.

Despite the success his canvas was having at the Salon, Matisse remained down. "The truth is that Painting"—he wrote it with a capital P—"is a very disappointing thing," he told his dear pal Camoin in a November 1913 letter, while the Salon was still running. "By the way, my painting (the portrait of my wife) is a great success among the progressives. But it hardly satisfies me: it is the beginning of a very great painful effort."

As soon as the Salon closed, the pivotal painting headed to Moscow to join Shchukin's large collection, the thirty-seventh—and ultimately final—Matisse canvas to hang in his palatial home.

With autumn, the light in Issy-les-Moulineaux dulled, the days shortened, and rain clouds blustered overhead, and the studio soon turned frigid. Camoin was still in Marseille, where Matisse advised him to stay and not return to Paris, "which at this time is equivalent to *demi-suicide*." They hadn't seen the sun in ages, Matisse wrote. "All last week the sky was gray and heavy and it made you disgusted with life. I hadn't worked for at least two weeks and, in order not to not get depressed, I got down to it yesterday Sunday. I took a model and did a nude. This morning, the second session and the beginning of the worries." He worked slowly. He struggled. He was anxious.

Matisse prepared to return to Tangier for a third consecutive winter.

He did so, though, with little excitement this time. He oscillated between going to Morocco and staying in France. "I wasn't very enthusiastic," he later explained to Swiss critic Pierre Courthion, "because I could see it all in advance: my arrival in Tangiers, setting up there, the same landscape motifs. I didn't want to go and had no ideas about going anywhere else, either."

If heading to familiar Tangier held little appeal for Matisse, then going to an unfamiliar destination appealed even less. After his two-week trip to Algeria in 1906, he wrote to Henri Manguin, "As a painter I saw many interesting subjects, but of course my stay was too short. The Biskra oasis is very beautiful, but I know that one must spend several years in these countries in order to extract something new and that one cannot just take one's palette and one's system and apply it." His system at the time was a bright fauve one with blasts of intense colors and bold brushwork.

Matisse had been unusually productive during his two Morocco stays and managed to "extract something new" for his art quite quickly—within just weeks and months rather than "several years." This was particularly the case during his second stay when he returned not just to the same city and same hotel, but to the same room with the same bed and the same view out the windows.

If he went back to Tangier, he could at least begin working straight away. The place would be familiar while far from home's routines.

He hesitated, though, and flirted with taking a studio in Paris. "You will probably be astonished to hear that I've made plans to spend a few months in Paris, subletting a studio in Montparnasse," he wrote to Camoin in November. "Judging that my present task demands concentration and that a trip, a change of climate and excitement of new things—whose first impact on us is always how picturesque they are—would lead my attention to be dispersed, so that the excitement of Paris is sufficient for me now."

He seems to be trying to convince himself. In the next sentence, he added: "But the sadness of the sky has acted contrary to my reason, and the short stay I'm going to make in the South will certainly decide me to leave." The self-aware Matisse knew he was going on too much about it, even to his closest friend. *"Je m'étends longuement sur mon cas."* ("I dwell at length on my case.")

By December, temperatures in Paris fell well below freezing, and the grass and weeds around the villa's garden turned stiff with hoarfrost. The light faded in his studio by 3:00 P.M. The French art historian Robert Rey visited that winter and captured the frigid working conditions. "In the studio was a canvas that seems very large in my memory: a white wall in front of which sits a Moroccan in a green djellaba," Rey recalled a decade later, referring to the unsold *Seated Riffian*. "Again it was the soul of a Moroccan that was there, indifferent to the studio's six degrees below zero."

Either that plan to sublet a studio in Montparnasse fell through or Matisse had had enough of Paris and its inclement winter weather. In Tangier, the Hôtel Villa de France would be waiting for him and perhaps the glass studio in the medina. The light would be good, and there would be Zorah to paint and Amido to help with translations.

He changed his mind again, and was soon packing his luggage for Morocco.

He was returning to Tangier for a third winter.

Before departing, Matisse went to visit Marquet in Paris. His fifth-floor studio on the Left Bank of the Seine at 19 quai Saint-Michel had previously been Matisse's.

In the early 1890s, Matisse opened his first studio in this Latin Quarter apartment block, under the roof and without a view. A year later he rented small rooms on the fifth floor with a view out over the Seine. He lived here with Camille Joblaud after their daughter, Marguerite, was born in 1894. A few months after marrying Amélie in January 1898, the newlyweds moved in and eventually lived there with their children. It was the busy, crowded heart of Paris. Voices carried up from the quai below, the noise of barking dogs and passing motor omnibuses, hawkers offering vegetables and, in summer, ice cream from two-wheeled pushcarts. In the winter the smell of roasting chestnuts floated up from a corner stall along with the coal smoke of the long, tubular river barges that slid under the low Pont Saint-Michel. The family moved out in 1905, though Matisse kept the studio for two more years until Marquet took it over.

Marquet had been the one to encourage Matisse to go to Morocco, and now, somewhat ironically, he offered his old friend a reason *not* to return to North Africa: the apartment below his studio was available.

Matisse went to see it. One of the windows looked out over the stone Petit Pont bridge and Notre-Dame Cathedral, the other upstream to Pont Saint-Michel, the Gothic royal chapel Sainte-Chapelle, and, in the distance, the long slate-gray mansard roof of the Louvre's riverside wing. Having spent many years of his adult life in the building, the views were familiar.

Matisse liked the way the low ceilings of the rooms caught the warm light reflecting off the imposing, honey-colored Préfecture de Police building on the Île de la Cité. Despite being a worn, early nineteenth-century building, with a narrow, gloomy entrance, rickety wooden staircase, and cantankerous concierge, he took it straight away without apparently showing, or even consulting, Amélie.

"So instead of leaving for Tangiers," Matisse told Courthion, "my luggage traveled to the quai Saint-Michel."

29

On January 1, 1914, the day after his forty-fourth birthday, Matisse and his wife installed themselves in their new Paris digs. Apart from a double bed, piano, some beloved paintings, and his violin, they brought little else beyond a few household items and what Matisse would need to work.

If the move out to Issy-les-Moulineaux from Paris in 1909 had been something of a withdrawal, this was a determined return. Having spent much of the last five years largely in the suburbia of Issy or further afield, he was returning at a time when Paris dominated the art world and remained the undisputed global epicenter of artistic revolution and innovation.

For the arts in Paris, 1913 had been a monumental, boundary-pushing year. Igor Stravinsky's *The Rite of Spring* caused a near riot when Sergei Diaghilev's Ballets Russes company performed it with choreography by Nijinsky at the opulent Théâtre des Champs-Élysées; Marcel Proust published *Swann's Way*, the first volume of his epic novel *In Search of Lost Time*; and the poet Blaise Cendrars and abstract painter Sonia Delaunay jointly produced their "simultaneous" work *La Prose du Transsibérien et de la Petite Jehanne de France* on a single, accordion-folded vertical sheet of paper that merged text and image and is now considered one of the century's most important artist's books. Cubism was at its zenith, while Apollinaire published *Les Peintres cubistes*, the essential work on the movement. But cubism's two principal drivers—Picasso and Braque—were already moving beyond shattered viewpoints; they were incorporating collage and newspaper into their works, and beginning to reassemble reality using cardboard, paper, and string. With his playful guitars, Picasso essentially reinvented sculpture.

Across the Atlantic, the International Exhibition of Modern Art at the 69th Regiment Armory—better known as the Armory Show—opened in New York in February 1913 and then traveled to Chicago and Boston. With some 1,300 works by over three hundred avant-garde artists, it offered Americans their first in-depth glimpse of impressionism, fauvism, and cubism, movements that had largely been centered in Paris. From Matisse, the show included thirteen paintings, three drawings, and one sculpture. *The New York Times* called his paintings ugly, coarse, narrow, and revolting in their inhumanity, while students at the Art Institute of Chicago, aghast at their abject horridness, burned copies and put Matisse on mock trial for crimes against art when the show came to their city.

The Armory Show's greatest sensation was Marcel Duchamp's *Nude Descending a Staircase, No 2*, a clever mixture of cubism and futurism that had caused outrage at the Salon des Indépendants (even the cubists rejected it). In Paris, Duchamp pushed the boundaries significantly further when he mounted a bicycle fork and wheel upside-down on a wooden stool in his studio and presented it as the first "readymade" art. An everyday object, Duchamp seemed to imply, became art simply because it was selected by an artist; that is, *chosen* rather than *made*. Beauty of the image and centuries of traditions were being further pushed aside for the idea, the concept, the conceit—for cleverness.

While lacking Picasso's voracious devouring of different styles, or Duchamp's extremism, Matisse, with his cool, organized talent, prodigious work ethic, and two winters in Tangier behind him, was ready to continue his incessant experimenting in the new studio.

January 1914 was dry and exceptionally cold in France, with frigid temperatures unseen for decades. Lakes and even rivers froze. Snow buried parts of Provence. In Paris, the mercury dropped to as low as 14°F (-10°C). Public sculptures were entombed in ice. Violent storms raked the country in February, March was exceptionally wet and rainy, and in May rare late snowstorms swept across the high plateau. In June, the capital saw the worst thunderstorms in fifty years. Sewers burst, a gas main exploded, cellars flooded, and buildings collapsed. Gaping holes in the pavement along the Seine opened, killing eleven.

Cocooned in his new studio while the extreme weather raged, an energized Matisse produced nearly a dozen important canvases in just six months. His windows looked out over the Cité, the island heart of ancient Paris. He painted and repainted the view of the river and the iconic twin-towered façade of Notre Dame, the very symbol of French tradition. He was refiguring his approach to these classical subjects, and continuing his rebellion against the French Academy that had erupted so loudly with his chromatic fauve assault in 1905.

That spring, he took back up the goldfish theme and painted what is widely considered one of his seminal works, *Interior with a Goldfish Bowl*, a complex and sumptuous meditation on interior and exterior space. In a room filled with blueish twilight, a large cylindrical aquarium holding a pair of floating orange fish sits on a small table. Out the window, the old city glows in the last of the afternoon light as people move across the Petit Pont. The plant's long shoots appear to be arching right through the window. This is Matisse's miniaturized world, separated from the city below by glass, and trapped within the stillness of his own tank-like room.

He painted it for Shchukin. For the Russian he also completed *Woman on a High Stool*, a seated portrait of Germaine Raynal, the wife of the poet and critic Maurice Raynal, backed by flat geometric planes of rather severe grays.

Unbeknownst to either Matisse or Shchukin, these would be the last two paintings that the artist would do for his loyal patron, though they would never reach him.

Meanwhile, across Paris in Montmartre, Charles Camoin was again suffering an artistic crisis. In Tangier with Matisse and Amélie, he seemed to have improved. But back in France, doubts returned. "I feel all my misery and resign myself to my modest job, telling myself that after all there are no lesser professions (I say this without joking)," he had written Matisse that past November while still in the South of France. As well, he continued to be tormented by his relationship with Émilie Charmy. Before returning to Paris, he told Matisse that he wasn't completely over her yet.

In Paris, in his Montmartre studio late one mid-June evening, he began to remove canvases from their stretchers with a penknife and then attack them with a larger knife and scissors. Camoin cut up nearly everything he found. Hundreds of colorful pieces littered the studio floor. He gathered them up, took them down to the street, and stuffed the scraps into trash cans on rue Lepic.

Camoin later explained the dramatic action rather matter-of-factly and attributed it fully to artistic motives: "When I returned from Tangiers, I had destroyed eighty canvases that no longer pleased me. During my stay in Morocco, in contact with Matisse, my approach had truly evolved."

There would be no neat discarding his pre-Moroccan past with the extreme act, though. A ragpicker salvaged the pieces and sold them to a priest in the flea market, the beginning of the scraps passing through a lengthy succession of hands and sewn back together in various levels of expertise. The poet, novelist, and art critic Francis Carco acquired a number of the pieces and had them relined and stitched back together. In 1925, Carco decided to sell some of the canvases, and Camoin sued to stop it. *Camoin v. Carco* (Affaire Camoin) was an important early French legal case in *le droit de divulgation*, the moral right of artists and authors to control how and when their works may be made public. After the lengthy trial and final judgment in 1931, four of the restitched canvases were burned before bailiffs in an oven of the Grand Palais where Camoin (and Matisse) had first come to public notice a quarter of a century before.

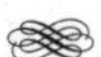

The buzz of Paris was quickly smothered in the summer of 1914 and the period that would later be known as La Belle Époque came to an abrupt end as World War I engulfed Europe. Nightmarish violence was soon consuming the continent and beyond.

Mobilization posters appeared across Paris, and many of the international art set found themselves swapping brushes for rifles and smocks for uniforms of various armies. Camoin was first sent to the Vosges Mountains on the Western Front as a stretcher-bearer and later painted canvases of camouflage by the kilometer. Braque was made an officer and sent to the front lines at Somme. Derain joined up the day after the general mobilization and spent years in the artillery. Jean Puy served in the army. Fernand Léger became a stretcher-bearer, Oskar Kokoschka a cavalryman, Max Beckmann a medic, and Otto Dix a machine gunner. Jean Cocteau joined the Red Cross Ambulance Corps as a driver. Giorgio de Chirico left for Italy, where he enlisted, but, deemed unfit, was assigned to work in a hospital. Apollinaire was also an Italian national, but was so keen to fight for his beloved France that he set about getting French nationality, joined an artillery unit after training, and fought in the trenches on the Western Front.

Picasso and Juan Gris, from neutral Spain, were not called up. Anticipating a collapse of the market for his work and the closing of Kahnweiler's gallery, Picasso rushed to Paris from Avignon to withdraw all of his money from the bank. Instead of returning home to Spain, Picasso went back to Avignon. Modigliani, whose advanced tuberculosis kept him from being drafted, was unable to get his monthly allowance from his family in Italy, lost his source of stone for sculpting, and turned back to sketching portraits of friends in Parisian cafés against abstract backgrounds, often with their eyes closed.

Although already forty-four years old, Matisse was keen to enlist and bought soldier's boots. He was rejected for service after failing his medical exam due to a weak heart. Crushed, he and Marquet (who was nearly forty) turned to Sembat, who had been made minister of Public Works in the French government. "Derain, Braque, Camoin, Puy, are at the front, risking their lives," an exasperated Matisse told Sembat. "We are sick of staying at home. . . . How can we serve the country?"

Sembat's reply was succinct and unequivocal: "By continuing to paint as well as you do."

After spending August 1914 in Issy-les-Moulineaux, Matisse and Amélie evacuated their children to the southwest of the country with her family in Toulouse and then headed together to Collioure, arriving on September 10. Marquet was already there, and so was an ill and broke Juan Gris with his wife.

Collioure, a steep, picturesque fishing village bounded by hills of vineyards, dry-stone walls, and olive trees in the South of France near the Spanish border where the Pyrenees Mountains tumble into the Mediterranean, had been key to Matisse's artistic development. It was here a decade before that he had painted his explosive fauve works.

This time his palette was very different. Banishing such fiery tones, he painted *French Window at Collioure* (called *Porte-fenêtre à Collioure* in French), a dark and abstract canvas (see figure 26). Framing a great vertical void of black are three panels: a softish bluish with some white and gray and etched with black marks on the left side and to the right, a gray one and then, edging the canvas, a luminous turquoise strip that in the Centre Pompidou's fifth-floor gallery has an almost eerie glow to it. Louis Aragon called it "the most mysterious picture ever painted."

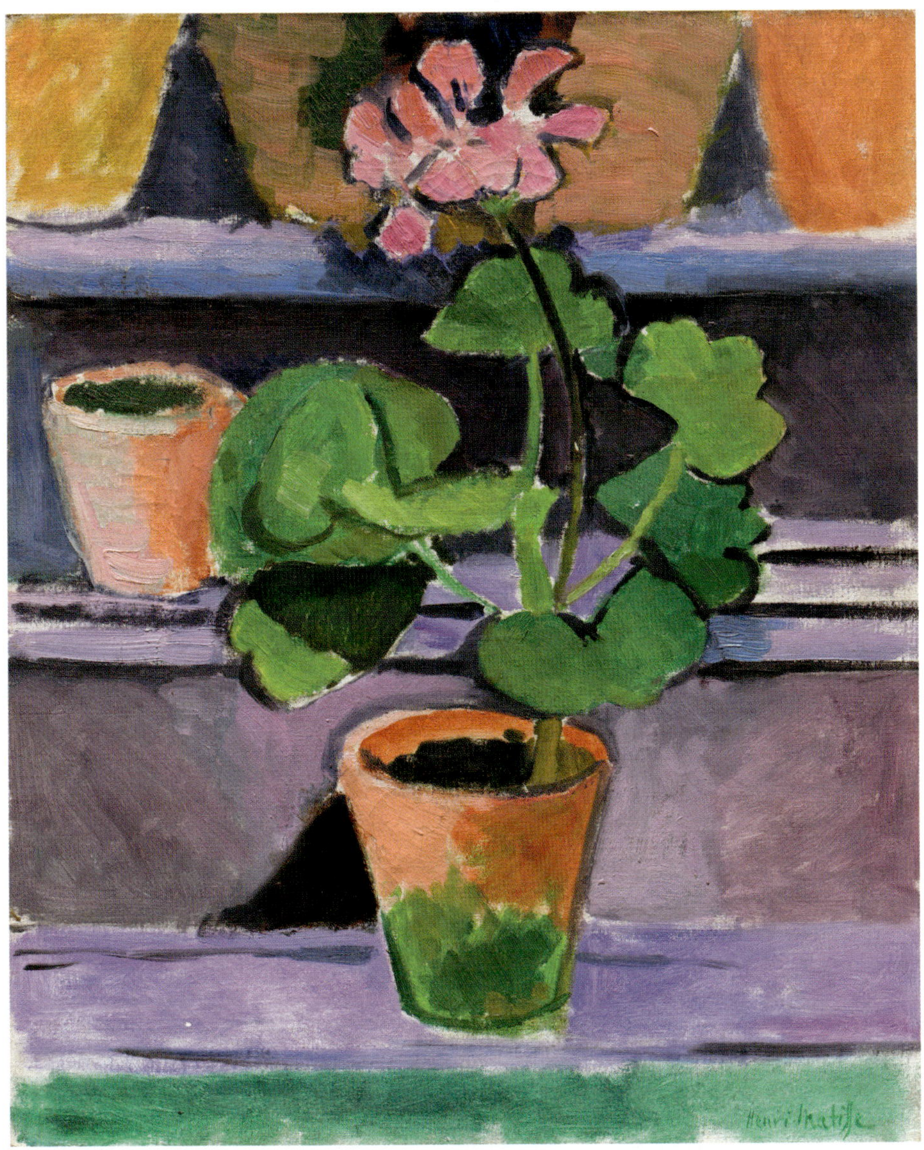

Figure 10. Henri Matisse, *Pot of Geraniums*, 1912

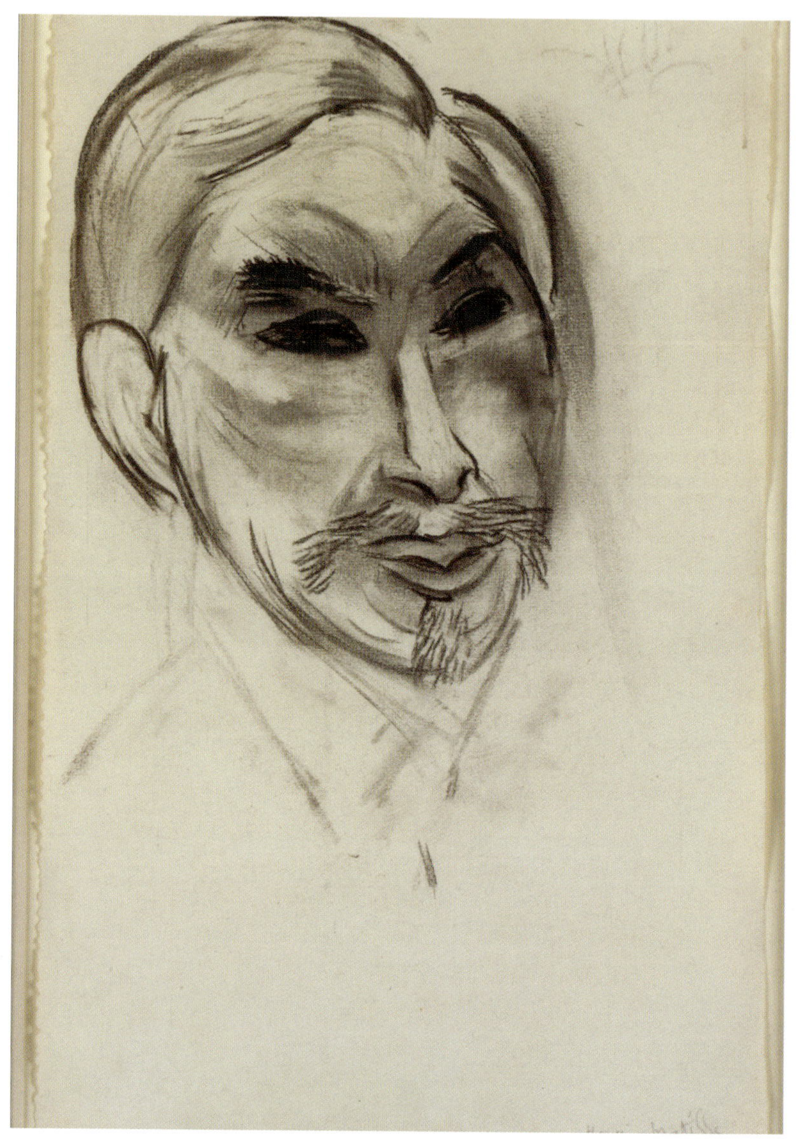

Figure 11. Henri Matisse, *Sergei Ivanovich Shchukin*, 1912

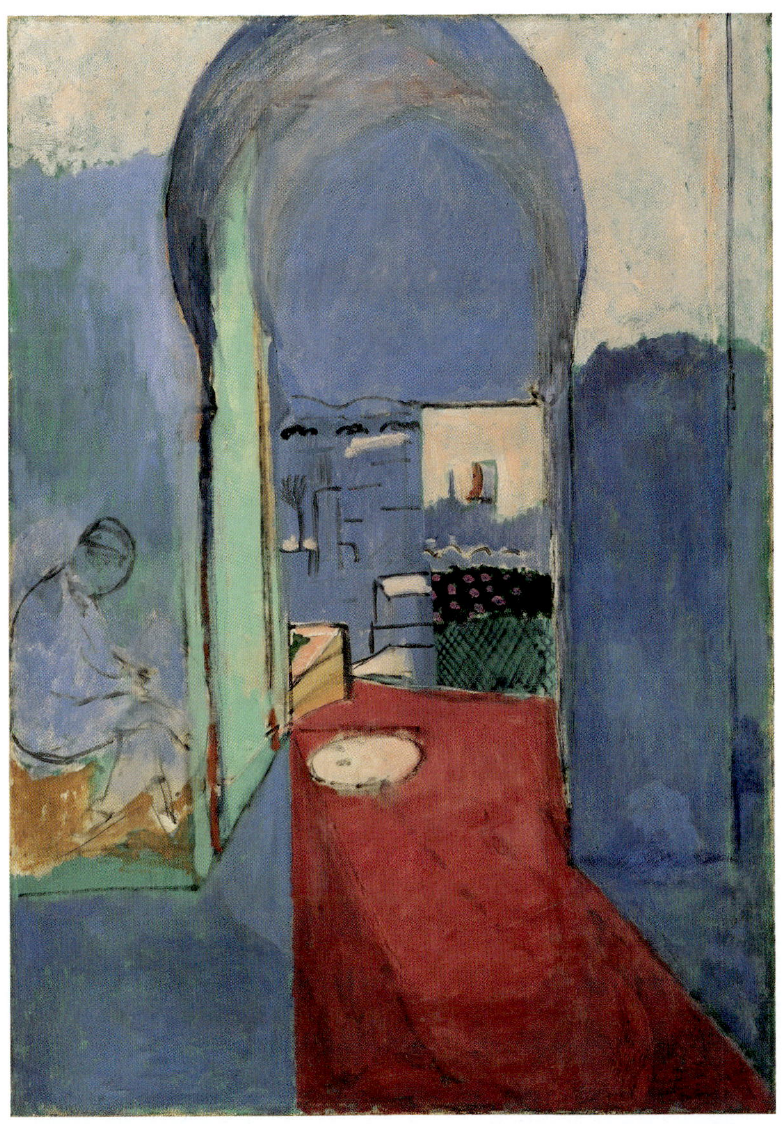

Figure 12. Henri Matisse, *The Kasbah Gate* or *Entrance to the Kasbah*, 1912

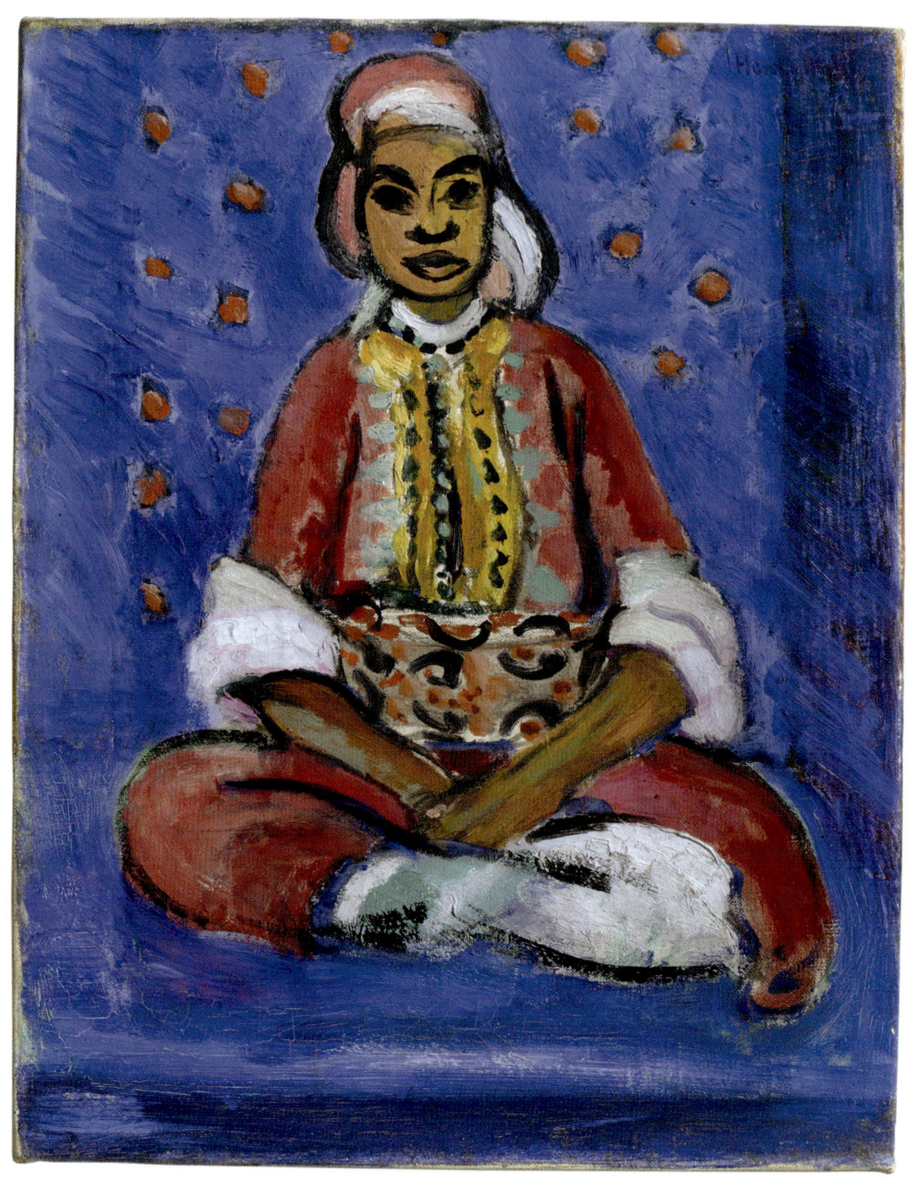

Figure 13. Henri Matisse, *The Small Mulatto Woman*, 1912

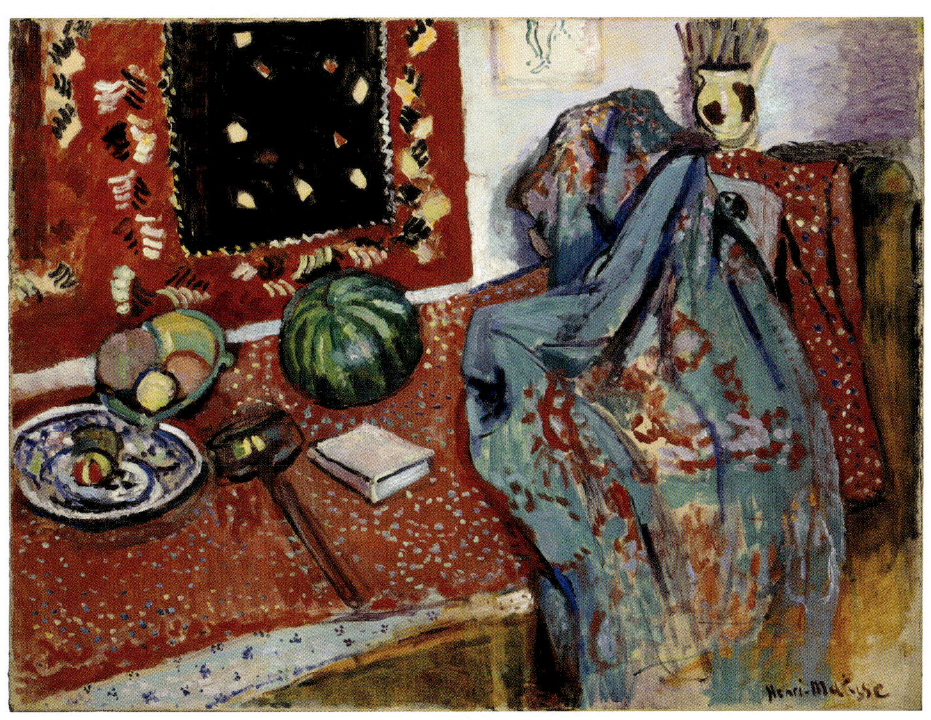

Figure 14. Henri Matisse, *The Red Carpets*, 1906

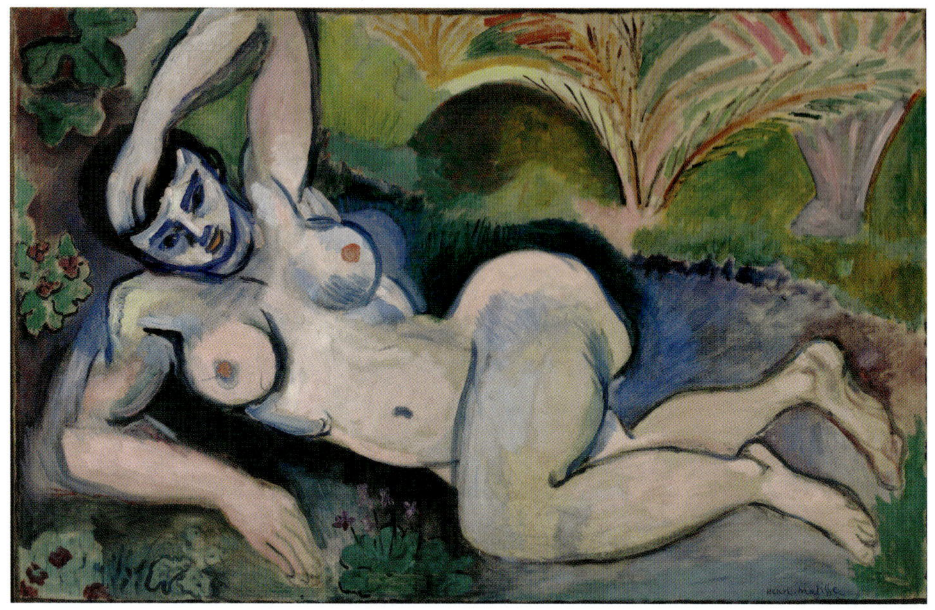

Figure 15. Henri Matisse, *Blue Nude (Memory of Biskra)*, 1907

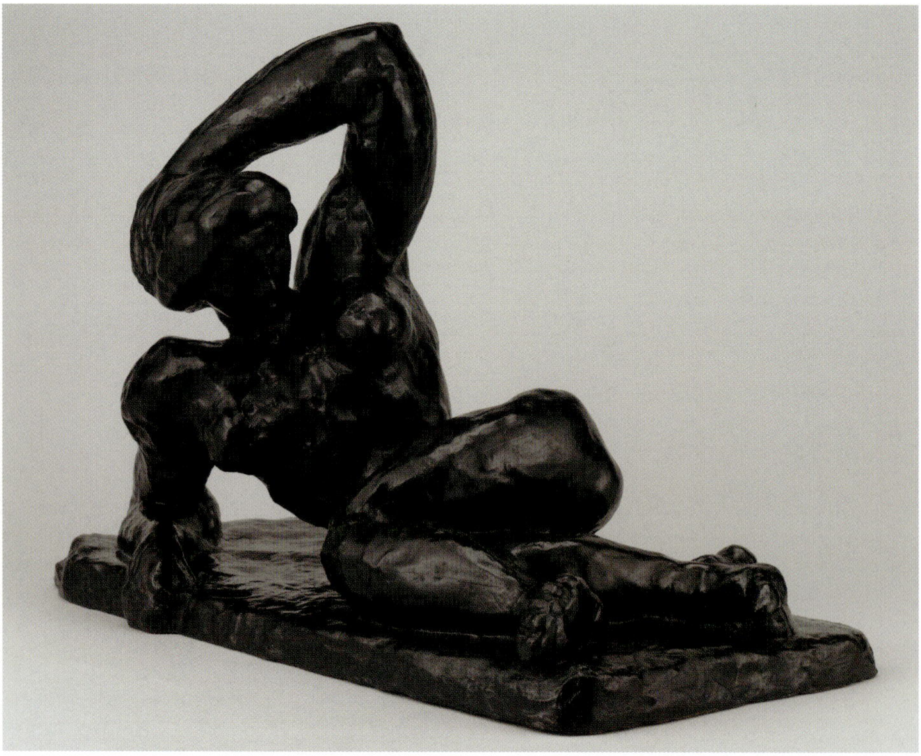

Figure 16. Henri Matisse, *Reclining Nude I (Aurore),* orig. 1907, this cast c. 1930

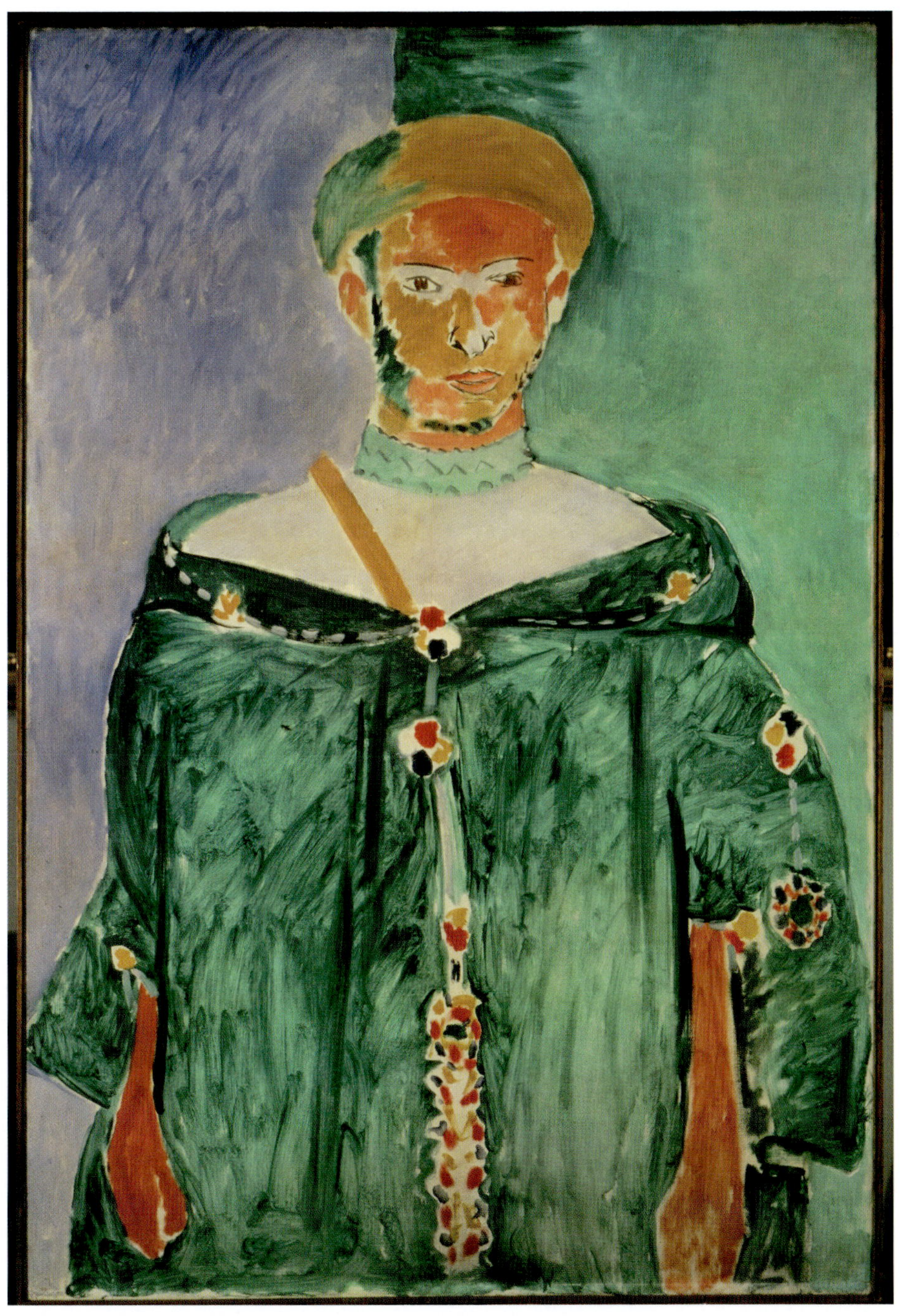

Figure 17. Henri Matisse, *The Standing Riffian*, 1912

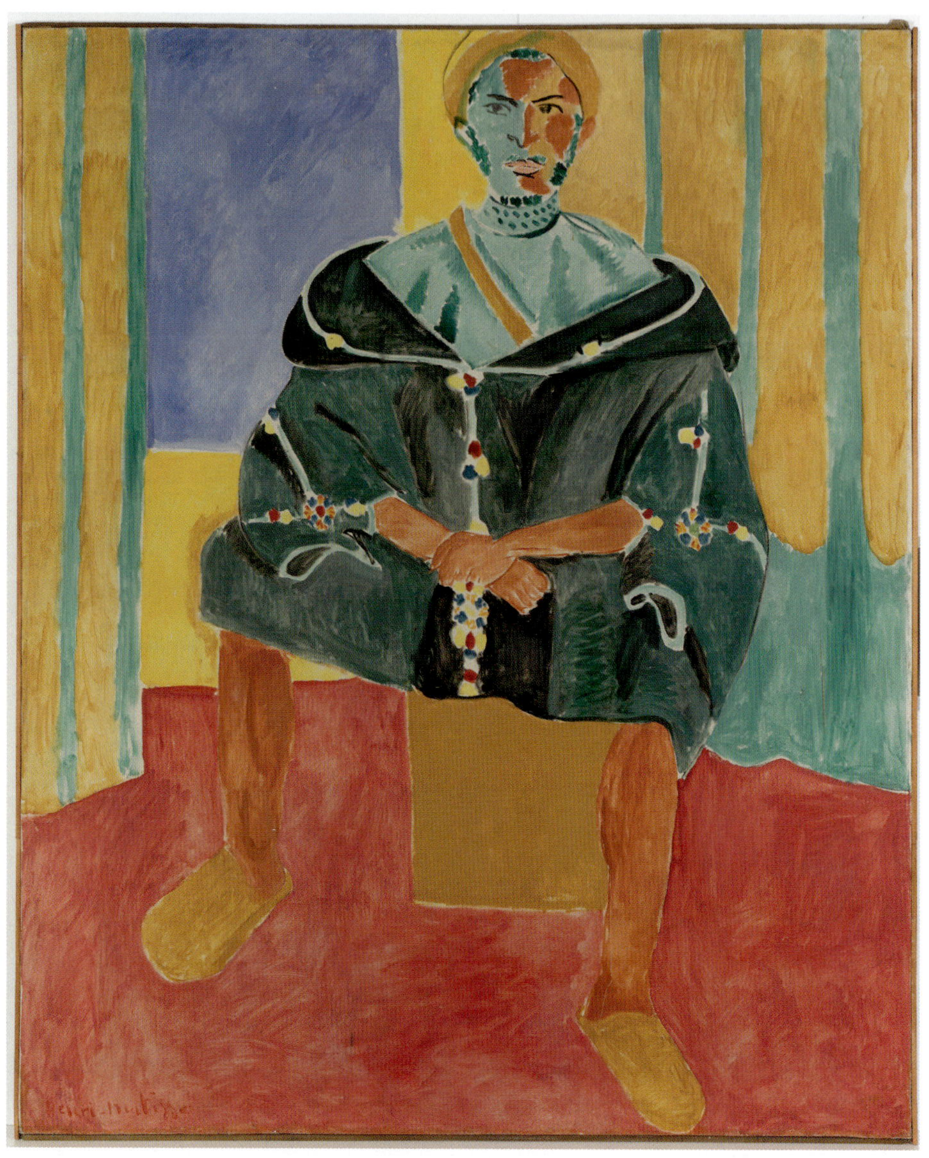

Figure 18. Henri Matisse, *The Seated Riffian*, 1912

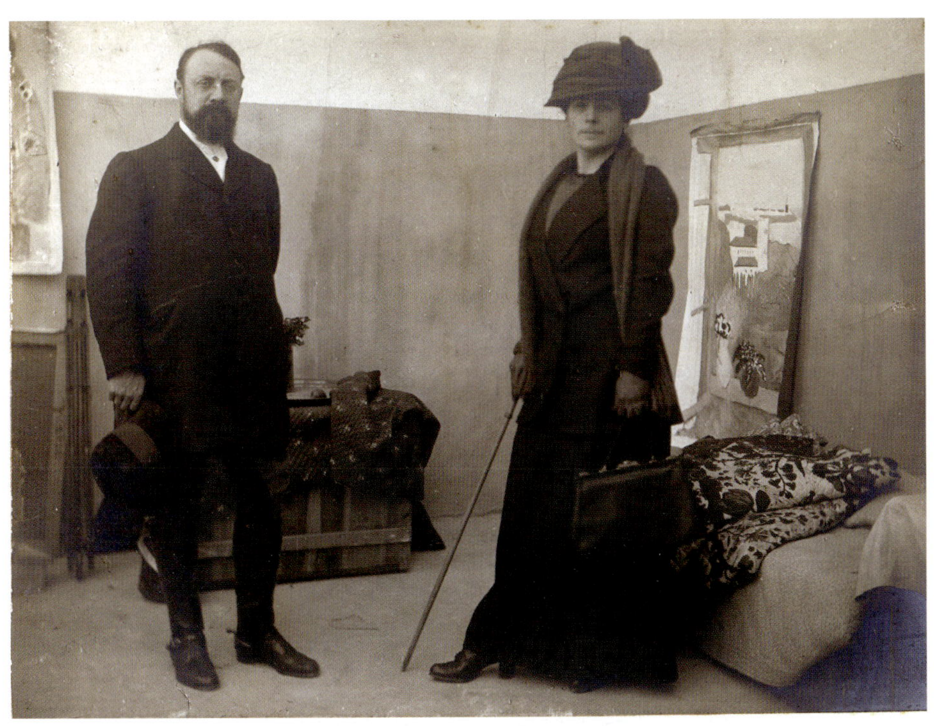

Figure 19. Henri and Amélie Matisse, Hôtel Villa de France, Tangier, 1912

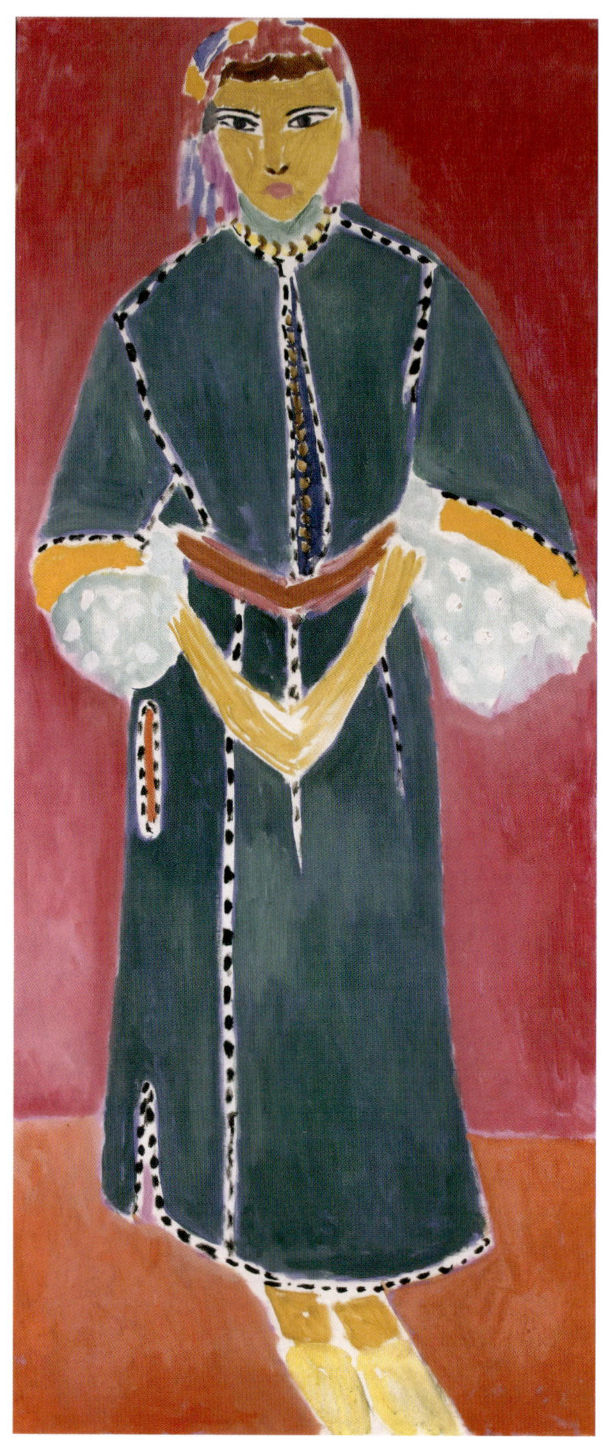

Figure 20. Henri Matisse, *Zorah Standing*, 1912

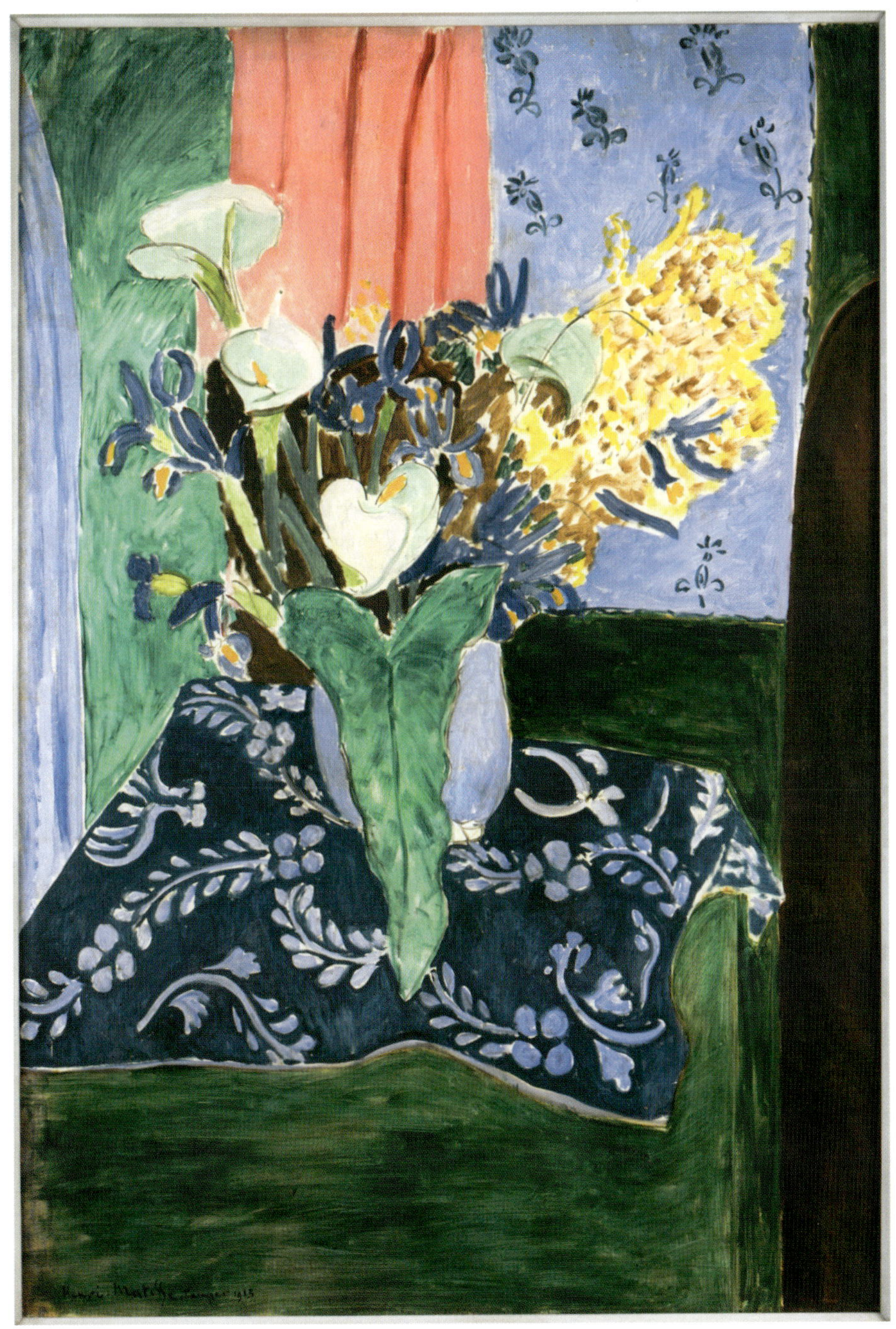

Figure 21. Henri Matisse, *Arums, Iris, and Mimosas*, 1913

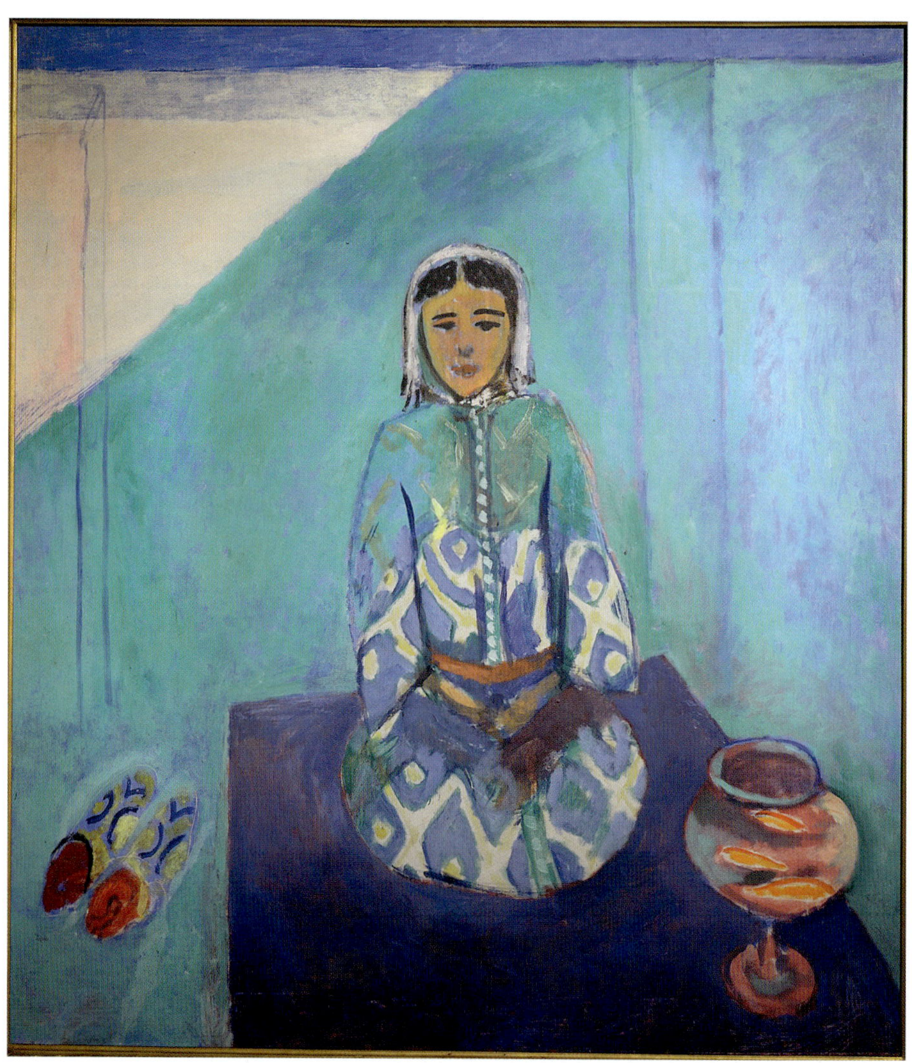

Figure 22. Henri Matisse, *Zorah on the Terrace*, 1912

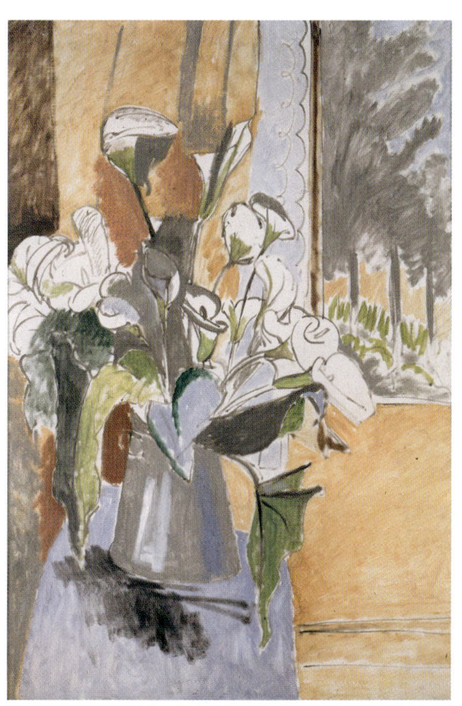

Figure 23. Henri Matisse, *Bouquet of Flowers on a Veranda or Arums (Calla Lilies)*, 1912

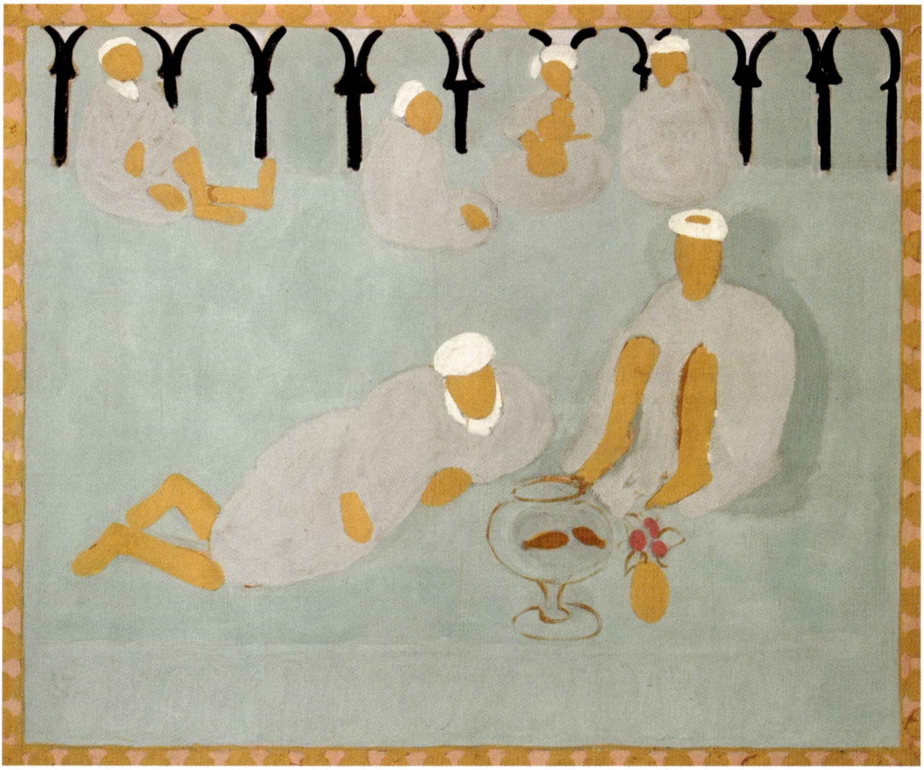

Figure 24. Henri Matisse, *Moroccan Café*, 1913

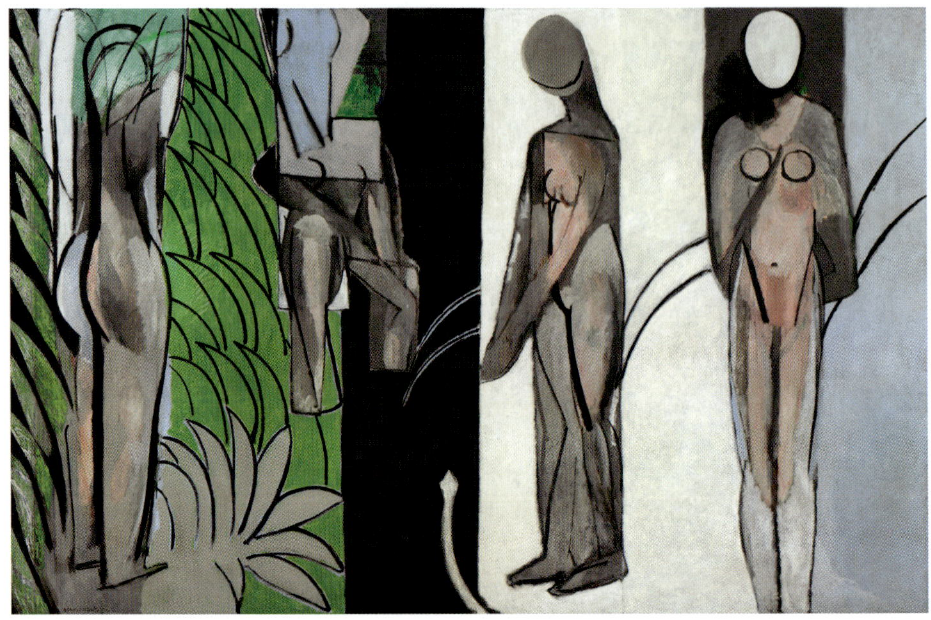

Figure 25. Henri Matisse, *Bathers by a River*, 1917

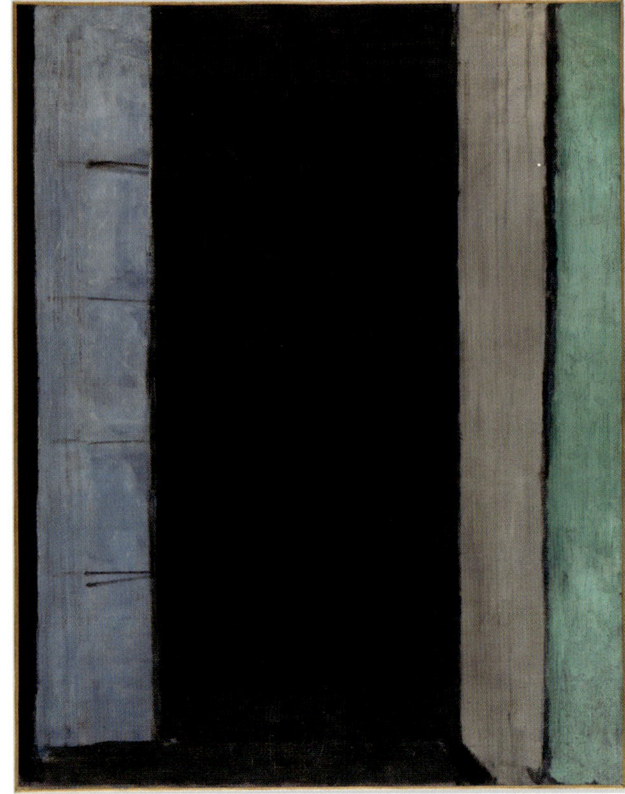

Figure 26. Henri Matisse, *French Window at Collioure*, 1914

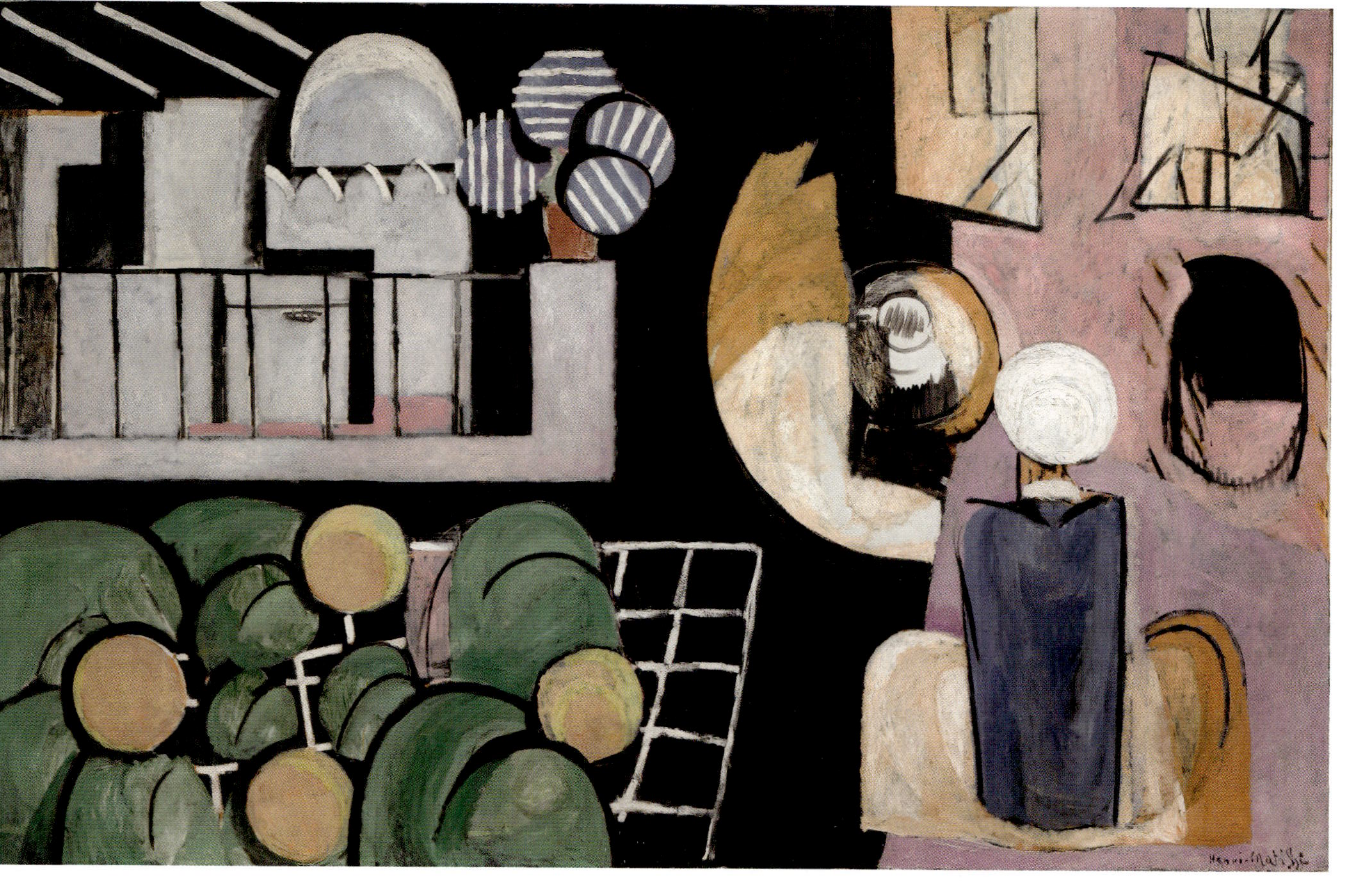

Figure 27. Henri Matisse, *The Moroccans*, 1916

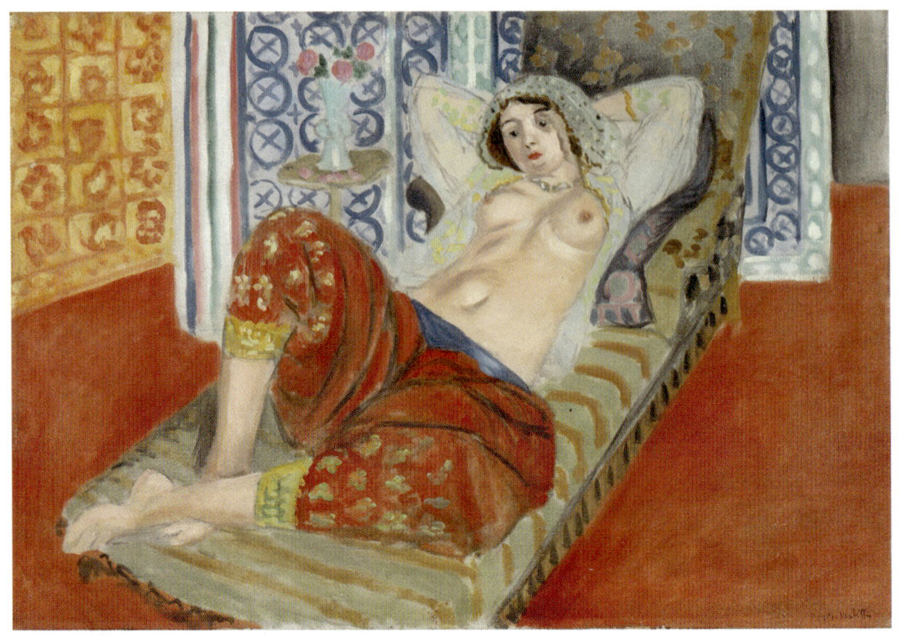

Figure 28. Henri Matisse, *Odalisque in Red Culottes*, 1921

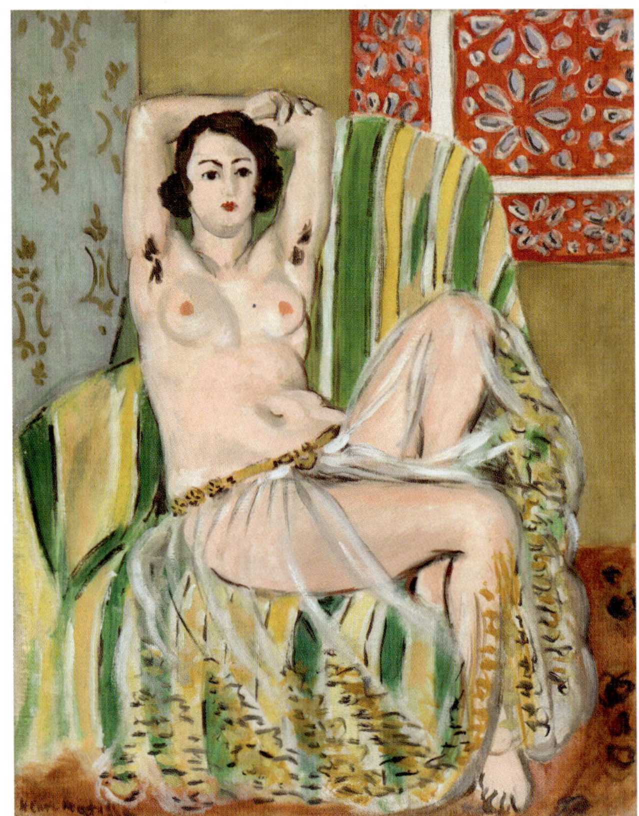

Figure 29. Henri Matisse, *Odalisque Seated with Arms Raised, Green Striped Chair*, 1923

In Collioure during the summer of 1905, Matisse had painted his groundbreaking *The Open Window*, with its intoxicated (and intoxicating) colors. This sober, gloomy one painted almost a decade later could not appear more dissimilar. It was the same view. (X-rays and raking light have revealed that he originally painted a decorative balcony railing and landscape in the central black panel.) But Matisse's world had changed. His hometown was one of the first in France to be overrun by the German army, and his brother and elderly, ailing mother were trapped in an occupied zone. His native region had become a major battleground.

Rather than of a sparkling, glistening sea, the new Collioure window view looks into dark nothingness: just the silence and darkness of a void.

He didn't feel the canvas was done before he returned to Paris with it toward the end of October, and left it unsigned. Back in his studio on quai Saint-Michel, Matisse never completed *French Window at Collioure*. The canvas remained unsigned.

The painting is now considered a forerunner to American abstract painting. Ab Reinhart hailed it as one of the two most important artist events of 1914—though that can be said only in hindsight. Matisse didn't exhibit the painting that year nor at any time during his life. After Matisse died in 1954, the damaged canvas was rediscovered, restored, and finally exhibited for the first time in Los Angeles in 1966. Its impact on a generation of painters is hard to overstate. For Richard Diebenkorn it was something of an epiphany seeing the canvas in California. "Undoubtedly, the hinge-point in Diebenkorn's career," wrote art critic Robert Hughes, the experience led to the Californian artist's celebrated *Ocean Park* series ("surely," according to Hughes, "one of the most distinguished meditations on landscape in painting since Monet's waterlilies"). When Reinhart, Diebenkorn, and company saw it in the sixties, the work still seemed explosively radical a staggering half century after Matisse had painted it.

Back in Paris from Collioure, Matisse's work came to a virtual halt. From his studio, he could sometimes hear the distant thump of shelling. His mother and brother remained stuck between war fronts; his oldest son, Jean, would soon be called up for service; and the military had requisitioned the villa in Issy-les-Moulineaux for French army officers, who would remain there until spring.

The art market contracted. Dealers fled Paris, galleries were shuttered, museums closed, and the two annual Salons were suspended. (The Grand Palais was taken over by the military and became a hospital.) Artists lost places to exhibit but also ways to receive money from clients, patrons, and family.

Poverty and dullness blanketed the city. Headlights and streetlamps were dimmed, bomb-proof tape covered shop windows, and coal for producing electricity was limited. There were food shortages and rationing, and the cost of living shot up. Coal for heating a home became hard to get, and for a painting studio virtually impossible. Winter snow piled up along the wide boulevards, as there was no one to shovel it. There were few lamps on the streets. Like a country hamlet, Paris became a city lit by moonlight.

Matisse tried to work. He eagerly awaited news about his family behind German lines and his friends fighting on the front. "Marquet and I ended up getting back to work—I made a painting, it's my painting of *Les Poissons rouges* [*Goldfish*] which I am redoing with a character who has the palette in hand and observing (brown-red harmony). Marquet continues his painting from last year. I do a lot of etchings," he wrote to Camoin in December 1914. The etchings were sold for the exclusive benefit of the Society of Prisoners of War. "Like it or not, you can't spend all day waiting for news bulletins."

In the letter, Matisse included a sketch, a self-portrait of the artist sitting in a chair with a palette in hand beside a table with a large bowl of goldfish and a plant. In the final version of *Goldfish and Palette* (also called *Artist and Goldfish*), the artist has virtually disappeared. Only a thumb looped through the palette can be seen. Reflecting Matisse's sense of isolation, there are no views of the city below, no glimpses of brilliant golden light, or even any other people. In his studio in the heart of Paris, the artist is fully cut off. Made of black bands, hard angles, and few curves, it is as if Matisse was trying to organize his thoughts in face of the senseless war around him. Far from the jolly colors, seductive arabesques, and relaxing mood of the original 1912 *Goldfish* that he told Camoin he was "redoing," it is the most intense canvas with goldfish.

It is also one of his most personal works. "I've examined this picture twenty times," André Breton would write almost a decade later, hailing it as one of the three or four most important works produced by the modern movement. "In truth it possesses at once unheard-of freedom, intelligence, discrimination and audacity. Formal innovation, profound penetration of every object by the artist's own life, magical colours, it has everything . . . I'm convinced Matisse has never put so much of himself into any other painting." It feels that way, even if just a thumb of the painter remains on the canvas.

30

In the fall of 1915, after virtually not painting for a year and focusing on his family surviving the war, Matisse returned for the only time to Morocco as a subject. The idea for the work, though, was not new. Conceived in Tangier, the painting that would ultimately become *The Moroccans* (see figure 27) had a lengthy period of gestation. He originally sketched it out in a letter to his wife from the Hôtel Villa de France on October 25, 1912, a couple weeks after arriving for his second stay in Morocco. Upon his return to Issy-les-Moulineaux in 1913, he stretched a canvas for the picture but did little else. Two years later he enlarged the composition and finally began concerted work on it.

"I start again with another canvas of the same size, it's a memory of Morocco, it's the terrace of the little café with the languid lazy people chatting towards the end of the day," he wrote in November 1915 to Camoin, serving on the Western Front. "We can see the little white marabout at the bottom, [but] the bad sketch won't tell you much. This bundle represents an Arab lying sideways on his burnous, the two hooks are the legs. I am writing to you tired, without energy, but I think I will do it better soon." The sketch he added shows a broader view of the same café and figures from *Moroccan Café* but as seen from inside the café at the back rather than the front, in an inverted viewpoint.

In January 1916, he sent an update to Camoin at the front. "I am very late in writing to you, excuse me, my head has been completely overwhelmed for a month, with a painting of Morocco that I am working on at the moment (2.80 x 1.80 m), it is the terrace of the little Kasbah café that you know well," he told Camoin. "I hope to get through it, but what a pain. I'm not in the trenches but I still worry all the same." He felt he was in a battle with this work.

Matisse spent much of the summer and autumn of 1916 working and reworking the picture as it became progressively more abstract. It moved away from a recognizable café scene and companion of *Moroccan Café* to being the finale of his Moroccan period and one of the most important paintings in his long and storied career. Measuring six feet by just over nine feet (181.3 x 279.4 cm), it was even larger than *Moroccan Café*, and significantly more abstract. While lacking the hazy heat and tranquility of that earlier work painted in Tangier, *The Moroccans* contains a similar stillness from the figure's rigid pose and hunched shoulders. Squatting on his haunches, his knees drawn up, the man appears in deep contemplation.

The canvas is divided into three distinct parts with solid black areas between them and the forms arranged into a series of related but separate tableaux: the upper left quarter is dominated by a terrace, roof, and marabout; the bottom left quarter by melons and leaves (or gourds or cactus); and the right third by a squatting turbaned figure facing a wall that shifts from rosy pink to a deep lavender as it becomes a floor. Black was the first color he applied, before adding paint so liquidly that in places—the celadon green and overlapping touches of pink on the leaves, for instance—it was essentially blotted onto the canvas.

It is a complex painting directed by a series of circular and semicircular shapes: the dome and crenelated fence of the marabout, melons that Matisse had seen sold from wooden handcarts in Tangier, pots holding four blue flowers reduced to discs with broad white stripes, the back of a man's turbaned head, and the curving hunch of his shoulders and jutting knees. These revolve around the picture's center, a great expanse of black that is nearly empty.

As the painting progressed, Matisse simplified elements from the compositional sketches, but did not entirely remove anything, even a pair of figures—the title of the work is in plural—who got reduced to a series of marks in the upper right. Matisse was, he explained to a German who visited his studio in Issy-les-Moulineaux while at work on the canvas, eliminating everything that wasn't contributing to the rhythm and balance, "constantly stripping the work down, as you would prune a tree."

The Moroccans is harder to read than basically anything of his that came before, or even after. There are multiple points of view—or no real point of view. It is among Matisse's most cubist work. Cubism was a topic on his mind when he began working on the painting. One of cubism's foremost figures, Juan Gris, had stayed with Matisse in Collioure during the autumn of 1914, and the men discussed their art at length and with passion. "We argue so heatedly about painting that Marquet can hardly sit still for boredom," Gris wrote to Daniel-Henry Kahnweiler, his dealer, exiled in Switzerland because of the war.

When looking at a reproduction of *The Moroccans* in a book or on a screen, the eyes flit back and forth across the entire scene. But standing before the massive canvas at the Museum of Modern Art in New York, one's eyes are drawn to the back of the man's nearly life-size head, and then follow his gaze straight ahead into a mass of pinks, tangled structural lines, and a gaping, tunnel-like hole in the wall, the densest, most abstract part of the picture that Matisse had scraped down and repainted.

Stepping back from the canvas several paces in the MoMA gallery, allowing the focus to shift away from the head, blacks and lines begin to dominate as the whole painting slowly unfolds and exudes deep tension. No wonder. It was done during one of the darkest periods of World War I. The Battle of Verdun, near where Matisse grew up, and the even more deadly Battle of the Somme, where over one million were killed or wounded, took place in 1916. Many painters tried to escape the chaos of the war with their artistic search for order, soothing repetition, or in the abstraction of cubism, creating ways to distance themselves from the miserable realities with the precision and angular purity of lines.

Matisse finished *The Moroccans* in November 1916, the month the brutal Battle of the Somme ended. He sold the painting to the Paris dealer Léonce Rosenberg but immediately bought it back. Perhaps for the dark, personal nature of the work, Matisse kept it largely out of sight. He didn't show it in public for a decade. And then, apart from appearing in the MoMA's 1931 *Henri-Matisse Retrospective Exhibition,* it disappeared again until being included in the MoMA's groundbreaking 1951 Matisse retrospective. Matisse agreed to sell the canvas the following year, though with the stipulation that it would be donated to the museum, where it remains among the permanent collection's highlights.

In *The Moroccans*, Matisse reversed the light of Tangier from clear to black and used it to join the different parts of the composition. He had experimented with the black on his unfinished *French Window at Collioure*. As he explained to the painter André Masson, "The Impressionists had banished black from their palette; I put it back—and prominently—and a painter as in love with color and light as Renoir had the honesty to confirm it: Black is not only a color but also a light." Black had long been used in shadow, where color was lost. Matisse altered that concept. While he is considered the finest colorist since Delacroix, one of his greatest influences on other artists is using black in their works.

Alfred Barr, the MoMA's founding director and author of the first substantial monograph on Matisse, called *The Moroccans* one of Matisse's "most magnificent achievements." Matisse himself named it among the most pivotal of his long career. It stands out as a particularly demanding, experimental, and enigmatic work.

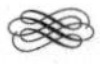

The war, in the meantime, did not spare the avant-garde. Not all of the artists who left to fight returned. Two key German expressionists were killed—August Macke in the opening months of the war and Franz Marc in the Battle of Verdun in 1916—while the Italian futurist Umberto Boccioni died during cavalry training.

Those that did make it back home were often not the same. "On 2 August 1914, I took Braque and Derain to the station at Avignon. I never saw them again," Picasso famously quipped. The pair may have survived, but were changed. Braque received a head wound and was left for dead on the battlefield. Rescued the following day and taken to a hospital, he had a hole drilled in his skull, causing him to go temporarily blind and fall into a coma. Braque returned to the easel finally in 1918. Apollinaire was also wounded in the head. The war-weakened poet and champion of the avant-garde would die from influenza in November 1918, just two days before Armistice.

The teenage André Masson, who, at sixteen years old, had won the Grand Prix de l'Académie for painting, joined the French infantry and fought in the Battle of the Somme. Later an important surrealist, Masson sustained a serious chest wound, had a lengthy recovery in a military hospital, and then was confined for a time to an institution for shell shock. André Breton observed firsthand the traumatizing effects of shell shock. Just out of school, Breton was a vocal dissenter against the war and worked in the neurological ward as a medical orderly in a hospital in Nantes, an experience that would prove fundamental in the development of surrealism, which he would cofound.

The war's collateral damage impacted everyone. The Australian Hilda Rix had not long returned to Étaples, just south of Calais, from her second winter painting in Tangier when war broke out, and was immediately evacuated to London with her mother and her sister, Elsie. On the Channel crossing, her mother became ill with typhoid and was taken from the ship to a hospital upon arrival in England. Elsie also contracted typhoid and died that September of 1914. Their mother never fully recovered and passed away in the spring of 1916.

It was a period when Rix painted almost nothing. That following September, she met an army major who had been stationed at Étaples.

(Family lore says he saw some of her canvases left behind in her studio and tracked her down in London.) Wounded at Gallipoli, he was in London to receive the Distinguished Service Order at Buckingham Palace. Rix accompanied him. They married three days later. In another three days, her new husband returned to the Western Front. Within a month he was shot and killed. She had little more to remember him by then a sketch done the day before he departed. Devastated and, the thirty-two-year-old Rix wrote in her journal, losing a will to live, she painted a number of dark, morbid pictures in deep contrast to the vibrancy and jaunty colors of her recent Tangier works. In the spring of 1918, she sailed back home to Australia.

In recent years, Rix has become an icon in twentieth-century Australian art as one of the few, and perhaps the only woman, from the country to have triumphed in Paris during those heady pre–World War I days when the city was the undisputed global capital of art. That success came from work done among the crowds of Tangier's Grand Socco while wintering at the Hôtel Villa de France, especially during the first stay that coincided with Matisse's.

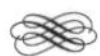

With *The Moroccans*, Matisse had reached an endpoint, and drew the dense, rich period of his work to a close. He was soon packing up his studio to move south.

"Paris is a city one enters with elation, but leaves without regret," wrote Malcolm Cowley, the American author, editor, and noted member of Paris's Lost Generation. Matisse had come to Paris for the artistic riches—first from the northern provinces as an aspiring artist and then later from the suburbs—and left them in the fall of 1917, escaping the city's wartime austerities and also perhaps guilt of not fighting himself. Of this, he was reminded constantly by the shelling, by the soldiers in Paris going to or from the front at times so close they traveled by taxi, by the walking wounded who ghosted along the city's streets, and, in the pale blue sky at dusk, the brown specks above the horizon that were airplanes guarding the French capital. Matisse was also facing another cold winter in his studio with coal difficult to obtain. He would shortly be turning forty-eight.

He craved the light and colors of the Mediterranean. With the war still raging, Tangier was not an option. Instead, he went to the South of France.

31

Matisse arrived in Nice in the middle of December 1917. Taking a room at the Hôtel Beau-Rivage, along the wide waterfront promenade, he initially found, as he had that first winter in Tangier, unexpected rain. It went on for a month. "It never stopped raining. Forced to work in a gloomy hotel room, I was reduced to painting my umbrella standing in the slop jar," he later recalled. Wearied, his patience exhausted, he packed up his luggage to return to Paris. "Finally I decided to leave. The next day the mistral chased the clouds away and it was beautiful. I decided not to leave Nice." The shift altered everything. As his contemporary Proust put a few years later in *The Guermantes Way*, "A change in the weather is sufficient to create the world and ourselves anew."

Matisse was soon extolling the virtues of Nice's light to Camoin. "What a gentle and soft light in spite of its brightness! . . . Here it is silvered. Even the objects that it touches are very colored, such as the greens for example," he told his old pal in spring, recalling similar descriptions he had given of Tangier's light. "I have often fallen on my face. After having written this declaration, I am looking around the room where some of my daubs are hanging, and I think I've hit it sometimes—but it isn't certain."

Light was everything to Matisse. It drove his paintings and dictated where he would travel and ultimately live. Paris soon became a place to visit; Nice would be home until the end.

In the four and a half years between returning from his second winter in Morocco and leaving for Nice, Matisse created the most abstract and geometrical works of his life, canvases weighty with black, grays, and muted tones. That period was over. Settled in Nice, Matisse turned away from such austere images, subdued colors, and angular forms. Any abstraction that had seeped into his work disappeared. "A will to rhythmic abstraction was battling with my natural, innate desire for rich, warm, generous colors and forms in which the arabesque strove to establish its supremacy," Matisse later explained. His vivid, pre-war tones came back, dense patterns covered his canvases, and the first odalisque paintings appeared as he turned to smaller figurative work.

"The odalisques were the fruits of a happy nostalgia, a lovely, lively dream and the almost ecstatic, enchanted experience of those days and nights, in the incantation of the Moroccan climate," Matisse explained in 1951. "I felt an irresistible need to express that ecstasy, that divine nonchalance, in corresponding colored rhythms, rhythms of sunny and lavish figures and colors. . . ." For the next dozen years, they were his main motif.

In 1921, Matisse painted *Odalisque in Red Culottes* of a topless model lounging on a divan in red harem pants and bare torso (see figure 28). The woman is sensually relaxed, with her arms raised and hands knitted behind her head to better show off her bared breasts. She's available and easy for the voyeur to look at, to fully take in. There is no blurring in the brushwork. The French state bought it the following year for the Musée de Luxembourg in Paris (later it became the Musée National d'Arte Moderne, today housed in the Centre Pompidou). A decade before, the same institution had bought one of Hilda Rix's market scenes done in Tangier's Grand Socco when both artists were staying in the Hôtel Villa de France. *Odalisque in Red Culottes* was the first painting of Matisse's purchased for a public French museum collection.

"Such a phenomenon may bear two interpretations," Roger Fry noted in *The Burlington Magazine* at the time of the official purchase. "It may be a criticism of Henri-Matisse's latest work or it may be the sign of a new era in the state patronage of art in France." It was more likely that the painting fell recognizably within the Orientalist tradition, something that his earlier Moroccan paintings did not. The Musée de Luxembourg was, after all, still being run by Léonce Bénédite, founder of the Société des Peintres Orientalistes Français.

The odalisques were an imaginary Orient, the fantasy East of the Orientalists, and done in the Orientalists' tradition of hedonism and passive women. *Odalisque Seated with Arms Raised, Green Striped Chair*, from 1923, is one of the many typical examples (see figure 29). If the portraits of Zorah and Fatma had been descendants of Eastern art, rooted in decorative textiles and Islamic traditions of color and pattern, along with Orthodox iconography, the odalisques of Nice were of Ingres and Delacroix. In comparison to the nineteenth-century canvases of these two predecessors, they lacked a certain emblematic heft, according to the American critic Guy Davenport. "When Delacroix and Ingres painted odalisques, the harem constituted a critique of the body, its governance, the sources of power over it," Davenport wrote in 1989. "An odalisque by Matisse is simply a model in a chair."

With a career and reputation built on shock and innovation, some of Matisse's supporters saw the odalisques as an artistic betrayal, a selling out with frivolous, decorative works rather than continued experimentation, a retreat from the front edges of the avant-garde. Or they at least seemed self-indulgent and certainly not forward looking. The years of brave experimentation appeared over.

Even Matisse's longtime champion, collector, and dear friend Marcel Sembat was disappointed with the shift, writing to Paul Signac when the French state bought *Odalisque in Red Culottes*, "He's given in, he's calmed down, the public is on his side." The poet Jean Cocteau, who had known Matisse for years, was more acerbic with the appearance of the odalisques: "The sun-drenched wild beast of Fauvism has turned into one of Bonnard's kittens."

The criticism stuck. But it didn't make Matisse stop. He continued to paint them until 1930. "Did I paint too many Odalisques, was I carried away by excessive enthusiasm in the happiness of creating those paintings, a happiness that swept me along like a warm ocean ground swell?" he said to an interviewer in the early 1950s, a few years before he died. "I still don't know."

On September 5, 1922, six months after making his comments to Signac, Sembat, the sixty-year-old politician, journalist, and faithful friend and supporter of Matisse, collapsed from a massive cerebral hemorrhage. He was at his home in Chamonix and preparing to go on an excursion with his wife, Georgette Agutte. By 12:30 P.M. he was declared dead.

For Agutte, the shock of his sudden death was immense. Distraught and alone that evening, she wrote a number of letters, with her handwriting becoming almost illegible at times. Three were addressed to her nephew, André Varagnac. She had no children of her own and was close to her nephews and nieces (and also to Marguerite Matisse). "I am writing all this to you in a jumble, you can imagine what state I am in, my dear André." She wanted him to carry out her last wishes and gave him instructions on the properties and what to do with their art collection. "As for the paintings, I would like to donate the best ones to a museum in the province, the Matisse, Marquet, Cross, etc. . . . and finally, a few of mine, the best ones with the Metthey's potteries."

Agutte had been with Matisse, Camoin, and Marquet in the studio of Gustave Moreau at the École des Beaux-Arts, a place reserved at the time for male students. "For Georgette, these training years were also ones of emancipation," according to Hélène Vincent in her authoritative work on the couple's art collection. Agutte divorced her first husband, the art critic Paul Flat, in 1893, despite strong family (and cultural) resistance and the scandal that it caused, and reverted to her maiden name. Three years later, she married Sembat. While the politician offered her financial freedom to dedicate herself to painting, she taught him about art and he went on to write the first monograph on Matisse.

The couple divided their time between Paris; Bonnières-sur-Seine, a town northwest of Paris near Monet's Giverny; and Chamonix at the base of Mont Blanc in the Alps, where they built a chalet. As Sembat rose to the top ranks of French politics, she continued with her art and in the past twenty-five years had completed around eight hundred paintings. She showed regularly at the big spring and autumn Salons and had five solo exhibitions at leading Parisian galleries—Georges Petit (1908), Druet (1910, 1921), and Bernheim-Jeune (1914, 1919). Critics wrote of her "fearless" and "fierce" character, her "courage" and "tenacity."

But now, she was afraid, alone, and consumed with grief. "André, tell mom how much I love her, if I can't see her again. Without this, I would no longer have the courage, and I want to join my loved one," Agutte wrote that night. "Think of the two of us in love, I love you, but I know that I cannot live without him."

In another letter, she wrote, "My poor friend, my life is finished without him. Through him, I had happiness, I had it in abundance, I have no reason to complain, but without him the light is dead. Farewell." At the bottom, she added: *"Minuit. Voilà—douze heures qu'il est parti. Je suis en retard."* ("Midnight. It's been twelve hours since his death. I am late.") She then took a handgun and fatally shot herself in the throat. She was fifty-five.

Agutte and Sembat were buried beside each other in the cemetery of Bonnières. The following year, the couple's art collection was transferred to the Musée de Grenoble, where Matisse himself had donated his large decorative masterpiece *Interior with Aubergines* (1911) the previous year. (After it was hung, the local newspaper called it "*papier peint pour salon de réception des fous*"—wallpaper for a crazy person's receiving salon.)

Their collection was a rich one, with works by Gauguin, Van Dongen, Signac, Vuillard, Vlaminck, Puy, Manguin, Roualt, and others. Among the canvases by Matisse were *View of the Bay of Tangier* and *The Small*

Mulatto Woman from Morocco; *The Red Carpets*, the first time he explicitly used Islamic decorated elements on canvas; and the stunning portrait of his daughter, *Marguerite Reading*. The collection also included Tangier paintings from Camoin—the bold and colorful *Minaret in Tangier*—and a small oil on cardboard of the kasbah by Marquet.

The forty-four paintings, two dozen drawings, twenty ceramics, and pair of sculptures they bequeathed altered the museum in Grenoble, and today forms the core of its modern art collection. For pieces by Agutte herself, Signac helped in making the choice of which should go to the museum. The most striking one is an intimate picture of her husband Marcel Sembat reading in their garden.

Thanks to the donation, Musée de Grenoble became what is considered the first museum of modern art in France.

The odalisques gave Matisse, finally, the public popularity that had so long eluded him, even if they were lacking in critical acclaim. Their blend of the exotic and erotic, their ravishing colors and sense of wonder appealed to the freewheeling postwar era with a hearty appetite for pleasure and little concern for the future. It was borrowed time with no new war in sight to scuttle the enjoyment.

During the 1920s, Matisse's prices rose significantly. In 1917, medium-size canvases went for 5,000 French francs, but by 1928 they were worth 30,000–50,000 francs. That year, a picture painted in 1921 sold for 121,000 francs, the highest amount for a living artist at the time. (The appeal of canvases from this period remains. In 2018, *Odalisque couchée aux magnolias* from 1923 sold for $80.75 million at Christie's, shattering the old record of $48.8 million for a Matisse work.) In 1930 and 1931, there were important exhibitions in Paris, Berlin, Basel, and New York, and publications about his work. He had made it.

❧

Since withdrawing to Nice in 1917, Matisse had lived a largely cloistered life. Newfound popularity and money did little to change his habits. He remained in Nice with his cats and large cages of birds, living at first along the seafront promenade in a series of hotel rooms and apartments.

Amélie did not initially follow him on the move south. For the next decade, she was between Nice and Paris, much to the displeasure of Matisse, whose letters to her are filled with pleading for her to come down. She was ill, with back and kidney issues, and for a time bedridden. Eventually, she settled more permanently with him in Nice.

In 1938, they moved into the converted Hôtel Régina. The sprawling, six-story Belle Époque property, built at the end of the nineteenth century overlooking Nice in a neighborhood called Cimiez, went broke after the 1929 stock market crash, and its owners converted four hundred hotel rooms into ninety-eight generous apartments with views over well-tended public gardens and onto the sea. Matisse bought one on the third floor, a high-ceilinged suite with three studios, two that faced south and one, with large black and white floor tiles, that faced north. Studio and home overlapped. ("He works, sleeps, and eats in any one of the studios, moving around like a tidy gypsy," noted a guest.) A quartet of black cats that he fed pieces of brioche in the morning nosed around the airy apartment.

"He lived the way he painted—when you entered the house," said Françoise Gilot, who visited Matisse in Nice with her partner, Picasso, "you were in his universe." Filling the apartment were items seen in his paintings: familiar patterned tapestries and pieces of cloth, the zebra-skin-covered lounge and red-and-white striped bergère chair, glass cases filled with knickknacks, and large bouquets of cut flowers.

But, among the recognition and move to Cimiez, the Matisses' marriage collapsed after four decades. They separated in 1939. He was seventy and she was sixty-seven. The final motive was the Russian refugee, Lydia

Délectorskaya, who was forty years younger than the painter. Orphaned at twelve in Siberia, she fled the country after the Russian Revolution. Wanting to be a doctor like her father, she applied to the Sorbonne and was accepted, but could not afford the fees. She drifted south to Nice, and at twenty-two was hired to help care for Amélie. She soon became Matisse's assistant, then, after three years, model. Madame Lydia—as Matisse always called her—took over running his studio, a role that had largely been Amélie's throughout their marriage. This proved to be too much of a threat. Amélie gave her husband an ultimatum: either the Russian or her. He chose Amélie, and dismissed Délectorskaya. But it was too late. His wife left him. Ten days later, Délectorskaya, distraught, shot herself in the chest with a pistol. The bullet lodged in the breastbone but caused little damage. With nowhere to go, she returned, at Matisse's invitation, to the studio, and was with him until his death fifteen years later as his muse, secretary, and, later, nurse.

Those late, last years were creatively fertile. With his paper cut-outs, Matisse again sailed back to the forefront of art and became a new hero to the avant-garde, exerting strong influence on a new generation of artists such as David Hockney and Robert Rauschenberg. Official appreciation and a full embrace by the establishment also came. The French government elevated him to the rank of Commander of Legion of Honor in 1946 and began collecting his work. At the 1950 Venice Biennale, Matisse won—at the seasoned age of eighty—a first prize.

In those late years, he also worked on the Chapelle du Rosaire de Vence, usually called the Vence Chapel or the Matisse Chapel, in the hilltop town of Vence about a half hour north of Nice. He designed every detail of the project, from the building's architecture, stained-glass windows, and decorative tiles to the priestly vestments worn during religious services. It was an impressive feat, considering it required taking up an entire new kind of art so late in life. He was nearly eighty when he began work on it. He continued to push himself forward to the end.

Matisse never returned to Morocco, or even North Africa, after those winters of 1912 and 1913. But, as with his great predecessor Delacroix, it never left him, and it inspired him to turn a corner and push forth with his art in his own unique and inimitable way.

32

On the last day of 1951, Matisse was turning eighty-two. He had aged and grown heavy, and fretted about his weakening vision from working with such strong colors for so long. Debilitating insomnia still plagued his nights. And while the surgeries for intestinal cancer performed a decade before had saved his life, they permanently weakened his stomach muscles and allowed him to only be up on his feet for a few hours a day. Largely confined to the trio of rooms of his apartment overlooking Nice, Matisse spent much of the day in (or on) his narrow bed. Yet these ailments did little to slow his prodigious output in a late creative flowering. He had been gifted, he told Marquet, "a second life."

Working on a custom-made mobile table that could tip up like an easel above his bed, he sketched almost continually—birds, flowers, fruits, seashells, faces—with his hand moving fluidly across sheets of paper, even while talking to visitors. For larger drawings he used a long bamboo pole with a piece of charcoal or crayon affixed to the end to sketch on paper attached to the wall. He was also actively producing paper cut-outs, wielding large scissors with startling delicacy to create sinuous shapes. Assistants pinned up the stiff sheets painted in gouache for him to study as he balanced their shapes and hues and allowed the arrangements to evolve. The pinholes that riddle surviving pieces are testaments to how frequently the assistants moved them around until he found their final composition. And in early summer that year, after a few years of work, he had completed the magnificent convent chapel in Vence.

In the copper slot on his apartment door, the visiting card read:

Henri Matisse
Artiste-Peintre

Yet Matisse hadn't painted on the easel in a few years. His oil work that had made his name and his fame had essentially finished.

That October of 1951, though, he took back out his oil paints, clamped a canvas on an easel, and returned to the medium that had defined him for decades to paint Katia, the tall, statuesque Swiss that was his favorite model at the time. (Her name was actually Carmen Leschennes, though he called her Katia or else *Le Platane*, *The Plane Tree*.) Hanging up around the apartment were numerous drawings of her face and some nude portraits done with charcoal or in broad, confident brushstrokes with Indian ink. In a trimmed beard and crown of white hair, his attentive eyes darting behind the thick lenses of his glasses, the heavyset Matisse sat before a lowered easel. Sitting on an upholstered chair, Katia wore a blue and yellow gandoura, a short-sleeve North African gown that he had in his collection of garments and tapestries picked up over the years.

Matisse dabbed paint on the china plate he was using for a palette, and captured the ample, flowing robe in azure and Moroccan blues with shards of sunflower yellow. As with most of his Moroccan portraits done decades before, Katia breaks out of the canvas, her hair grazing the top frame. Her neck is thick and bullishly powerful, like a column—or a totem to vitality. Fat, oval smears of blue eyes beam out. Though her mouth lacks any sort of expression, she looks straight at the painter, chin up, full of confidence. Backing her is a field of fiery reds and oranges applied with a thick brush, textured and layered colors unnerving in their intensity and energy. *Femme à la gandoura bleue* (*Woman in a Blue Gandoura*) is a symphony of tones orchestrated in a masterful gestural freedom and bursting forth with exuberance.

In mid-November the following month, the Museum of Modern Art in New York opened a landmark Matisse retrospective. To coincide with it, Alfred Barr, the MoMA's director, published *Matisse: His Art and His Public*, offering the first historical framework of the painter's career. The six-hundred-page work took writing about Matisse from art criticism to art history. The exhibition included three canvases Matisse painted in Morocco—*Acanthus*, *Periwinkles* (*Moroccan Garden*), and *Zorah in Yellow*—and Matisse had fielded questions about them beforehand from Barr.

Matisse clearly had *Zorah in Yellow* on his mind when he took back out his oil paints in December as the MoMA show was running to do a second portrait of Katia. This time he had her put on a yellow smock. And, as with Zorah's portrait, he named her, and called the painting *Katia à la chemise jaune* (usually rendered in English as *Katia in a Yellow Dress*).

Sitting on an upholstered armchair, Katia wears a deep green skirt with waves of blue and a single strand of red zigzagging across it; the rest of her is yellow with a background of scrubbed Tangier blue.

While the color of Zorah's robe has faded over time in the picture, the original brilliance can be glimpsed in the background of *Studio with Goldfish,* where the canvas hangs on the wall in the background. The young Moroccan's gown is the identical bright sunflower hue of the one Katia wears in Nice forty years later.

For some reason, Matisse didn't seem to complete *Katia in a Yellow Dress*. Putting his paints back away, he left Katia's face a featureless oval filled in with the same brilliant yellow as her smock and arms.

"You left with the naked light of Morocco and you installed it on the sky of France. Whether it is the theme of the odalisques or that of some portraits, the Orient, your Orient insinuates itself or clearly takes its place in the canvas," wrote Ben Jelloun. Numerous paintings done in the decades that followed were "entirely 'occupied' by your Moroccan memories." These, the novelist noted, included those last portraits of Katia, whose links to Morocco four decades before could hardly be more explicit. "Thirty-eight years after your return to Tangier, you are still (bewitched) under the spell of Zorah." Memories of Zorah, Matisse's favorite Moroccan model, had not disappeared, and with them, Ben Jelloun wrote, he painted Katia. "You are in Nice. Tangier is on the other side of the sea. You miss Tangier. You are content to retain its light within you. You spread it everywhere. You summon it even when all the skies are gray."

Matisse would not paint again. His farewell to oil painting was also a final farewell to Tangier, a final summons and nod to the most fertile period he ever had at the easel.

"In this winter of 1912, Matisse sought above all to get away from the effervescence of Paris, to find a place conducive to meditation nourished by the contributions of his previous stays in Algeria and Andalusia, and his visits to exhibitions of Islamic art in Paris and Munich or Byzantine art in Moscow," wrote Brahim Alaoui, the Moroccan art historian and ex-director of the Museum and Exhibitions at the Institut du Monde Arabe in Paris. "This dialogue with the Orient, already initiated in the work and reflection of the painter, will take on its full measure in Morocco and will now be present in the rest of his œuvre."

As experts and critics like Alaoui have widely noted, the Tangier sojourns permanently marked Matisse and his art. "From 1913 to his last works Henri Matisse was always 'returning' to Morocco. And until he departed this earth, Matisse never left the many special qualities and impressions so enthusiastically gathered during his Moroccan period, as he pursued the search for his artistic self through the exploration of various motifs," wrote Jack Cowart, curator of twentieth-century art at the National

Gallery of Art, head organizer of the four-stop 1990–1991 *Matisse in Morocco* exhibition, and lead author of its catalogue.

In his review of that exhibition, John Russell, the esteemed head art critic for *The New York Times*, wrote, "To say that Matisse found himself in Morocco would not be quite true, for Matisse was never the man to lose himself. But to say that he made himself in Morocco might not be an overstatement. It was in Morocco that he broke new ground, learned what to leave out, and allowed free rein to the alternations of tyranny and passivity in human relations that seemed to bring out the best in him as an artist." His colleague Michael Kimmelman wrote after seeing the show, "As it did for Delacroix, North Africa liberated his imagination."

Colorful and exotic but not picturesque, the Moroccan canvases relied on a repetition of forms and used the intricate designs he discovered in Islamic art. While Delacroix had focused on "ready-made" themes, Matisse paid attention to the shapes of the buildings, the patterns of the textiles, and the varied foliage, with the repetitions of colors and shapes aligning to his decorative instincts, Kimmelman noted in *The New York Times*. "Decoration in Morocco was not like decoration in France. It was not secondary to an image; it was the principal subject. By painting the patterns and flowers and costumes he saw around him, Matisse realized that he could elevate decoration to something weightier and more evocative than it had been in certain of his earlier works."

Decoration was no longer inferior; he gave it meaning, importance. To describe a work as decorative is, in general, to debase it, to imply that it lacks something human—that it is not infused, or suffused, with the feelings or emotions. Even today, according to an ex-director of Sotheby's and Christie's auction houses, in artspeak, the definition of "decorative" is "devoid of intellectual substance." If there is an exception to this, it is Matisse.

By the end of his long career, the profound role that Morocco had played over the decades since his two stays was evident. "By character, Matisse is a complex mixture of hot and cold—a mélange of his dominant, stabilizing intelligence and the flaming, luminous sensibilities of his genius as a colorist," wrote Janet Flanner in a lengthy, two-part *New Yorker* profile with the opening of the 1951 MoMA retrospective of the artist. Morocco "gave his brain and eyes what he needed for his balanced excess. His mastery of this controlled extravagance became his typical style."

That is, Matisse fully became the Matisse that we know.

His lengthy honeymoon stay on Corsica and early ones in Collioure furnished Matisse's palette with the tenor of the Mediterranean. And then he went to Tangier. He didn't go to just paint exotic scenes and leave in the colonial manner of extracting resources (in this case subject matter), but rather something quite the opposite. "Other French painters of his generation traveled in North Africa and, despite their ocular excitements, were still French tourists when they left," wrote Flanner. "Through his North African visits, Matisse, as an artist, became colonialized."

Fauvism had been a new and more personal way for Matisse to respond to nature as he followed the poet Stéphane Mallarmé's dictum, "Paint, not the thing, but the effect it produces." But that ultimately made him withdraw from nature. He reconnected with nature in Tangier, where its tones turned smoother and more seductive. "An artist must possess Nature," Matisse wrote in a letter to a young artist in 1948. "He must identify himself with her rhythm, by efforts that will prepare the mastery which will later enable him to express himself in his own language."

That language—so distinctively Matissean, so immediately identifiable, so profoundly original—surged with fluency and pulsating vibrancy.

"Morocco bridged the gap between the reality and the dream," wrote the British artist, teacher, and curator Lawrence Gowing. "There was something of his imaginary ideal in the place and the light and his brush moved more freely there than ever before."

Matisse's Morocco stays had replenished his art, and he had managed to draw from it until he put down his brushes.

Matisse died in November 1954, at the age of eighty-four. Lydia Délectorskaya packed her suitcase and left the apartment. Amélie returned as a widow for the funeral. Amélie died four years later and was buried in the same tomb as her husband in the cemetery of the Monastère de Cimiez, on the hill above Nice. On a verdant lower terrace under a gnarled olive tree, the tomb—unadorned gray stone inscribed with their two names—sits on a grassy spot surrounded by flowers.

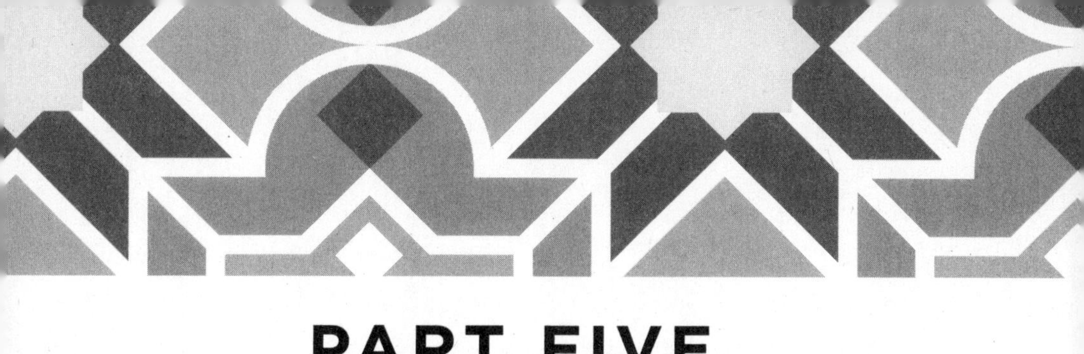

PART FIVE

THE COLLECTIONS

33

Matisse never again saw the Moroccan canvases that went to Shchukin and Morozov after sending them off to Moscow. In the last part of his life, he didn't even know if they—or any of the other fifty-plus works by him that two Russians had acquired—even still existed.

The uncertainty of the collections began with the onset of World War I. Shchukin cabled Matisse in September 1914 informing him that he would not be able to have transported to Moscow the last two paintings he reserved, *Interior with a Goldfish Bowl* and *Woman on a High Stool*. "Impossible send [money] Moscow exchange closed bank and post office refuse transfer money France hope send when contacts restored greetings, Sergei Shchukin."

When Russian banks halted remissions abroad, Shchukin and Morozov lost their ability to pay artists and dealers in France, and their collecting came to an abrupt halt.

For Morozov's Tver Textile Mill Company, the outbreak of war meant a boomtime. In one year, the spinning factory processed some 22 million pounds (10 million kilograms) of cotton and produced over 17.5 million pounds (8 million kilograms) of finished yarn, making as much money as in the previous twenty years. But in terms of adding to his collection of Western art, the windfall meant nothing to its director.

Rallying behind Tsar Nicholas II, Russia entered the war with the world's largest army. Russian soldiers, fighting on the side of the Allies, battled along the Eastern Front. Losses came quickly—the Second Army was annihilated by the Germans in just four days at the Battle of Tannenberg in East Prussia during the first month of fighting. War soon exhausted the Russian economy. There were shortages of food and fuel, transportation broke down, manufacturing output dwindled, inflation rose, morale fell. People were hungry and cold. By the spring of 1917, the Romanovs had lost their grip on power after ruling Russia for over three centuries, forcing the tsar to abdicate. A month later, Lenin returned from exile to a devastated country on the verge of collapse.

Throughout the conflict, Shchukin's art collection hung undisturbed on the walls of Trubetzkoy Palace, a bubble of beauty in a horrendous war. He even continued to receive visitors on Sunday mornings to view the works. (Morozov, conversely, moved his paintings into a fireproof storeroom.)

That changed with the 1917 October Revolution. Once Lenin and the Bolshevik Party seized power, the property of wealthy citizens like Shchukin and Morozov became targets. Authorities nationalized all major industrial enterprises. The collections of the country's merchant princes were in their sights.

In a decree dated March 5, 1918, the government nationalized all works of art. On November 15, a seal was placed on the door of Shchukin's home. Lenin himself had signed the order. Hanging on the walls were over three dozen Matisse paintings, representing every stage of the painter's career, right up to *Portrait of the Artist's Wife*, which arrived in Moscow in mid-March 1914, just a few months before the outbreak of fighting. It was, by a significant margin, the most important Matisse collection in the world. Of course, the collection went far beyond Matisse. Stacked three, four, even five high on the walls of Shchukin's home, it was unparalleled in its richness and depth of modern European paintings, with some 275 works, nearly all considered major. There were eight canvases by Cézanne, sixteen by Gauguin, thirteen by Monet, seven by Rousseau, four by Van Gogh, sixteen by Derain, and a staggering fifty-one by Picasso. The world's greatest collection of modern European art now belonged to the state. For fifteen years, Shchukin had steadily built the collection, and in a stroke lost it all. His only consolation was that it was safe from looting mobs who rampaged through Moscow's streets.

Shchukin himself had already fled Russia by the time the seal appeared on the door of his home. In August, Shchukin's second wife, Nadejda, a piano teacher he had discretely married during the war, had left the country for Kiev and then Germany with their two-year-old daughter and a governess. The girl carried her favorite doll, into which had been sewn diamonds and gold. Shchukin quietly followed them a month later, arriving in Weimar in mid-September 1918. They managed to get to Switzerland and then France. (Shchukin's daughter from his first wife and her husband remained behind to watch the collection. They eventually left Moscow in 1922.)

Shchukin never saw his collection again. He spent the next eighteen years in exile in France. For his large apartment in Auteuil, near the Bois de Boulogne on the west side of Paris, he bought seven paintings by Henri Le Fauconnier, plus a few by Raoul Dufy and the figurative Catalan painter Pere Pruna. While not financially destitute like many other Russian émigrés in Paris (he had managed to transfer money to a bank in Stockholm before the war), he didn't collect art again.

Nor did his relationship with Matisse return to its old footing. The balance of power had shifted. When the two met after the war, there was an awkwardness between them. Unable to now buy from his favorite artist, the proud Russian kept his distance. Perhaps meeting Matisse face-to-face was too harsh a reminder of all he had lost.

Matisse was living in the South of France by then, and often visited the aging Renoir in Cagnes-sur-Mer. One day he persuaded Shchukin to come and meet the distinguished painter who, though suffering from debilitating rheumatoid arthritis, was still managing to paint with a brush strapped to his hand. Matisse went to the train station to meet the Russian, looking for him in the first-class carriages. Shchukin wasn't there. Searching, Matisse found him sitting in a second-class wagon. He was waiting for Matisse, likely to make a point on his change of circumstances: his new position was without the money, power, or even respect that he had once so lavishly and unquestionably enjoyed.

The two didn't meet again. Shchukin died in Paris in January 1936, at age eighty-two, and was buried in Montmartre Cemetery in the family tomb he had bought after the suicide of his younger brother, Ivan, nearly three decades before.

It was a similar story with Morozov, Russia's richest manufacturer.

In the summer of 1918, Morozov personally handed over the account books and keys to the safes of his factories to a representative of the workers and waited for the Bolsheviks to take control of his house and art collection. The rooms of his palatial Moscow home on Prechistenka Street held about the same number of modern European paintings as Shchukin's did, with major works by Manet, Renoir, Cézanne, Van Gogh, and Matisse, plus another three hundred or so by Russian artists. On December 19, a month after a notice had been stuck on Shchukin's door, a decree appropriating Morozov's property appeared. The government appointed a *saveduichi* (manager) and made Morozov his deputy. Humiliatingly for the deeply private man, Morozov was given three rooms in his home—the remainder were opened to the public—and tasked with leading tours of the art hanging on the walls.

Constantly under threat of being arrested, Morozov was keen to leave the country. In June 1919 he finally managed to flee with his wife, daughter, and niece to Europe, although precisely how remains unclear, or where they crossed the border to Finland by paying smugglers. He had hoped to settle in France, but passed away before he could do so. He died in the summer of 1921, during a family visit to Karlovy Vary (Carlsbad), a spa town in the Bohemia region of today's Czech Republic, at the age of forty-nine.

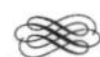

The two art collections in Moscow became known as the First (Shchukin) and Second (Morozov) Museums of New Western Painting. In the spring of 1923, authorities decided to combine them into a single body. Five years later the paintings were finally taken down from the walls of Shchukin's home and transferred to Morozov's neoclassical villa. While larger, it was already overcrowded with canvases. It now had to somehow hold six hundred canvases. (Shchukin's home became the Ministry of War, and still belongs to the Defense Department.)

These formed the core of the newly named State Museum of Modern Western Art. It was an unparalleled collection. (The Museum of Modern Art in New York wouldn't open until November 1929.)

But these artistic riches in Moscow soon vanished from public view. Authorities deemed the paintings anti-working class and cosmopolitan, decadent works against the cultural policies of Joseph Stalin, and hid them away in storage.

While the merged collection virtually disappeared, it did remain almost entirely intact, with only a few of the works sold off. An exception came in 1933 with the sale of four paintings for hard currency to the American art collector Stephen Carlton Clark, heir to the Singer Sewing Machine Company fortune, founder of the Baseball Hall of Fame in Cooperstown, New York, and founding trustee of the MoMA. Among them were two from Morozov, Cézanne's *Madame Cézanne in the Conservatory* and Van Gogh's *The Night Café*. (Morozov had first acquired Gauguin's *Café at Arles*, painted during the summer he lived with Van Gogh in Arles, and then bought the latter's counterpoint, *The Night Café*, as a companion.)

At the end of June 1941, five days after Germany invaded Russia, the State Museum of Modern Western Art went into war mode. The collection's paintings were removed from their frames, hastily crated up, and sent by rail on a special museum train to the Siberian capital of Novosibirsk for safekeeping in the vaults of the opera house. The journey and then cold damaged some of the works, but ultimately the move likely saved them from Nazi bombings that hit the State Museum of Modern Western Art building in Moscow. Of particular concern would have been *Moroccan Café*. Done in delicate tempera on a canvas that had not been properly primed, it was stored without a stretcher, aggravating the flaking of the brittle paint.

In 1944, the paintings returned to Moscow, where, still in their wooden crates, workers moved them back into storage.

The State Museum of Modern Western Art did not reopen, and on March 6, 1948, Stalin signed a decree to dissolve it. "The Council of Ministers of the USSR considers that the collection of the State Museum of Modern Western Art in Moscow is composed mainly of ideologically inadequate, anti-working class, formalist works of Western bourgeois art devoid of any progressive, civilizing value for Soviet visitors," it read.

Just ten days were given to liquidate the collection. One minister suggested that because the works were not realist or socialist, and thus of no use to the state, they should be destroyed.

Politburo member General Voroshilov, in charge of purging the state collections, inspected the paintings with Alexandr Gerasimov, a prominent Soviet artist and the new president of the Academy of Arts, the party's mouthpiece in art. Gerasimov considered the paintings by Matisse and his contemporaries "enemies of Soviet realistic art" and "progenitors of decadent bourgeois art." Despising the museum, and, aware of what he was doing, he began by showing Voroshilov the panels Matisse painted to hang above Shchukin's stairwell, *Dance* and *Music*. Sneering, Voroshilov looked at *Dance* unspooled from its roller and laughed. "He, he," he chuckled at the primitive, whirling figures stretched out across the floor. The rest of his entourage joined in. "He, he, he." So beneath their contempt, it was not even worth the effort of destroying.

In the disused museum, workers pried open the wooden crates and removed canvases to choose which to save and which to destroy. It was a stunning gathering of art, dominated by the century's two titans: there were fifty-three canvases by Matisse and the same number by Picasso. (Following these was a hefty gap: twenty-nine by Gauguin, twenty-six by Cézanne, twenty-two by Derain, nineteen by Monet, fourteen by Bonnard, eleven by Renoir, ten by Van Gogh, nine by Degas, and so on.)

Most of Matisse's paintings from his sublimely fertile spell in and around the two winters in Morocco were present. Laid out on the cold ground, frameless and curling, the paintings lost their aura as masterpieces. But how splendidly they glowed in the pale March light! Alongside the innocent face of Zorah kneeling on the blue carpet and standing against the red wall is Amido in his lilac-purple jodhpurs, the powerful Riffian robed in dazzling emerald, and the shimmering blues of Tangier as seen from his hotel room window. Unrolled in impressive splendor, the nirvanic *Moroccan Café* radiated heat in the frigid building.

The most conservative paintings were sent to the Pushkin State Museum of Fine Arts in Moscow, some three hundred works. The State Hermitage Museum in Leningrad (Saint Petersburg) received the ones deemed more extreme, 316 canvases to be used to demonstrate bourgeois decadence. The ones with little value were to go to the provinces, and the most openly risky or dangerous ones were to be destroyed.

While, in the end, none seemed to have been destroyed and nearly all were split between those two museums, a few from Shchukin's collection were scattered elsewhere. One of his three paintings by Maurice Lobre (*Bibliothèque du dauphin*) went to Lviv, Ukraine; one of his three by Firmin Maglin (*Le printemps à Bouchet*) went to Odessa, Ukraine; and two others went to Baku, Azerbaijan, Emile Giran's *Intérieur* and Charles Milcendeau's *Fruiterie*. Shchukin had acquired all of these in the early stages of his collecting.

The Matisses were divided up. Some two dozen of the most challenging went to the Hermitage, along with nearly all of Picasso's work. From Matisse's Morocco stay were Shchukin's *Moroccan Café*, the standing portraits of Zorah, Amido, and the Riffian, and the bouquet of irises. The remainder went to the Pushkin. Morozov's triptych was split up, with *The Kasbah Gate* heading to the Hermitage and *Zorah on the Terrace* and *Landscape Viewed from a Window* to the Pushkin.

But the works did not return to public display at either institution. Authorities immediately placed them in storage, where they would remain largely unseen for years to come.

While some of the collection could be viewed with special permission, the Matisse and Picasso works remained off limits. Certain foreign visitors, art researchers, and a select few who could pull strings could get a glimpse of the works once owned by Shchukin and Morozov. But exhibiting such art was unimaginable.

In 1951, the Museum of Modern Art mounted a major Matisse retrospective. Alfred Barr, the director of the MoMA's collections, curator of the exhibition, and author of the catalog, published a pioneering critical biography on the painter to coincide with the show.

The MoMA exhibition, the short catalog noted, "is designed first of all to present a highly selective review of Matisse's painting by means of some seventy-five of his most important or characteristic works ranging from 1890 to his recent magnificent still lifes." That was a profound and knowing overstatement by Barr. The exhibition included no paintings from Russia, which Barr acknowledged held the most important Matisse collection in the world.

While the MoMA did include *Red Studio* and the liquidy blue *Goldfish with Sculpture*, many of the pieces in the show from that extremely important period just before World War I were secondary ones: rather than *Dance* or *Music* were studies of them; present was *Nasturtiums and "La Danse" I*, a preparatory sketch done quickly for the far superior *Nasturtiums and "La Danse" II*. *Zorah in Yellow* was included, but not the other two more accomplished portraits of the Moroccan girl.

These missing masterworks were in Russia. Or at least so many hoped. Not one person in the West could say if they even still survived, or if they had been destroyed.

34

When Matisse died in November 1954, Janet Flanner wrote a "Letter from Paris" dispatch in *The New Yorker* on his passing. In it, she referred to the missing Russian works. "Their whereabouts was lost in mystery until last summer, when the magazine *Nouveau Femina* printed recent snapshots of the collection, and in particular of the Matisses, showing them unframed, hung by the dozen on portable racks, like washing, and kept locked from the public eye in the attic of the Hermitage Museum, in Leningrad." The Hermitage's catalog, Flanner added, didn't even mention Matisse's name.

The reemergence of Matisse's work from the Shchukin and Morozov collections finally happened in the 1960s in the Soviet Union and the 1970s in the West. Stalin died in 1953, and the canvases only began to slowly reappear with Khrushchev's "thaw" that followed.

In 1955, some pieces by Monet, Cézanne, Gauguin, and Renoir were finally exhibited at the Pushkin Museum. Authorities green-lighted a few by Picasso and Matisse for public showing, though none that were cubist or fauvist.

When Beverly Kean, the future biographer of Russia's two supreme collectors, went to the Soviet Union in 1959 as one of the first Western tourists, she found three Matisses in a "small inaccessible back room." There was no indication of the provenance on what she saw. Shchukin's and Morozov's names had been erased from history.

In the early 1960s, the Hermitage showed works from the two collections, with some Matisse paintings hanging among them. By the mid-sixties, the storerooms had been nearly emptied. In 1968, *The Kasbah Gate* was returned to Moscow, reuniting the Moroccan Triptych. And in 1969, *Moroccan Café* was exhibited, some four decades after it had last been seen in public.

Matisse's paintings from Russia showed in the West during the large centennial exhibition in 1970 at Paris's Grand Palais, where he and his fellow fauves had stormed the fortress of academy art sixty-five years before with their garish colors and provocative disregard of tradition. Conceived by André Malraux while France's Minister of Culture, the retrospective filled three floors and included 249 paintings, sculptures, and gouaches, with twenty pieces from Soviet museums never seen before in the West. The Moroccan Triptych was displayed together for the first time in France since hanging for five days at the Galerie Bernheim-Jeune exhibition in 1913, nearly six decades before. *Moroccan Café* was deemed too fragile to be moved. (It has never left Russia.)

By then Matisse had been dead for a decade and a half.

Matisse's Moroccan paintings finally got their own show in the spring of 1990 with an exhibition called *Matisse in Morocco: The Paintings and Drawings, 1912–13*. Spearheaded by the National Gallery of Art in Washington, DC, it opened in Washington, moved to the MoMA in New York for the summer, and then headed to Russia, first to the Pushkin in Moscow and finally the Hermitage in Saint Petersburg (still called Leningrad), closing in mid-February 1991. With twenty-three paintings and forty-five drawings, the exhibition gathered together virtually everything Matisse had done in Morocco. Twelve of the paintings had never been exhibited in the United States before and forty-two of the drawings had never been shown publicly anywhere. The exhibition catalog offered the first detailed look at the artist's two stays in Tangier.

Successfully mounting the show was a significant achievement, and a substantial piece of soft diplomacy between the United States and the USSR. It was the first time an exhibition had been jointly worked out in every phase by Western and Soviet curators. The entire exhibition went on view in all four of the museums involved in organizing it. It was a comprehensive show dedicated to this pivotal period in Matisse's long career that the National Gallery's director J. Carter Brown called "one of the most dazzling moments in twentieth-century art."

The lead curator was Jack Cowart, head of the department and curator of twentieth-century art at the National Gallery. After it opened in Washington, Cowart began advocating for the addition of a fifth and final stop of the traveling exhibition in Tangier, where the works themselves had been painted.

The Moroccan ruler, King Hassan II, was keenly interested and offered his full support. The monarch suggested the show come to Tangier in March 1991, after the Hermitage, and include paintings as well as drawings. This would require extending the loans, namely from the Soviets. The Pushkin and Hermitage held half of the canvases on show and most of its highlights.

After a meeting at the end of April 1990 with the Moroccan ambassador Ali Bengelloun, Cowart sent a lengthy interoffice memorandum. "Bengelloun strongly replied that, when the King spoke, problems are solved, that finances are not a problem, security (using his own royal security forces) is not a problem, the catalogue (at my suggestion that an Arabic edition be considered) would not be a problem, since there may be a French edition forthcoming, anyway. He said he was sure environmental and display conditions could be made satisfactory . . . having in mind the Forbes Palais Mendoub or the Tangier American Legation Museum or perhaps a third site." In pencil across the top of a copy, the National Gallery of Art's director, who had been in the meeting, wrote, "I am for doing what we can."

Time was tight, and the American organizers were having last-minute issues with the Soviets and working out a few final kinks for the Russian legs of the exhibition. But Cowart was enthusiastic and pushing ahead with the idea. An essay about the show that could be used as an introduction essay in the planned Arabic-language catalog was solicited from Tahar Ben Jelloun, whose Prix Goncourt–winning novel *L'Enfant de sable* (*The Sand Child*) had been published in English a couple of years beforehand.

But as memos found among Jack Cowart's papers in the archives of the Baltimore Museum of Art show, there was significant pushback against the idea from some of his colleagues at the National Gallery.

D. Dodge Thompson, head of exhibitions, sent Roger Mandle, the museum's deputy director, a short handwritten memo in June: "Since my admonitions have gone unheeded, suggest you ask Jack to 'cool it.' We should not be viewed as promoting a Matisse exhib. in Tangiers, when there is no suitable facility." A couple of days later, Mandle relayed the message to Cowart: "Both Dodge and I have expressed reservations to you about the Moroccan venue for Matisse—Why persist," he wrote in a handwritten memo, with sharp underlining. "It is more trouble than it will ever be worth. Let's discuss—but please back off."

Cowart's lengthy response to Mandle, written on June 20, the very day of the exhibition's opening in New York City, was suitably diplomatic. "At the risk of throwing gasoline on a smoldering coal, let me respond (as I am here briefly today before going up to the opening of Matisse/Morocco at the MOMA), to my interpretation of both the attitude and tone of Dodge's buckslip to you and its direct/indirect admonishment," Cowart's memorandum opened. He noted Brown's support and that the meetings between the head of the Hermitage and the Moroccan ambassador with the National Gallery's director had gone well. This meant, Cowart assumed, that they should be throwing the institution's weight behind the idea to the Soviets in order to extend the loans and to complete a formal evaluation of potential venues. "Dodge is not correct at this preliminary stage in saying that 'there is no suitable facility,' since we don't know that until we survey the recently proposed Mendoubia," he wrote. At the time of

Matisse's stays, the building was the German consulate, but later became the Mendoubia, the house of the Sultan's representative in Tangier. "Is it more trouble than it will ever be worth? . . . that depends entirely on one's point of view about experiences with real works of art in a country whose history have deprived them of much of their cultural tradition."

For Cowart, such resistance seemed premature. "So until we can get some more hard facts like: might the USSR be interested; what might a space be; could we send just the drawings and/or a selection of paintings with drawings—I wonder why the dust up?" It was, Cowart felt, "quite within the overall objectives of our involvement with Matisse in Morocco." He concluded: "This memo is offered very much in the spirit that the experience of Matisse in Morocco should be communicated to a broader audience, indeed perhaps to a culture that so specially marked the artist for the rest of his life. As educators and curators it would seem to try to do less is an unfortunate turn."

It would be then, both a tribute to a place that so deeply impacted Matisse, and a chance for those in Tangier to see the art that their city had inspired—how their city, their people, and their traditional art had impacted the artist.

For reasons that are unclear, the show never made it to Tangier.

In the fall of 1999, nearly a decade later, a belated version of the *Matisse in Morocco* exhibition opened in Paris at the Institut du Monde Arabe under the title *Le Maroc de Matisse.* One element of Cowart's plan for Tangier materialized in France. Tahar Ben Jelloun wrote the opening essay in the exhibition's catalog.

35

In his extended piece on Matisse in 1913 after seeing the Bernheim-Jeune exhibition of Moroccan works, Marcel Sembat lavished the most attention on *Moroccan Café*, Matisse's greatest single achievement from his time in Morocco and the culmination of two winters of gradual abstraction and influence from Islamic art. "All of Matisse is in it!" wrote Sembat. "Take a good look at it and you will see everything in it."

But the three paintings that comprise the Moroccan Triptych—*Landscape Viewed from a Window*, *Zorah on the Terrace*, and *The Kasbah Gate*—are what fully tells the story of his journey in Tangier.

Matisse insisted that the trio should be viewed as a group and hang together at the Bernheim-Jeune show and also in the home of Morozov, who bought them. "The three paintings have been combined with the intention that they should be hung together in a particular order—that is, that the view from the window should be on the left, the kasbah gate on the right, and the terrace in the middle, as the sketch indicates," Matisse wrote to the Russian collector. He added a schema to ensure that there was no doubt to their order. Matisse, then, was very specific on how they should not only hang, but also how they should be read.

Matisse starts, then, as a tourist in Morocco, looking out from the top floor of a luxurious European-owned hotel in *Landscape Viewed from a Window*. The flowerpots sitting on the windowsill in the foreground are familiar and comforting anchors in the exotic, unknown city outside. While the English church and the blue of the Mediterranean are clearly recognizable, the roofs in the kasbah and medina are indistinct and, from his window, nonthreatening. The city is not empty, but the lone figure is at first barely noticeable and done with a few choppy dashes of thick white paint. A large flag flies from a tower in the citadel: the ruler is in control; the government is stable; the area is peaceful. The minaret flanking the other side of the citadel shows that it is a godly place. In the comfortable and reachable distance beyond are the hills of Spain: Europe remains close. It is a distant vantage point of security; Matisse is safe, perhaps even hesitant.

Matisse started the canvas not long after arriving on his first stay while trapped in the hotel by the rains, and the kasbah and medina, where he wanted to paint, remained out of reach, and the city itself still, at least when he began the painting, under the sultan's rule.

In the right panel, on an identical-size canvas, the journey moves toward the deeper, mysterious center with *The Kasbah Gate*. The artist peers through the horseshoe arch into the medina where there is little sign of European life.

It is a gate rather than a window that the painter stands before this time. It is in the shape of a keyhole, which immediately identifies it as being in the Islamic world. He is on the verge of passing into the dense residential quarter, a place whose narrow alleys and tangle of dead ends and vaulted passageways are, still today, best explored with a local guide. ("In a hundred years, Tangier has changed a lot. It has grown, scattered. A certain modernity has imposed itself in its architecture," wrote Ben Jelloun of his home city in 2012, exactly a century after Matisse had explored its lanes. "The streets of the medina have kept their secret. The alleys draw a labyrinth worthy of a dream of Borges.") A shadowy man lingers just inside the arch, a vague, mysterious figure that literally melts into the wall.

The Kasbah Gate is sketchy and somewhat abstract, and the viewer only slowly picks out elements through the arch. Details gradually begin to emerge—the palm tree done in a couple of simple black lines, a minaret even more rudimentarily depicted—just as the city was gradually revealing itself to the artist. Matisse painted it during his second stay, as he was gaining a deeper understanding of Morocco. No longer fully an outsider, the artist, standing on the inviting red pathway, is about to leave the fortified citadel for the sinuous heart of the ancient city.

His arrival comes with the center panel of Zorah.

Zorah on the Terrace is the same height as the other two canvases, but almost square. The nonstandard size as well as the positioning follows the Renaissance tradition of the center panel being the most important. X-rays show that the kneeling figure was originally half the size. Matisse rubbed out the image with solvent and enlarged her to make Zorah the focus, in the manner of the Virgin in the triptychs of Christendom.

If his presence is implied in the side panels, the painting of Zorah connects Matisse to this world. Where the left panel includes just a hint of other people, and the right one only the outline of a spectral guard, Zorah is in tight focus. Or rather, she *is* the focus: she anchors him to Tangier. It is a hymn to the human figure—to his young model who had already lived too much.

Matisse has arrived, finally, into the depths of North Africa. From a window to a city gate to a young woman in the medina is, as Jack Flam noted, "from a vista to a passage to an offering." Zorah has slipped off her shoes, and kneels as if in prayer or in submission, embodying, wrote Flam, "much of the sumptuousness and mystery—the paradoxical sensually spiritual—that drew Matisse to Morocco."

The paintings depict a journey from outside—by an outsider—to the core of North Africa. It is the journey of Matisse in Morocco.

The Moroccan Triptych in particular, along with *Moroccan Café* and the portraits of Zorah, Fatma, Amido, and Riffian, have come to define not just Tangier—few could actually specifically place them in this city—or even

Morocco, but more generally North Africa to the Western world. Though most of Matisse's Morocco paintings took many decades to reach a wider public, once they did, they quickly became iconic images of the region. "It is now almost impossible for any European painter to approach North Africa except through Matisse's vision," wrote Britain's best-known expert of the region, Barnaby Rogerson, noting that the Moroccan Triptych "has become a triple archway into North Africa."

Why did they so indelibly mark the area? Why *do* they still? Why has their power remained?

Is it because the canvases of Morocco were done in Morocco and not in hindsight, like Delacroix, who did his paintings in the years that followed his stay? Matisse captured not an imagined ideal looking back from his studio at home, but rather offered a clear and anchored sense of place in Tangier where he was able to complete them, capturing the light and inspiration of the moment while in city itself.

Or is it because Matisse captured Morocco in the final moments of independence, before European colonialism and modernity had overtaken it? That they reflect a more innocent time before two world wars broke up traditional cultures across much of the globe? A sense of perceived innocence in them before full European encroachment?

Delacroix visited the region as it was just beginning to fall under colonial rule, and his notebook sketches and paintings depict a glorious, powerful Moroccan civilization seemingly unfazed by European influence: surrounded by his entourage at the gate of the imperial city, the sultan sits on his magnificent stallion in undiminished strength. Eighty years later, Matisse witnessed North Africa's final capitulation with the signing of Treaty of Fez while in Morocco. He not only saw the French delegation gather to present their terms to the sultan, but was invited to join the journey to Fez to witness the surrender.

Yet Matisse didn't offer any sort of wistfulness for that closing period, as many other artists did. There is no trace of nostalgia or of sentimentality in the paintings. Nor did he offer a vision of vanishing nobility, with the painterly equivalent of Edith Wharton's Gothic tone after her trip to Morocco as a guest of France's Resident-General Hubert Lyautey four years after Matisse's stay. "We visited old palaces and new, inhabited and abandoned, and over all lay the same fine dust of oblivion, like the silvery mould on an overripe fruit. Overripeness is indeed the characteristic of this rich and stagnant civilization," Wharton wrote in her classic travelogue *In Morocco*. "Buildings, people, customs, seem all about to crumble and fall of their own weight: the present is a perpetually prolonged past."

Matisse avoided the typical Orientalists' tropes, subjects, and standard anecdotes popular at the time for painters in North Africa, something rare. From the 1913 Bernheim-Jeune exhibition, Apollinaire singled out *Moroccan Café* and *The Kasbah Gate* as "among the rare tolerable works inspired by contemporary North Africa." Instead of the anecdotal realism that defined nineteenth-century Orientalist paintings or even the exotic naturalism of many of his exact contemporaries like Hilda Rix, he developed in Tangier a lush, sensual abstraction.

That was part of their attraction for Apollinaire—and for many people since. It is what also makes them so appealing to many North Africans.

"Nothing in your work, in your remarks, or in your correspondence suggests that your view of those who were called the natives was colonial, condescending, or folkloric," wrote Abdelkader Djemaï, one of Algeria's most distinguished and decorated writers, in a deeply personal, novella-length appraisal of Matisse's Morocco paintings. "Despite their often invisible or erased arms or hands, your characters exist." They were not types like those found on postcards for sale in the city. (Such postcards, he added, were often not made in Morocco but in Spain.) "Your women do not undulate their bellies, and the men do not have the hieratic posture of village elders who seem a little too wise or permanently resigned," Djemaï wrote. "Devoid of jewelry and trinkets, but dressed in rich clothes, the people of Tangier—men and women—are not there to hide a real and daily misery in this city which is theirs and where foreigners, generally well-off, live in isolation. Their costumes and looks emphasize their dignity and simply highlight their personality."

For Djemaï, the magnificence of the Riffian's robe—as with Zorah's or Fatma's gowns—was not an exoticizing act but a celebration of distinctiveness that didn't perpetuate fantasies, clichés, or prejudice. Rather, it gave the man from the Rif a singular identity.

Matisse wasn't capturing "types" but *people* in these portraits, something rare at the time for European artists in North Africa, the Algerian author wrote. And it ultimately didn't feel indulgent or exploitative in getting these people to pose because Matisse brought empathy and respect to their portraits.

By downplaying localizing details, Matisse avoided historical context. The backgrounds of the portraits of Zorah, Fatma, Amido, and the Riffian are flat planes of color scrubbed of specificity, stripped to a broader universality. With so little to place most of the canvases in Tangier, he achieved a generalized regional aesthetic.

While the Morocco paintings have drama and emotion, they are devoid of any obvious narrative or allegory. Matisse lacks that driving impulse that writers and some painters—Delacroix comes to mind—have for storytelling. In the paintings he did in Tangier, their mystery is merely suggested, *felt* rather than explicitly expressed.

Maybe the reasons for their lingering power, and popularity, are less thematic, though, and more technical. Matisse's Moroccan pictures have an impeccable balance and careful alignment of every object on the canvas so that they obtain pictorial rhythm.

And then there are the colors! The sublime coloring vibrates off the canvas. "If one were to compare Henri Matisse's work to something, it would have to be an orange," Apollinaire wrote in 1918. "Like the orange, Matisse's work is a fruit bursting with light." Light and energy seems to radiate from within the colors of the Moroccan canvases.

Matisse was the greatest colorist of his generation. It was not merely in the colors but how he combined him. As Proust put it in an answer to his famous questionnaire, "Beauty lies not in colours but in their harmony." Matisse was unparalleled in his ability to balance colors and find that harmony. No one, stressed John Berger, who has not painted themselves can fully appreciate Matisse's mastery of this. "It is comparatively easy to achieve a certain unity in a picture either by allowing one colour to dominate or by muting all the colours. Matisse did neither. He clashed his colours together like cymbals and the effect was like a lullaby."

But maybe it is something more basic, something found on the final page of Delacroix's journal. Delacroix began keeping one at twenty-four, and over the next four decades, the extraordinary and profound document is filled with sensitive observations and astute criticism. In the very last entry, made six weeks before he died, Delacroix wrote in pencil, *"Le premier mérite d'un tableau est d'être une fête pour l'œil."* After decades as France's greatest artist and the hinge between Romanticism and modernism, after over nine thousand works attributed to him, Delacroix distilled his wisdom to a single thought: "The first merit of a painting is to be a feast [or celebration] for the eye."

Perhaps it is, simply, because Matisse's paintings from Morocco are so beautiful. As with Islamic art, they require no historical background or knowledge of art to enjoy. They are splendid visual gifts. There is no need to rationalize or justify anything about them, no need to find a reason to appreciate them. There is pure joy in the two dozen canvases, pure sensual pleasure in simply looking at them. They are, above everything else, feasts for the eye.

ACKNOWLEDGMENTS

The germ of this book dates back decades to the winter of 1990–1991 when, during my last year of university, my mom gave me the catalogue for the *Matisse in Morocco* exhibition which had opened the previous spring in Washington, DC, and was showing in Russia at its fourth and final stop when I received my copy for Christmas. The story of those paintings and those winters in Morocco eventually became an obsession, a quest, and, ultimately, a book.

I want to thank a handful of writers whose works have deepened my knowledge and appreciation of Matisse and his art, namely Tahar Ben Jelloun, Roger Benjamin, Jack Cowart, Abdelkader Djemaï, Jack Flam, Claudine Grammont, Jeanette Hoorn, Rémi Labrusse, Natalya Semenova, and Hillary Spurling.

My research was significantly aided by the collections of a dozen libraries on three continents. I want to thank the staffs at the Institut National d'Histoire de l'Art (INHA) and Bibliotheque Fondation Custodia in Paris. Sincere thanks to Latifa Samadi at the Tangier American Legation Institute for Moroccan Studies (TALIM) as well as to its director, Jennifer Rasamimanana. At the Musée de Grenoble, thanks to Estelle Favre-Taylaz for aiding my research in the archives and library. And at the Baltimore Museum of Art's Ruth R. Marder Center for Matisse Studies, thanks to its director Katy Rothkopf, senior curator and department head of European Painting and Sculpture; Laura Albans, curatorial research associate; and Sarah Dansberger, head librarian and archivist.

Key to this project was understanding, and capturing, the city of Tangier itself. Frequent stays over the past fifteen years have gifted me with lasting friendships, and I want to particularly thank Aziz Begdouri, Souleiman Berrada, Vincent Coppée, Stéphanie Gaou, Philippe Guiguet-Bologne, and Serena Van Buskirk for teaching me so much about Tangier. And thank you to the staff at Hôtel Villa de France where I have been able to stay over the years and glimpse that captivating view through Matisse's *chambre* 35.

Many thanks to a number of others who have offered support and helpful conversations about Matisse's time in Morocco: Pascal Poignard, Valeria Judkowski, and Lena Poignard; José Abete and Fabrizio Ruspoli; Mohammed El Baroudi; Mouna Mekouar; Chakib Ghadouani; Dave Besseling; Alan Rapp; and Madison Cox. Particular thanks to Rebecca Staffel for her thoughts, wisdom, and support over the years on this project.

My agent, Maria Whelan at InkWell Management, was instrumental and without her diligent work and enthusiasm this book would have remained just an idea.

At Pegasus Books, a deep thanks to Claiborne Hancock and Jessica Case, who immediately shared my passion for the idea. From the first email I knew that this book had found its perfect home, and from Jessica's first notes, its perfect editor. Many thanks to the rest of the team at Pegasus, including Maria Fernandez for her beautiful design and hard work on guiding it through production, Meghan Jusczak for publicity, Mary O'Mara for copyediting, Lori Paximadis for proofreading, and Julie Grady for indexing.

As with each of my books, my biggest thanks go to three at home in Barcelona—Eva, Alba, and Maia. This could not have been written without your support.

ILLUSTRATION CREDITS

Front cover. Henri Matisse (1869–1954), *The Kasbah Gate or Entrance to the Kasbah*, 1912, oil on canvas, 31 ½ x 45 11⁄16 in. (80 x 116 cm), Pushkin Museum of Fine Arts, Moscow, Russia. Photo: Archives Henri Matisse. Copyright © 2024 Succession H. Matisse / Artists Rights Society (ARS), New York.

Figure 1. Henri Matisse (1869–1954), *Vase with Irises*, 1912, oil on canvas, 46 7⁄16 x 39 ⅜ in. (118 x 100 cm), Hermitage, St. Petersburg, Russia. Image photography by Roman Beniaminson / Art Resource, New York. Copyright © 2024 Succession H. Matisse / Artists Rights Society (ARS), New York.

Figure 2. Henri Matisse (1869–1954), *Basket with Oranges,* 1912, oil on canvas, 37 x 32 11⁄16 in. (94 x 83 cm), Musée national Picasso, Paris, France. Image photography by Mathieu Rabeau / Art Resource, New York. Copyright © 2024 Succession H. Matisse / Artists Rights Society (ARS), New York.

Figure 3. Henri Matisse (1869–1954), *Landscape Viewed from a Window*, 1912, oil on canvas, 45 ¼ x 31 ½ in. (115 x 80 cm), Pushkin Museum of Fine Arts, Moscow, Russia. Photo: Archives Henri Matisse. Copyright © 2024 Succession H. Matisse / Artists Rights Society (ARS), New York.

Figure 4. Henri Matisse (1869–1954), *View of the Bay of Tangier*, 1912, 18 ⅛ x 21 ⅝ in. (46 x 55 cm), Ville de Grenoble / Musée de Grenoble–J. L. Lacroix. Copyright © 2024 Succession H. Matisse / Artists Rights Society (ARS), New York.

Figure 5. Henri Matisse (1869–1954), *Moroccan Landscape (Acanthus)*, 1912, oil on canvas, 45 ¼ x 31 ½ in. (115 x 80 cm), Moderna Museet, Stockholm. Copyright © 2024 Succession H. Matisse / Artists Rights Society (ARS), New York.

Figure 6. Henri Matisse (1869–1954), *Periwinkles (Moroccan Garden)*, Tangier, 1912, oil, pencil, and charcoal on canvas, 46 x 32 ½ in. (116.8 x 82.5 cm), Museum of Modern Art, New York, United States. Gift of Florene M. Schoenborn. Image photography by SCALA / Art Resource, New York. Copyright © 2024 Succession H. Matisse / Artists Rights Society (ARS), New York.

Figure 7. Henri Matisse (1869–1954), *Palm Leaf, Tangier*, 1912, oil on canvas, 46 ¼ x 32 ¼ in. (117.5 x 81.9 cm) National Gallery of Art, Washington, DC, United States. Copyright © 2024 Succession H. Matisse / Artists Rights Society (ARS), New York.

Figure 8. Henri Matisse (1869–1954), *Open Window, Collioure*, 1905, oil on canvas, 21 ¾ x 18 ⅛ in. (55.3 x 46 cm), Collection of Mr. and Mrs. John Hay Whitney, National Gallery of Art, Washington, DC, United States. Copyright © 2024 Succession H. Matisse / Artists Rights Society (ARS), New York.

Figure 9. Henri Matisse (1869–1954), *Moroccan Amido*, 1912, oil on canvas, 57 11⁄16 x 24 ⅛ in. (146.5 x 61.3 cm), Hermitage, St. Petersburg, Russia. Photo: Archives Henri Matisse. Copyright © 2024 Succession H. Matisse / Artists Rights Society (ARS), New York.

Figure 10. Henri Matisse (1869–1954), *Pot of Geraniums*, 1912, oil on linen, 16 ¼ x 13 ⅛ in. (41.3 x 33.3 cm), National Gallery of Art, Washington, DC, United States.

Figure 11. Henri Matisse (1869–1954), *Sergei Ivanovich Shchukin*, 1912, charcoal on paper, 19 ½ x 12 in. (49.5 x 30.5 cm), The Pierre and Maria-Gaetana Matisse Collection, Metropolitan Museum of Art, New York, United States. Image photography © Metropolitan Museum of Art, provided by Art Resource, New York. Copyright © 2024 Succession H. Matisse / Artists Rights Society (ARS), New York.

Figure 12. Henri Matisse (1869–1954), *The Kasbah Gate or Entrance to the Kasbah*, 1912, oil on canvas, 31 ½ x 45 11⁄16 in. (80 x 116 cm), Pushkin Museum of Fine Arts, Moscow, Russia. Photo: Archives Henri Matisse. Copyright © 2024 Succession H. Matisse / Artists Rights Society (ARS), New York.

Figure 13. Henri Matisse (1869–1954), *The Small Mulatto Woman*, 1912, 14 x 10 13⁄16 in. (35.5 x 27.5 cm), Ville de Grenoble / Musée de Grenoble–J. L. Lacroix. Copyright © 2024 Succession H. Matisse / Artists Rights Society (ARS), New York.

Figure 14. Henri Matisse (1869–1954), *The Red Carpets*, 1906, oil on canvas, 35 1⁄16 x 45 11⁄16 in. (89 x 116 cm), Ville de Grenoble / Musée de Grenoble–J. L. Lacroix. Copyright © 2024 Succession H. Matisse / Artists Rights Society (ARS), New York.

Figure 15. Henri Matisse (1869–1954), *Blue Nude* (*Memory of Biskra*), 1907, oil on canvas, 36 ¼ x 55 ¼ in. (92.1 x 140.3 cm), Baltimore Museum of Art: The Cone Collection, formed by Dr. Claribel Cone and Miss Etta Cone of Baltimore, Maryland, United States. Image photography by Mitro Hood. Copyright © 2024 Succession H. Matisse / Artists Rights Society (ARS), New York.

Figure 16. Henri Matisse (1869–1954), *Reclining Nude I (Aurore),* original model 1907, this cast c. 1930, bronze, 13 $\frac{9}{16}$ x 19 ⅝ x 11 in. (34.4 x 49.9 x 27.9 cm), Baltimore Museum of Art: The Cone Collection, formed by Dr. Claribel Cone and Miss Etta Cone of Baltimore, Maryland, United States. Image photography by Mitro Hood.

Figure 17. Henri Matisse (1869–1954), *The Standing Riffian*, 1912, oil on canvas, 57 $\frac{11}{16}$ x 38 ⅜ in. (146.5 x 97.5 cm), Hermitage, St. Petersburg, Russia. Image photography by Erich Lessing / Art Resource, New York. Copyright © 2024 Succession H. Matisse / Artists Rights Society (ARS), New York.

Figure 18. Henri Matisse (1869–1954), *The Seated Riffian* (*Le Rifain assis*), 1912, oil on canvas, 78 ⅞ x 63 ¼ in. (200.3 x 160.7 cm), Barnes Foundation, Philadelphia, Pennsylvania, United States. Image from the Barnes Foundation. Copyright © 2024 Succession H. Matisse / Artists Rights Society (ARS), New York.

Figure 19. Charles Camoin, "Henri and Amélie Matisse, Hôtel Villa de France, Tangier," 1912, photograph, © Archives Camoin. Used with permission.

Figure 20. Henri Matisse (1869–1954), *Zorah Standing*, 1912, oil on canvas, 57 $\frac{11}{16}$ x 24 in. (146.5 x 61 cm), Hermitage, St. Petersburg, Russia. Image photography by Art Resource, New York. Copyright © 2024 Succession H. Matisse / Artists Rights Society (ARS), New York.

Figure 21. Henri Matisse (1869–1954), *Arums, Iris, and Mimosas (Blue Vase with Flowers on a Blue Tablecloth),* 1913, oil on canvas, 57 ¼ x 38 ¼ in. (145.5 x 97 cm), Pushkin Museum of Fine Arts, Moscow, Russia. Photo: Archives Henri Matisse. Copyright © 2024 Succession H. Matisse / Artists Rights Society (ARS), New York.

Figure 22. Henri Matisse (1869–1954), *Zorah on the Terrace*, 1912, oil on canvas, 39 ⅜ x 45 ¼ in. (100 x 115 cm), Pushkin Museum of Fine Arts, Moscow, Russia. Photo: Archives Henri Matisse. Copyright © 2024 Succession H. Matisse / Artists Rights Society (ARS), New York.

Figure 23. Henri Matisse (1869–1954), *Bouquet of Flowers on a Veranda* or *Arums (Calla Lilies)*, 1912, oil on canvas, 57 ½ x 38 3⁄16 in. (146 x 97 cm), Hermitage, St. Petersburg Russia. Image Alamy stock. Copyright © 2024 Succession H. Matisse / Artists Rights Society (ARS), New York.

Figure 24. Henri Matisse (1869–1954), *Moroccan Café* or *Arabian Coffee House*, 1913, glue colours on canvas, 69 5⁄16 x 82 11⁄16 in. (176 x 210 cm), State Hermitage Museum, St. Petersburg, Russia. Copyright © 2024 Succession H. Matisse / Bridgeman Images.

Figure 25. Henri Matisse (1869–1954), *Bathers by a River*, 1917, oil on canvas, 102 ½x 154 3⁄16 in. (260 x 392 cm), Charles H. and Mary F. S. Worcester Collection, The Art Institute of Chicago, Chicago, United States. Image photography by The Art Institute of Chicago / Art Resource, New York. Copyright © 2024 Succession H. Matisse / Artists Rights Society (ARS), New York.

Figure 26. Henri Matisse (1869–1954), *French Window at Collioure*, 1914, oil on canvas, 45 ⅞ x 35 1⁄16 in. (116.5 x 89 cm), Musée National d'Art Moderne, Centre Georges Pompidou, Paris, France. Image photography by Philippe Migeat. Digital image © CNAC/MNAM, Dist. RMN-Grand Palais / Art Resource, New York. Copyright © 2024 Succession H. Matisse / Artists Rights Society (ARS), New York.

Figure 27. Henri Matisse (1869–1954), *The Moroccans*, 1916, oil on canvas, 71 ⅜ in. x 9 ft. 2 in. (181.3 x 279.4 cm), Gift of Mr. and Mrs. Samuel A. Marx, The Museum of Modern Art, New York, United States. Digital image © The Museum of Modern Art / Licensed by SCALA / Art Resource, New York. Copyright © 2024 Succession H. Matisse / Artists Rights Society (ARS), New York.

Figure 28. Henri Matisse (1869–1954), *Odalisque in Red Culottes*, 1921, oil on canvas, 25 9⁄16 x 35 7⁄16 in. (65 x 90 cm), Musée National d'Art Moderne, Centre Georges Pompidou, Paris, France. Image photography by Philippe Migeat. Digital image © CNAC/MNAM, Dist. RMN-Grand Palais / Art Resource, New York. Copyright © 2024 Succession H. Matisse / Artists Rights Society (ARS), New York.

Figure 29. Henri Matisse (1869–1954), *Odalisque Seated with Arms Raised, Green Striped Chair*, 1923, oil on canvas, 25 ⅝ x 19 ¾ in. (65.1 x 50.2 cm), National Gallery of Art, Washington, DC, United States. Copyright © 2024 Succession H. Matisse / Artists Rights Society (ARS), New York.

NOTES

Chapter 1

p. 3 "We have had a quiet crossing . . .": Hoorn, *Moroccan Idyll*, 64.
p. 4 "On a slightly rough . . .": *Le Maroc de Matisse*, 228; my translation.
p. 4 "sticks of dynamite . . .": Delaunay, *Le Fauvisme*, 6.
p. 5 "Here all description . . .": Barr, *Matisse: His Art and His Public*, 55.
p. 5 mimetic qualities: West, *Portraiture*, 195.
p. 5 from *pour trait* or *trait pour trait*: Klein, *Matisse Portraits*, 7.
p. 5 "a thing brilliant and powerful . . .": Kean, *All the Empty Palaces*, 162.
p. 5 "visitors howled and jeered": Stein, *Appreciation*, 158.
p. 6 high point: Clement, *Les Fauves*, xxv.
p. 6 "had become Picassoites . . .": Stein, *Autobiography of Alice B. Toklas*, 64.
p. 6 dipped the tail of a donkey: Flanner, "King of the Wild Beasts."
p. 6 "Henri Matisse's taste . . .": Flam, *Matisse: A Retrospective*, 129.
p. 7 "But in the final analysis . . .": Kostenevich and Semyonova, *Collecting Matisse*, 51.
p. 7 "It was Matisse who took the first step . . .": Flam, *Matisse: A Retrospective*, 21.
p. 7 "We may as well say . . .": *Matisse on Art*, 64.
p. 7 "You are charged . . .": Grossman, "In 1913."
p. 7 "sketched in a quarter of an hour": *Correspondance Matisse-Sembat*, 107; my translation.
p. 7 "Your two sketches . . .": *Correspondance Matisse-Sembat*, 107; my translation.
p. 8 "Matisse is alone": Antliff and Leighten, *Cubism Reader*, 366.
p. 8 "Matisse's influence . . .": Apollinaire, *Apollinaire on Art*, 217.
p. 8 no fixed date of return: Spurling, *Matisse the Master*, 107.
p. 9 "like a white dove . . .": Borrow, *The Bible in Spain*, 221.
p. 9 "all is white . . .": Borrow, *The Bible in Spain*, 221.
p. 10 "jump the ditch": *Matisse in Morocco*, 207.

Chapter 2

p. 12 "a city with walls of bronze . . .": Stuart, *The International City of Tangier*, 3.

p. 12 "a jewel . . .": Hamilton, *Tangier*, 54.

p. 12 1,750 vessels a year: Ducruet, "Maghreb Port Cities."

p. 13 "The average tourist . . .": Holt, *Morocco the Piquant*, 4–5.

p. 13 passports not required: *Baedeker's The Mediterranean*, 98.

p. 14 Tangier's population: *Baedeker's The Mediterranean*, 99.

p. 15 "Oh my dears . . .": Hoorn, *Moroccan Idyll*, 64–65.

p. 16 "We got caught . . .": Kostenevich and Semyonova, *Collecting Matisse*, 135.

p. 16 prices were negotiable: *Baedeker's The Mediterranean*, 98.

p. 17 "On Friday . . .": *Al-Moghreb Al-Aksa*, February 5, 1912.

p. 17 "Shall we ever see . . .": *Matisse in Morocco*, 17.

p. 17 "Ever since we arrived . . .": *Matisse in Morocco*, 17.

p. 17 who persuaded Matisse: *Matisse in Morocco*, 18.

p. 17 "Ah my friend! . . .": *Matisse-Marque: Correspondance*, 85; my translation.

p. 17 "While I am writing . . .": *Matisse-Marquet: Correspondance*, 86; my translation.

p. 18 "Ah, Tangier, Tangier! . . .": *Matisse in Morocco*, 17.

Chapter 3

p. 19 "his inability to relax . . .": Gowing, *Matisse*, 34.

p. 19 "Keep reading": Herrera, *Matisse: A Portrait*, 31.

p. 19 "I went for a month and a half . . .": Matisse, *Chatting*, 121.

p. 19 "My bed shook . . .": Spurling, *Matisse the Master*, 59.

p. 20 "Boredom by day . . .": Spurling, *Matisse the Master*, 106.

p. 20 left the two in Belle-Île: Spurling, *The Unknown Matisse*, 142.

p. 20 "Mademoiselle, I love you dearly . . .": Spurling, *The Unknown Matisse*, 148.

p. 21 family's main source of income: Barr, *Matisse: His Art and His Public*, 41.

p. 21 "His marriage . . .": Escholier, *Matisse from the Life*, 91.

p. 21 "She was a very straight dark woman . . .": Stein, *Autobiography of Alice B. Toklas*, 36.

p. 22 "Madame Matisse . . .": "Testimony Against Gertrude Stein."

p. 22 "*Travailler, toujours travailler*": Corbett, *You Must Change Your Life*, 93.

p. 22 "Matisse worked every day . . .": Stein, *Autobiography of Alice B. Toklas*, 39.

p. 22 "He found refuge in intensely working": Flam, *Matisse: The Man and His Art*, 18.
p. 22 *"J'ai commencé": Matisse in Morocco*, 55.
p. 25 "Black blinders . . .": Gilot, *Matisse and Picasso*, 8–9.
p. 25 "Dismayed by the weather . . .": Celdran and Vidal y Plana, *Triangle*, 49–51.
p. 26 "I prefer the [wider] composition . . .": Celdran and Vidal y Plana, *Triangle*, 55.
p. 26 prison of vertical bars: see image in *Matisse in Morocco*, 116.
p. 26 "and in front of it . . .": Labrusse, *Matisse: La Condition*, 275; my translation.
p. 26 "mustered the courage . . .": Gilot, *Matisse and Picasso*, 28.
p. 27 "Transcending personal doom . . .": Gilot, *Matisse and Picasso*, 28.

Chapter 4
p. 29 "But the moment I had the paint box . . .": Matisse, *Chatting*, 30.
p. 29 "That was the seed . . .": Matisse, *Chatting*, 30.
p. 29 "It means starvation . . .": Spurling, *Henri Matisse, Man of the North*, 74.
p. 30 "I am in a wonderful place . . .": *Matisse-Marquet: Correspondance*, 21; my translation.
p. 31 "I was quite dazed . . .": *Matisse on Art*, 176.
p. 31 "as if by an epileptic . . .": Flam, *Matisse: A Retrospective*, 31.
p. 31 "They did not alter . . .": Flanner, "King of the Wild Beasts."
p. 32 "a pot of colors flung . . .": Elderfield, *The "Wild Beasts,"* 43.
p. 32 "There were a number of attractive . . .": Stein, *Autobiography of Alice B. Toklas*, 34.
p. 32 "People were roaring . . .": Stein, *Autobiography of Alice B. Toklas*, 35.
p. 32 "As for me . . .": Spurling, "Matisse and His Models."
p. 33 "It is very difficult now . . .": Stein, *Autobiography of Alice B. Toklas*, 10.
p. 33 "Now I was confused . . .": Stein, *Autobiography of Alice B. Toklas*, 11.
p. 33 "In spite of everything . . .": Matisse, *The Vence Chapel*, 176.
p. 34 "decidedly cheap": Reynolds-Ball, *Mediterranean Winter Resorts*, 386
p. 34 down payment information: Spurling, *Matisse the Master*, 105.
p. 34 "work of a nervous man": Matisse, *Chatting*, 121.

Chapter 5
p. 36 "I've just arrived . . .": Delacroix, *Eugène Delacroix: Selected Letters*, 181.
p. 37 "This place is made for painters": Delacroix, *Eugène Delacroix: Selected Letters*, 186.

p. 37 "Rome is no longer . . .": Delacroix, *Eugène Delacroix: Selected Letters*, 194.

p. 37 "I have Romans . . .": Delacroix, *Eugène Delacroix: Selected Letters*, 193.

p. 37 "There's nothing finer . . .": Delacroix, *Eugène Delacroix: Selected Letters*, 188.

p. 37 "Here at once . . .": Drummond Hay, *Memoir*, 77.

p. 38 "I'm even sure . . .": Delacroix, *Eugène Delacroix: Selected Letters*, 187.

p. 38 "The picturesque . . .": Delacroix, *Eugène Delacroix: Selected Letters*, 192.

p. 38 "But I am learning . . .": Delacroix, *Eugène Delacroix: Selected Letters*, p 189.

p. 39 "I plan . . .": Delacroix, *Eugène Delacroix: Selected Letters*, 185.

p. 39 "From this place . . .": Djebar, *Women of Algiers*, 135.

p. 40 "About Tangiers . . .": *Matisse, Chatting*, 119.

p. 40 "as in Delacroix's paintings . . .": Matisse, *Chatting*, 117.

p. 40 "To touch . . .": Wharton, *In Morocco*, 85.

p. 41 "In spite of the splendor . . .": *Matisse in Morocco*, 209–10.

p. 41 "the rare and precious . . .": Delacroix, *Eugène Delacroix: Selected Letters*, 186.

p. 41 "a vast, silent . . .": Loti, *Au Maroc*, 16; my translation.

p. 41 "Although one distinguishes . . .": *Matisse in Morocco*, 33.

p. 41 *"C'est l'un des premiers ambassadeurs* . . .": various news service reports, July 12, 2021.

Chapter 6

p. 44 "preferred by most . . .": Reynolds-Ball, *Mediterranean Winter Resorts*, 401.

p. 44 "The Villa de France had once . . .": Reynolds-Ball, *Mediterranean Winter Resorts*, 401.

p. 45 "a superb view": *Matisse in Morocco*, 36.

p. 46 St. Andrew's Church: for detailed history, see Taylor, *The Sultan's Gift*.

p. 48 "Windows have always interested me . . .": *Matisse on Art*, 205.

p. 48 first automobile: Finlayson, *Tangier*, 59.

p. 49 "Today's the first . . .": *Matisse-Marquet: Correspondance*, 87; my translation.

Chapter 7

p. 51 "Tangier, which appears . . .": Loti, *Au Maroc*, 6; my translation.

p. 51 "like snow at twilight": Capote, *Dogs Bark*, 92.

p. 51 "We have blue shadows . . .": personal communication with Abdelaziz Bufrakech.

p. 53 "Its position . . .": Reynolds-Ball, *Mediterranean Winter Resorts*, 401.

p. 54 "There is nothing so noisy . . .": Dumas, *Tangier to Tunis*, 35.
p. 54 "Occasionally . . . a camel . . .": Dumas, *Tangier to Tunis*, 35.
p. 54 "The Grand Sok . . .": Groves, "Morocco as a Winter Sketching Ground."
p. 55 "wonderful picturesqueness . . .": Hoorn, *Moroccan Idyll*, 4.
p. 56 "See how most of them . . .": Hoorn, *Moroccan Idyll*, 81.
p. 56 "This artist has the ability . . .": Hoorn, *Moroccan Idyll*, 85.
p. 57 "the colonial process . . .": Rogerson, "The Exploration of Light."
p. 57 *"Le beau temps . . ."*: *Le Maroc de Matisse*, 234; my translation.

Chapter 8

p. 58 wild boar were plentiful: Tyrwhitt Drake, "Notes on the Birds of Tangier and Eastern Morocco."
p. 59 "It was immense . . .": Matisse, *Chatting*, 118.
p. 59 For details and images of Matisse's working in Villa Brooks, see Benjamin, "Matisse at the Senya el Hashti."
p. 59 rented one of the villa's outbuildings: Spurling, *Matisse the Master*, 104.
p. 59 "I worked in a spot . . .": Matisse, *Chatting*, 118.
p. 60 "I found them magnificent . . .": Matisse, *Chatting*, 118.
p. 60 Matisse forgot the instruction manual: Benjamin, "Matisse at the Senya el Hashti."
p. 60 "*morose*": Benjamin, "Matisse at the Senya el Hashti."
p. 61 "After having seen the rain fall . . .": *Correspondance Camoin/Matisse*, 25; my translation.
p. 61 "How new . . .": *Le Maroc de Matisse*, 228; my translation.
p. 61 Over a layer of pink: Flam, *Matisse: The Man and His Art*, 331.
p. 61 waits for something to happen: Flam, *Matisse: The Man and His Art*, 331.
p. 62 "The garden of the Swedish consulate . . .": Delacroix, *Journey to the Maghreb*, 52.
p. 62 "Criss-crossed by paths . . .": Delacroix, *Journey to the Maghreb*, 73.
p. 62 "was wild when he had eaten kif . . .": Delacroix, *Journey to the Maghreb*, 71.
p. 62 "I go for rides . . .": Delacroix, *Eugène Delacroix: Selected Letters*, 183.
p. 63 "Anything I may accomplish . . .": Delacroix, *Eugène Delacroix: Selected Letters*, 183.
p. 63 "The great interest . . .": *Le Maroc de Matisse*, 40; my translation.
p. 63 "I tend to express . . .": Celdran and Vidal y Plana, *Triangle*, 49.
p. 64 "And [how] could we take . . .": Antliff and Leighten, *Cubism Reader*, 373.
p. 64 "While Mr. Henri Matisse . . .": Vincent, *Collection Agutte-Sembat*, 13; my translation.

p. 64 "Can I send you this letter . . .": Celdran and Vidal y Plana, *Triangle*, 57.
p. 64 "*un chantier*": *Le Maroc de Matisse*, 41; my translation.
p. 65 "understanding a painting . . .": *Le Maroc de Matisse*, 41; my translation.
p. 65 ocher and yellow: Celdran and Vidal y Plana, *Triangle*, 51.
p. 66 "Leaves as big as swords": Celdran and Vidal y Plana, *Triangle*, 53.
p. 66 nowhere in Matisse's entire oeuvre: Barr, *Matisse: His Art and His Public*, 155.
p. 66 "Painting is always very hard . . .": Barr, *Matisse: His Art and His Public*, 144.
p. 66 "in a burst of spontaneous creation": Spurling, *Matisse the Master*, 115.
p. 67 "the exaltation of color": *Matisse on Art*, 204.
p. 67 "Fauvism at first . . .": *Matisse on Art*, 202.
p. 67 "Their harmonies . . .": Flam, *Matisse: The Man and His Art*, 215.
p. 67 more convincing version of Arcadia: *Matisse in Morocco*, 208.

Chapter 9

p. 68 "What interests me . . .": *Matisse on Art*, 41.
p. 68 "Yesterday I received your letter . . .": Labrusse, *Matisse: La Condition de l'Image*, 272; my translation.
p. 69 "Everyone says it's absolutely impossible . . .": Hoorn, "Letters from Tangiers," 46.
p. 69 "But it is really difficult . . .": Celdran and Vidal y Plana, *Triangle*, 45.
p. 69 "Mother you can't . . .": Hoorn, *Moroccan Idyll*, 149.
p. 69 "Of course many subterfuges . . .": Rix, "Sketching in Morocco."
p. 70 "I am gradually insinuating myself . . .": Delacroix, *Eugène Delacroix: Selected Letters*, 183.
p. 70 "Delacroix said one . . .": Matisse, *Chatting*, 47.
p. 70 "The Moors are fantastically jealous . . .": Delacroix, *Eugène Delacroix: Selected Letters*, 191.
p. 71 "The greatest hindrance . . .": Lavery, *Life of a Painter*, 101.
p. 71 "Mr. John Lavery . . .": *Al-Moghreb Al-Aksa*, February 5, 1912.
p. 71 to get a few aging women: Spurling, *Matisse the Master*, 110.
p. 71 "Veiled beauties are interesting . . .": Blackburn, *Artists and Arabia*, 66.
p. 72 the port's chief engineer: Delacroix, *Journey to the Maghreb*, 120.
p. 72 calmed with sorbets: Delacroix, *Eugène Delacroix: Selected Letters*, 16.
p. 72 "that most engaging . . .": Baudelaire, *The Salon of 1846*, 59.
p. 72 "When I speak to you about the joy . . .": Gasquet, *Cézanne*, 178; my translation.
p. 73 "*Les Femmes d'Alger, il n'y a pas . . .*": Vollard, *La vie*, 229.

p. 73 "Well Hilda and I . . .": Hoorn, *Moroccan Idyll*, 169.
p. 74 "It was one of the charms . . .": Bowles, *Let it Come Down*, 21.

Chapter 10

p. 76 Regnault's luggage: Porch, *The Conquest of Morocco*, 240.
p. 76 "The colour of their quaint saddles . . .": Hoorn, *Moroccan Idyll*, 67.
p. 76 "As for us . . .": Celdran and Vidal y Plana, *Triangle*, 43.
p. 77 "with almost indecent haste": Porch, *The Conquest of Morocco*, 241.
p. 78 "He lived through . . .": Hughes, *Shock of the New*, 134.
p. 78 "Matisse keeps his sorrows . . .": Flam, *Matisse: A Retrospective*, 149.

Chapter 11

p. 79 the two had a row: Spurling, *Matisse the Master*, 114.
p. 79 "After examining it . . .": *Le Maroc de Matisse*, 40; my translation.
p. 80 "You should realize . . .": *Le Maroc de Matisse*, 41; my translation.
p. 80 *"désorienté comme un enfant . . ."*: *Le Maroc de Matisse*, 40.
p. 80 prescribed much of the same regime: Spurling, *Matisse the Master*, 114.
p. 80 "How bitterly I regret parting . . .": Spurling, *Matisse the Master*, 114.
p. 80 called the steamship company: Spurling, *Matisse the Master*, 114.
p. 81 "Arab girl": *Matisse: Radical Invention*, 131.
p. 81 "After lunch . . .": *Morrice and Lyman*, 219.
p. 81 "It's small but it has a good light": Hoorn, *Moroccan Idyll*, 166.
p. 81 "Yesterday afternoon I would have liked . . .": *Le Maroc de Matisse*, 230; my translation.
p. 81 "was free and might pose": *Matisse: Radical Invention*, 131.
p. 82 "What did Hamidou . . .": Ben Jelloun, *Lettre à Matisse*, 24; my translation.
p. 83 did he superimpose them: *Matisse: Radical Invention*, 132.
p. 84 "This all or nothing . . .": *Matisse: Radical Invention*, 132.

Chapter 12

p. 85 "Shall I leave on Monday? . . .": *Matisse in Morocco*, 18.
p. 86 "I thought it right . . .": *Le Maroc de Matisse*, 62; my translation.
p. 86 "I'm getting ready to leave . . .": *Le Maroc de Matisse*, 230; my translation.
p. 87 bereaved man and his wife: Spurling, *Matisse the Master*, 116.
p. 87 "Mattisse": *Al-Moghreb Al-Aksa*, April 15, 1912.
p. 87–88 "I began making something passing . . .": *Matisse in Morocco*, 23.
p. 88 "This process of idealization . . .": Read, *The Meaning of Art*, 176.
p. 89 "is quite enchanting . . .": *Le Maroc de Matisse*, 62.
p. 89 "There came to me two ideas . . .": *Matisse in Morocco*, 56; my translation.

Chapter 13

p. 93 *"tout-à-fait exigu"*: Matisse, *Chatting*, 316.
p. 93 "what Matisse between pride . . .": Stein, *Autobiography of Alice B. Toklas*, 93.
p. 93 "Here, come look at my garden! . . .": Temkin and Aagesen, *Matisse: The Red Studio*, 183.
p. 94 "The flowers often give me . . .": *Matisse on Art*, 77.
p. 94 would need some time to readapt: Flam, *Matisse: The Man and His Art*, 337.
p. 95 "Matisse came to settle . . .": Potiron, "Il faut sauver la villa Matisse"; my translation.
p. 97 end-of-season sales of Parisian haute couture: Matisse, *His Art and His Textiles*, 16.
p. 97 *"ma bibliothèque de travail"*: Kropmanns, *Matisse à Issy*, 56.
p. 98 without galleries: Spurling, *Unknown Matisse*, 27.
p. 100 the yellow has faded: *Le Maroc de Matisse*, 44.
p. 102 "He always picked the best": Spurling, *Matisse the Master*, 99.

Chapter 14

p. 103 "I buy it . . .": *Matisse on Art*, 203.
p. 103 either liking a painting immediately: Read, *Meaning of Art*, 36.
p. 103 two lithographs and a drawing: Delocque-Fourcaud, "Elderly Gentleman."
p. 103 "he also gave him a drawing of himself as a fisherman": Kostenevich and Semyonova, *Collecting Matisse*, 44.
p. 104 "I was lucky . . .": *Matisse on Art*, 203.
p. 104 "He was good because . . .": Kean, *All the Empty Palaces*, 160.
p. 104 sleeping with the window open: Semenova, *Collector*, 65.
p. 104 "That drawing had an Asiatic character . . .": Matisse, *Chatting*, 128.
p. 105 treated by a specialist: Semenova, *Collector*, 18.
p. 105 virtually cornered the market: Kean, *All the Empty Palaces*, 135.
p. 105 "shrewd, subtle, and serious": Kean, *All the Empty Palaces*, 125.
p. 105 "The Russian Fricks . . .": Kean, *All the Empty Palaces*, p.63.
p. 105 Old Masters as the aristocracy: Bowlt, "Moscow Art Market," 110.
p. 106 the first Monet in Russia: Kean, *All the Empty Palaces*, 156.
p. 106 "If a picture gives you . . .": Kean, *All the Empty Palaces*, 157.
p. 106 Relying purely on his own intuition: Poznanskaya and Petukhov, "Sergei Shchukin."
p. 106 "His courage surely surpassed . . .": Barr, *Matisse: His Art and His Public*, 106.
p. 106 "a liberated expatriate . . .": Barr, *Matisse: His Art and His Public*, 106.

p. 107 "How many [of your canvases] . . .": *Correspondance Matisse-Sembat*, 107.
p. 107 5,400 square feet: Semenova, *Collector*, 68.
p. 107 defacing work: Ward, "How a Russian Collector Changed the Course of Modern Art."
p. 107 would act as guide: Kean, *All the Empty Palace*s, 212.
p. 107 into the pockets of his rumpled suit: Kean, *All the Empty Palaces*, 229.
p. 107 "The master of the house . . .": Semenova, *Collector*, 2.
p. 108 "No. 8 Bolsói Známenki Pereúlok . . .": *Baedeker's Russia*, 304.
p. 108 "an Asian town . . .": Matisse, *Chatting*, 128.
p. 108 "I keep the first pictures I bought": Matisse, *Chatting*, 120.
P.109 tipped sharply at 45 degrees: Barr, *Matisse: His Art and His Public*, 143.
p. 109 extended his first trip: Temkin and Aagesen, *Matisse: The Red Studio*, 54.

Chapter 15

p. 110 largely white-collar traders: Semenova, *Collector*, 139.
p. 111 weekly lessons: "Ivan Morozov Talks to Félix Fénéon in 1920."
p. 111 "I have to settle . . .": Semenova, *Morozov*, 72.
p. 111 devoted himself almost exclusively: Kostenevich and Semyonova, *Collecting Matisse*, 13.
p. 111 "as if assessing our taste (and pocket)": Barnes, "At the Fondation Louis Vuitton."
p. 112 "bluff, genial and kindly . . .": Kean, *All the Empty Palaces*, 121.
p. 112 "repulsed him": Kostenevich and Semyonova, *Collecting Matisse*, 14.
p. 112 "with the jealous love of a miser": Semenova, *Morozov*, 146.
p. 112 stripped of all decoration: Kostenevich and Semyonova, *Collecting Matisse*, 15.
p. 114 Moscow's first private commercial gallery: Bowlt, "The Moscow Art Market," 110-111.
p. 114 "It was an incredible place . . .": Stein, *Autobiography of Alice B. Toklas*, 30.
p. 115 his real pride: Kostenevich and Semyonova, *Collecting Matisse*, 15.
p. 115 "the Russian who doesn't haggle": Kostenevich and Semyonova, *Collecting Matisse*, 14.
p. 115 capable of waiting years: Semenova, *Collector*, 140.
p. 116 "When Morozov would go . . .": *From Russia*, 48.
p. 116 "chewing shards of broken glass": Semenova, *Collector*, 204.
p. 116 "Constantly cautious and restrained . . .": Kostenevich and Semyonova, *Collecting Matisse*, 13.
p. 116 "unstable times": Tugendhold, "S. I. Shchukin's French Collection."
p. 117 "It took sheer nerve . . .": Kean, *All the Empty Palaces*, 267.

Chapter 16

p. 118 Vollard moved through the crowd: Semenova, *Collector*, 100–101.
p. 118 telegram reached Shchukin: Delocque-Fourcaud, "Elderly Gentleman."
p. 119 "Matisse, whose attempts . . .": Whitfield, *Fauvism*, 119.
p. 119 not a single new painting: Delocque-Fourcaud, "Elderly Gentleman."
p. 119 caravan consisting of: Shchukin, "Travel Diary."
p. 119 not generally the meditative type: Kean, *All the Empty Palaces*, 149.
p. 119 "In a short time . . .": Kostenevich and Semyonova, *Collecting Matisse*, 11.
p. 120 "One afternoon, as he was exploring": Kean, *All the Empty Palaces*, 149.
p. 121 were forgeries: Flam, *Matisse: The Man and His Art*, 224.
p. 121 not to be fake after all: Wullschlager, "The Russians Are Coming."
p. 121 "The canvases hang side by side": Semenova, *Collector*, 130.
p. 121 "A madman painted it . . .": Hook, *Modern*, 279.
p. 121 "a very rich Russian Jew": Olivier, *Loving Picasso*, 211.
p. 122 "I see the painting all the time . . .": Wullschlager, "The Russians Are Coming."
p. 122 "You are going to simplify painting": *Matisse on Art*, 79.
p. 123 "The least that one can say . . .": Flam, *Matisse: The Man and His Art*, 291.
p. 123 "Considered while traveling . . .": Kostenevich and Semyonova, *Collecting Matisse*, 167.
p. 123 "While traveling . . .": Kostenevich and Semyonova, *Collecting Matisse*, 167.
p. 124 Insomnia set in: Spurling, *Matisse the Master*, 59.
p. 124 "All artists have . . .": Hook, *Modern*, 143.
p. 124 "Your panels have arrived . . .": Kostenevich and Semyonova, *Collecting Matisse*, 168.
p. 124 "It is impossible . . .": Semenova, *Collector*, 183.
p. 125 shot himself in the heart: Semenova, *Collector*, 159.
p. 125 with a revolver: Bartlett, "The Revolutionary Collector Who Changed the Course of Russian Art."
p. 125 known how to soothe: Delocque-Fourcaud, "Elderly Gentleman."
p. 125 led his son to suicide: Spurling, *Matisse the Master*, 56.
p. 125 "A profoundly different Shchukin . . .": Giovannini, "A Bridge from Moscow to Paris."
p. 125 "aromatic hothouse . . .": Kostenevich and Semyonova, *Collecting Matisse*, 36.

Chapter 17

p. 126 4,269 works: Clement, *Les Fauves*, 8.
p. 126 1,625 works: Clement, *Les Fauves*, 13.

p. 127 "This group convenes . . .": Sembat, *Les Cahiers Noirs*, 418; my translation.
p. 128 "I did sculpture because . . .": Matisse, *Chatting*, 84–85.
p. 128 Not a single piece sold: Barr, *Matisse: His Art and His Public*, 144.
p. 129 "I have been thinking . . .": *Matisse in Morocco*, 263.
p. 129 "Dear Sir . . .": *Matisse in Morocco*, 264.
p. 130 "The insurgents marched . . .": *Morrice and Lyman*, 119.
p. 130 "The Treaty of Fez . . .": Pennell, *Morocco Since 1830*, 153.
p. 132 "The quality of the light . . .": Gide, *Immoralist*, 190.

Chapter 18
p. 135 just long enough to complete landscapes: *Matisse in Morocco*, 222.
p. 136 prices were stipulated: Flam, *Matisse: The Man and His Art*, 348–349.
p. 137 "my nostrils . . .": Selous, *Appointment to Fez*, 13.
p. 137 "All yellow, the earth tawny colored . . .": Matisse, *Chatting*, 117.
p. 137 "Everyone is desperate . . .": *Le Maroc de Matisse*, 235; my translation.
p. 138 "It's not like that . . .": Matisse, *Chatting*, 118.
p. 138 "smaller": Matisse, *Chatting*, 118.
p. 138 "Everything I thought lacking . . .": Matisse, *Chatting*, 118.
p. 139 "So what could be called . . .": *Le Maroc de Matisse*, 15; my translation.

Chapter 19
p. 141 "Don't imagine . . .": Spurling, *Matisse the Master*, 127.
p. 141 "Here, it's always the same . . .": *Le Maroc de Matisse*, 42; my translation.
pp. 141–42 "cliquey and socially oppressive": Fisher, "Bible Dream," 179.
p. 142 "Visitors do not . . .": Reynolds-Ball, *Mediterranean Winter Resorts*, 389.
p. 143 "M. Matisse himself . . .": MacChesney, "A Talk with Matisse."
p. 144 "Stripped of the legend . . .": Flam, *Matisse: A Retrospective*, 145.
p. 144 "there are no streets . . .": Reynolds-Ball, *Mediterranean Winter Resorts*, 386.
p. 145 "touts and alleged guides . . .": Fraser, *Land of Veiled Women*, 280.
p. 145 "Perhaps the Moor . . .": Holt, *Morocco the Piquant*, 3–4.
p. 147 "broad white stripes . . .": Hold, *Morocco the Piquant*, 20.

Chapter 20
p. 148 "stretched out like a panther": Spurling, *Matisse the Master*, 123.
p. 148 "When I thought . . .": *Matisse: Radical Invention*, 132.
p. 149 "I have just finished . . .": *Matisse: Radical Invention*, 132.
p. 150 "*une petite marocaine* . . .": *Correspondance Matisse-Sembat*, 113; my translation.

p. 150 "We are very happy . . .": *Correspondance Matisse-Sembat*, 126; my translation.
p. 151 "Her condition did not allow her . . .": Ben Jelloun, *Lettre à Matisse*, 33; my translation.
p. 151 "The painting is installed . . .": *Correspondance Matisse-Sembat*, 139; my translation.
p. 152 "It is in an old . . .": *Correspondance Matisse-Sembat*, 140; my translation.
p. 152 decorative porcelain tile: *Matisse in Morocco*, 92.

Chapter 21

p. 153 *"J'ai toujours beaucoup aimé l'Orient* . . .": Clévenot, "Matisse au Maroc"; my translation.
p. 153 *"La revelation* . . .": Clévenot, "Matisse au Maroc"; my translation.
p. 153 "the most beautiful ceramics . . .": Clévenot, "Matisse au Maroc"; my translation.
p. 154 "is not stylistic . . .": *Le Maroc de Matisse*, 31–32; my translation.
p. 154 "Nice place! . . .": Benjamin, *Orientalist Aesthetics*, 161.
p. 154 "a place full of light and shade . . .": Gide, *The Immoralist*, 49.
p. 155 "the light is blinding": Spurling, *Unknown Matisse*, 358.
p. 155 prepared to deal with strong desert light: Benjamin, *Orientalist Aesthetics*, 164.
p. 156 "It expresses the artist's leanings . . .": Labrusse, "Deconstructing Orientalism."
p. 156 "One day I was working on her . . .": *Chatting with Matisse*, 86.
p. 157 "I admit to not understanding . . .": Clement, *Les Fauves*, 28.
p. 159 "I will have the pleasure . . .": *Correspondance Matisse-Sembat*, 93; my translation.
p. 160 "What do you say . . .": *Le Maroc de Matisse*, 28; my translation.
p. 160 "Islamic pattern offers the illusion . . .": Hughes, *Shock of the New*, 139.
p. 161 It came at the right time: *Le Maroc de Matisse*, 17.
p. 161 "It is a rich language . . .": Sijelmassi, *Moroccan Painting*, 10.
p. 161 *"Le Maroc est encore plus riche que la luminière* . . .": *Le Maroc de Matisse*, 17; my translation.

Chapter 22

p. 162 *"Ici toutes les journées* . . .": Ben Jelloun, *Lettre à Matisse*, 26; my translation.
p. 162 "a magnificent mountaineer type . . .": Kostenevich and Semyonova, *Collecting Matisse*, 147.
p. 163 "My butt is . . .": *Matisse-Marquet: Correspondance*, 82; my translation.

p. 163 "They crouch . . .": Fraser, *Land of Veiled Women*, 277.
p. 163 "Here are a score . . .": Fraser, *Land of Veiled Women*, 278.
p. 163 "The very fact of posing . . .": Ben Jelloun, *Lettre à Matisse*, 26; my translation.
p. 164 "The firm torso . . .": Djemaï, *Zorah sur la terrasse*, 19; my translation.
p. 164 "In reality, this face . . .": Ben Jelloun, *Lettre à Matisse*, 27; my translation.
p. 166 "You see that without seeming excited . . .": *Le Maroc de Matisse*, 42; my translation.
p. 166 "Marquet and I . . .": *Correspondance Camoin/Matisse*, 36; my translation.
p. 166 "because she is terribly bored . . .": *Correspondance Matisse-Sembat*, 123; my translation.
p. 167 "She always placed . . .": Stein, *Autobiography of Alice B. Toklas*, 36.

Chapter 23

p. 169 "Therefore, by police order . . .": *Le Maroc de Matisse,* 66; my translation.
p. 170 "Over there, the girls . . .": Matisse, *The Vence Chapel*, p.155.
p. 171 "I won't tell you . . .": Matisse, *The Vence Chapel*, 155.
p. 172 "You should have seen . . .": Rusakov and Bowlt, "Matisse in Russia in the Autumn of 1911."
p. 172 "I spent ten years searching . . .": Kostenevich and Semyonova, *Collecting Matisse*, 36.
p. 173 "The individual character . . .": Hilton, "Matisse in Moscow."
p. 173 "They are really great art . . .": Flam, *Matisse: The Man and His Art*, 323.
p. 173 "The main task . . .": Rusakov and Bowlt, "Matisse in Russia: Autumn 1911."
p. 174 "The Byzantine principle . . .": Hilton, "Matisse in Moscow."

Chapter 24

p. 176 "You are used to having someone . . .": Ben Jelloun, *Lettre à Matisse*, 24; my translation.
p. 176 "That's where I painted Zorah . . .": *Le Maroc de Matisse*, 234; my translation.
p. 177 the key tenants of Orientalism: Wright, *Matisse and the Subject of Modernism*, 198.
p. 177 the idea of sexual availability: Benjamin, *Orientalist Aesthetics*, 167.
p. 177 "As for odalisques . . .": *Matisse on Art*, 205.
p. 178 "displaying themselves like late refugees from Delacroix": Hughes, *Shock of the New*, 146.

p. 179 "Matisse has almost done away . . .": Darwent, "The Moor in Matisse."
p. 179 "You have made her . . .": Djemaï, *Zorah sur la terrasse*, 19; my translation.

Chapter 25

p. 181 "For a week . . .": *Correspondance Matisse-Sembat*, 134; my translation.
p. 182 "The year is off . . .": *Le Maroc de Matisse*, 234; my translation.
p. 183 "You play chess . . .": *Matisse-Marquet: Correspondance*, 93; my translation.
p. 184 "I need friendship . . .": *Charles Camoin: Rétrospective*, 67; my translation.
p. 184 nursed him back to health: *Matisse in Morocco*, 43.
p. 184 "In recent years . . .": *Charles Camoin: Rétrospective*, 64; my translation.
p. 185 "Of this city crushed . . .": Vincent, *Collection Agutte-Sembat*, 83; my translation.
p. 185 "The beach embodies . . .": *Charles Camoin: Rétrospective*, 65; my translation.
p. 185 "I am very happy . . .": *Correspondance Camoin/Matisse*, 41; my translation.
p. 185 fifteen paintings: *Charles Camoin: Rétrospective*, 65.
p. 185 "*Période rare de santé* . . .": *Correspondance Camoin/Matisse*, 49.
p. 186 "He was travelling always . . . ": *Morrice and Lyman*, 221.
p. 186 "with a pate . . .": Maugham, *The Magician*, 20–21.
p. 187 the greatest North American painter: Lyman, *Morrice*, 14.
p. 187 "His knowledge of painting . . .": Vauxcelles, "The Art of J. W. Morrice."
p. 187 "Apart from our working sessions . . .": *Morrice and Lyman*, 221.
p. 188 "A painter should go South . . .": *Morrice and Lyman*, 58.
p. 188 "You only understand it . . .": *Morrice and Lyman*, 102.
p. 188 favorite word was "gusto": Fulford, "The Painter We Weren't Ready For."
p. 188 "You know the artist . . .": *Morrice and Lyman*, 221.
p. 188 "Whisky! Whisky!": *Morrice and Lyman*, 220.
p. 189 "I don't know where . . .": *Correspondance Matisse-Sembat*, 117; my translation.
p. 189 "I had to endure . . .": Matisse, *Chatting*, 117.

Chapter 26

p. 190 "Curiosity pushed me . . .": *Le Maroc de Matisse*, 92; my translation.
p. 190 "In the back . . .": Bowles, "Worlds of Tangier."
p. 191 "in the café that the foreign visitor . . .": Bowles, "Café in Morocco."

p. 191 Made to feel welcome: Spurling, *Matisse the Master*, 131.
p. 191 "It's a quiet café . . .": *Matisse: Radical Invention*, 135.
p. 192 "*C'est très intime*": *Le Maroc de Matisse*, 92.
p. 192 sketched together: Matisse, *Chatting*, 131.
p. 192 learned to draw with Delacroix-like rapidity: Spurling, *Matisse the Master*, 131.
p. 192 "[Your father] is currently doing . . .": *Le Maroc de Matisse*, 235; my translation.
p. 193 against the laws of color composition: Kostenevich and Semyonova, *Collecting Matisse*, 153.
p. 193 "the most Oriental . . .": *Henri Matisse: Paintings and Sculptures in Soviet Museums*, 22.
p. 193 "the landscape of the thousand and one nights . . .": Sembat, *Les Cahiers noirs*, 493; my translation.
p. 194 "A host of birds sang . . .": Flam, *Matisse: A Retrospective*, 149.
p. 194 "Retain only . . .": Herrera, *Matisse: A Portrait*, 193.
p. 194 "Why did he eliminate . . .": Flam, *Matisse: A Retrospective*, 148.
p. 195 "What I dream of . . .": *Matisse on Art*, 42.
p. 195 "Matisse had reached a pitch . . .": Spurling, *Matisse the Master*, 134
p. 196 "Since you left . . .": *Correspondance Camoin/Matisse*, 41; my translation.
p. 196 "We made a picturesque crossing . . .": *Correspondance Camoin/Matisse*, 40; my translation.
p. 196 "In Menton . . .": *Correspondance Camoin/Matisse*, 40; my translation.

Chapter 27

p. 200 counterattack against disparaging critics: Flam, *Matisse: The Man and His Art*, 360.
p. 200 "They have been a great . . .": *Matisse in Morocco*, 264.
p. 200 "I have just received . . .": Kostenevich and Semyonova, *Collecting Matisse*, 186.
p. 200 "Mr Morozov is ravished . . .": Kean, *All the Empty Palaces*, 122.
p. 201 "Every painting and drawing . . .": Apollinaire, *Chroniques d'art*, 430; my translation.
p. 201 "My most grave objection . . .": Wright, *Matisse and the Subject of Modernism*, 195.
p. 201 "Only an eye . . .": Wright, *Matisse and the Subject of Modernism*, 195–197.
p. 201 "Look at it! . . .": Flam, *Matisse: A Retrospective*, 146.
p. 201 "I think that you worked . . .": *Correspondance Camoin/Matisse*, 44; my translation.

p. 202 "We are turning them down . . .": Bois, *Matisse in the Barnes Collection*, 184.
p. 202 "the best thing . . .": Kostenevich and Semyonova, *Collecting Matisse*, 42.
p. 202 paying 10,000 francs: Barr, *Matisse: His Art and His Public*, 160.
p. 202 "The longer you look at it . . .": Barr, *Matisse: His Art and His Public*, 160.
p. 202 "It is the picture . . .": Barr, *Matisse: His Art and His Public*, 160.
p. 203 "meant to be felt and submitted to": Spurling, *Matisse the Master*, 148.

Chapter 28

p. 204 "I've wanted to write . . .": *Correspondance Camoin/Matisse*, 51; my translation.
p. 206 "Henri Matisse's portrait . . .": Apollinaire, *Apollinaire on Art*, 330–331.
p. 206 "If there is a masterpiece . . .": Flam, *Matisse: A Retrospective*, 151.
p. 207 young André Breton: Kostenevich and Semyonova, *Collecting Matisse*, 156.
p. 207 "I saw the Salon d'Automne . . .": *Correspondance Camoin/Matisse*, 57–58; my translation.
p. 207 "The truth is that Painting . . .": *Correspondance Camoin/Matisse*, 59–60; my translation.
p. 207 "By the way . . .": Kostenevich and Semyonova, *Collecting Matisse*, 156.
p. 207 "which at this time . . .": *Correspondance Camoin/Matisse*, 57; my translation.
p. 208 "I wasn't very enthusiastic . . .": Matisse, *Chatting*, 118.
p. 208 "As a painter . . .": Benjamin, *Orientalist Aesthetics*, 164.
p. 208 "You will probably be astonished . . .": *Matisse: Radical Invention*, 173.
p. 209 "In the studio . . .": Bois, *Matisse in the Barnes Collection*, 181.
p. 210 without showing Amélie: Spurling, *Matisse the Master*, 145.
p. 210 "So instead of leaving . . .": Matisse, *Chatting*, 118.

Chapter 29

p. 214 "I feel all my misery . . .": *Correspondance Camoin/Matisse*, 55; my translation.
p. 214 "When I returned from Tangiers . . .": *Charles Camoin: Un Fauve en liberté*, 81.
p. 214 for details on cut canvases: *Charles Camoin: Un Fauve en liberté*, 76–81.
p. 215 Picasso rushed to Paris: Roe, *In Montparnasse*, 25.
p. 215 Modigliani, whose advanced tuberculosis: Roe, *In Montparnasse*, 26.
p. 216 "Derain, Braque, Camoin, Puy . . .": Escholier, *Matisse from the Life*, 96.
p. 216 "the most mysterious picture ever painted": Aragon, *Henri Matisse* (vol. 1), 303.

p. 217 X-rays revealed: *Matisse: Radical Invention*, 235.
p. 217 most important artist events of 1914: Flam, *Matisse: The Man and His Art*, 394.
p. 217 "Undoubtedly, the hinge-point . . .": Hughes, *Shock of the New*, 159.
p. 218 "Marquet and I ended up . . .": *Correspondance Camoin/Matisse*, 67; my translation.
p. 219 "I've examined this picture . . .": Spurling, *Matisse the Master*, 168.

Chapter 30
p. 220 "I start again . . .": *Correspondance Camoin/Matisse*, 89; my translation.
p. 220 The sketch he added: shown in Flam, *Matisse: The Man and His Art*, 414.
p. 220 "I am very late . . .": *Correspondance Camoin/Matisse*, 95; my translation.
p. 221 blotted onto the canvas: *Matisse: Radical Invention*, 293.
p. 222 "constantly stripping the work down . . .": *Matisse: Radical Invention*, 295.
p. 222 "We argue so heatedly . . .": Flam, *Matisse: The Man and His Art*, 394.
p. 223 "The Impressionists had banished black . . .": Schwabsky, "Black Is Also a Color."
p. 223 "most magnificent achievements": *Henri-Matisse: Retrospective Exhibition*, 19.
p. 224 "On 2 August 1914 . . .": Danchev, *Georges Braque*, 121.
p. 225 "Paris is a city . . .": Cowley, *Exile's Return*, 136.

Chapter 31
p. 227 "It never stopped raining . . .": "The National Gallery of Art to Present Paintings by Matisse."
p. 227 "A change of weather . . .": Proust, *The Guermantes Way*, Part II, 49.
p. 227 "What a gentle and soft light . . .": Cowart, *Henri Matisse: The Early Years in Nice*, 23.
p. 228 "A will to rhythmic abstraction . . .": *Matisse on Art*, 301.
p. 228 "The odalisques were the fruits . . .": *Matisse on Art*, 301.
p. 228 "Such a phenomenon . . .": Fry, "Henri-Matisse in the Luxembourg."
p. 229 "When Delacroix and Ingres . . .": Davenport, *A Balthus Notebook*, 40.
p. 229 "He's given in . . .": Spurling, "Matisse and His Models."
p. 229 "The sun-drenched wild beast . . .": Herrera, *Matisse: A Portrait*, 150.
p. 229 "Did I paint too many . . .": *Matisse on Art*, 300.
p. 230 "I am writing all this . . .": Lefebvre, *Marcel Sembat*, 164; my translation.
p. 230 "As for the paintings . . .": Celdran and Vidal y Plana, *Triangle*, 6.

p. 230 "For Georgette, these . . .": Vincent, *Collection Agutte-Sembat*, 10; my translation.
p. 231 "fearless" and "fierce": Vincent, *Collection Agutte-Sembat*, 13; my translation.
p. 231 "André, tell mom . . .": Lefebvre, *Marcel Sembat*, 164; my translation.
p. 231 "My poor friend . . .": Lefebvre, *Marcel Sembat*, 164; my translation.
p. 231 "*papier peint pour* . . .": Musée de Grenoble gallery label.
p. 232 medium-size canvases went for 5,000 francs: Herrera, *Matisse: A Portrait*, 150.
p. 233 "He works, sleeps . . .": Flanner, "King of the Wild Beasts—I."
p. 233 "He lived the way . . .": Wullschlager, "Matisse: Inside His Private Universe."

Chapter 32

p. 236 fretted about his weakening vision: Spurling, "Matisse and His Models."
p. 236 "a second life": Sooke, *Henri Matisse: A Second Life*, 6.
p. 236 sketched almost continually: Flanner, "King of the Wild Beasts—I."
p. 237 "Artiste-Peintre": Stewart, "Matisse."
p. 237 china plate: Flanner, "King of the Wild Beasts—I."
p. 238 "You left with the naked light . . .": Ben Jelloun, *Lettre à Matisse*, 36.
p. 239 "In this winter of 1912 . . .": *Le Maroc de Matisse*, 19; my translation.
p. 239 "From 1913 to his last works . . .": *Matisse in Morocco*, 148–149.
p. 240 "To say that Matisse found himself . . .": Russell, "Matisse and the Mark left on Him by Morocco."
p. 240 "As it did for Delacroix . . .": Kimmelman, "How the Spirit of Morocco Seized Matisse."
p. 240 "Decoration in Morocco . . .": Kimmelman, "How the Spirit of Morocco Seized Matisse."
p. 240 "devoid of intellectual substance": Hook, *Breakfast at Sotheby's*, 314.
p. 240 "By character, Matisse . . .": Flanner, "King of the Wild Beasts—I."
p. 241 "Other French painters . . .": Flanner, "King of the Wild Beasts—I."
p. 241 "Paint, not the thing . . .": *The Steins Collect*, 343.
p. 241 "An artist must possess . . .": Friedenthal, *Letters of the Great Artists*, 238.
p. 241 "Morocco bridged the gap . . .": Gowing, *Matisse*, 117.

Chapter 33

p. 245 "Impossible send [money] . . .": Kostenevich and Semyonova, *Collecting Matisse*, 177.
p. 245 Tver factory production numbers: Semenova, *Morozov*, 176.
p. 246 fireproof storeroom: Kostenevich and Semyonova, *Collecting Matisse*, 44.

p. 247 sewn diamonds and gold: Semenova, *Morozov*, 230.
p. 247 transfer money to a bank in Stockholm: Semenova, *Collector*, 250.
p. 247 Matisse went to the train station: Kostenevich and Semyonova, *Collecting Matisse*, 44.
p. 248 given three rooms: "Ivan Morozov Talks to Félix Fénéon in 1920."
p. 248 leading tours of the art: Kostenevich and Semyonova, *Collecting Matisse*, 44.
p. 250 to the Siberian capital of Novosibirsk: Kostenevich, "Sergei Shchukin: Modern Art Pioneer."
p. 250 "The Council of Ministers of the USSR . . .": Kostenevich, "Sergei Shchukin: Modern Art Pioneer."
p. 250 ten days were given: Kostenevich, "Sergei Shchukin: Modern Art Pioneer."
p. 250 "enemies of Soviet realistic art": Mileeva, "Utopia in Retreat."
p. 250 began by showing Voroshilov the panels: Kostenevich and Semyonova, *Collecting Matisse*, 45.
p. 250 "He, he, he": Kostenevich and Semyonova, *Collecting Matisse*, 45.
p. 251 So beneath their contempt: "Beverly Whitney Kean."
p. 251 numbers of works: Semenova, *Morozov*, 214.
p. 251 go to the provinces, and the most openly risky: Semenova, *Collector*, 246.
p. 252 Matisse and Picasso works remained off limits: Semenova, *Collector*, 247.
p. 252 "is designed first of all . . .": *Henri Matisse: Exhibition at the Museum of Modern Art*, 3.

Chapter 34

p. 254 "Their whereabouts was lost . . .": Flanner, "Letter from Paris."
p. 254 Hermitage's catalog didn't even mention Matisse's name: Flanner, "Letter from Paris."
p. 254 "small inaccessible back room": Kean, *All the Empty Palaces*, 162.
p. 256 All quotes from the Jack Cowart Papers in the archive of the Baltimore Museum of Art.

Chapter 35

p. 259 "All of Matisse is in it! . . .": Flam, *Matisse: A Retrospective*, 148.
p. 259 "The three paintings . . .": Kostenevich and Semyonova, *Collecting Matisse*, 184.
p. 260 "In a hundred years . . .": Ben Jelloun, *Lettre à Matisse*, 37; my translation.
p. 261 "from a vista . . .": Flam, *Matisse: The Man and His Art*, 349–50.
p. 262 "It is now almost impossible . . .": Rogerson, "The Exploration of Light."

p. 263 "We visited old palaces . . .": Wharton, *In Morocco*, 85.

p. 263 "among the rare tolerable works . . .": Benjamin, *Orientalist Aesthetics*, 168.

p. 263 "Nothing in your work . . .": Djemaï, *Zorah sur la terrasse*, 102–3; my translation.

p. 264 "If one were to compare . . .": Apollinaire, *Apollinaire on Art*, 457.

p. 265 "Beauty lies not in colours . . .": Maurois, *Quest for Proust*, 55.

p. 265 "It is comparatively easy to achieve . . .": Berger, *Portraits*, 282.

p. 265 *"Le premier mérite . . ."*: Delacroix, *Journal de Eugène Delacroix*, 438.

SELECT BIBLIOGRAPHY

Al-Moghreb Al-Aksa. Microfilm for 1912 and 1913 editions accessed at the Tangier American Legation (TALIM), Tangier, Morocco.

Antliff, Mark, and Patricia Leighten, eds. *A Cubism Reader: Documents and Criticism, 1906-1914*. Chicago: University of Chicago Press, 2008.

Apollinaire, Guillaume. *Apollinaire on Art: Essays and Reviews, 1902-1918*. New York: Viking, 1972.

———. *Chroniques d'art, 1902-1918*. Paris: Gallimard, 1960.

———. *The Cubist Painters*. Berkeley: University of California Press, 2002.

Aragon, Louis. *Henri Matisse: A Novel*. 2 volumes. New York: Harcourt Brace Jovanovich, 1972.

Baedeker's The Mediterranean: Seaports and Sea Routes, 1911. Leipzig: Karl Baedeker, 1911.

Baedeker's Paris and its Environs, 1913. Leipzig: Karl Baedeker, 1913.

Baedeker's Russia, 1914. Leipzig: Karl Baedeker, 1914.

Barnes Foundation. *The Barnes Foundation: Masterworks*. New York: Skira Rizzoli, 2012.

Barnes, Julian. "At the Fondation Louis Vuitton." *London Review of Books*, January 19, 2017.

Barr, Alfred H., Jr. *Matisse: His Art and His Public*. London: Secker & Warburg, 1975.

Bartlett, Rosamund. "The Revolutionary Collector Who Changed the Course of Russian Art." *Apollo*, October 17, 2016.

Baudelaire, Charles. *The Salon of 1846*. New York: David Zwirner, 2021.

Ben Jelloun, Tahar. *Lettre à Matisse et autres écrits sur l'art*. Paris: Gallimard, 2013.

———. "Tangier: Myths and Memories." *UNESCO Courier*, March 1997.

Benjamin, Roger. "Matisse at the Senya el Hashti: Diplomacy and Decoration in an Anglo-Moroccan Garden." *Art Bulletin* 101, no. 3 (September 2019).

———. *Orientalist Aesthetics: Art, Colonialism, and French North Africa, 1880-1930*. Berkeley: University of California Press, 2003.

Berger, John. *Portraits: John Berger on Artists*. London: Verso, 2015.

"Beverly Whitney Kean" (obituary). *The Telegraph*, August 19, 2011.

Blackburn, Henry. *Artists and Arabia, Or Sketching in Sunshine*. London: Sampson Low, Son, and Marston, 1868.

Bois, Yve-Alain. *Matisse in the Barnes Collection*. London: Thames & Hudson, 2015.

Borrow, George. *The Bible in Spain*. Philadelphia: James M. Campbell & Co, 1843.

Bowles, Paul. "Café in Morocco." *Holiday*, September 1968.

———. *Let it Come Down*. London: Penguin, 2000.

———. "Worlds of Tangier." *Holiday*, March 1958.

Bowlt, John. *Moscow & St. Petersburg, 1900–1920: Art, Life, & Culture of the Russian Silver Age*. New York: Vendome, 2008.

———. "Moscow Art Market." In *Between Tsar and People*, edited by E. Clowes et al. Princeton: Princeton University Press, 1991.

Brodskaya, Nathalia, and Nina Kalitina. *Claude Monet: Volume 2*. New York: Parkstone International, 2012.

Buchanan, Donald. *James Wilson Morrice*. Toronto: Ryerson Press, 1947.

Burgess, Gelett. "The Wild Men of Paris." *Architectural Record*, May 1910.

Capote, Truman. *The Dogs Bark: Public People and Private Places*. New York: New American Library, 1973.

Celdran, Françoise, and Ramon-R. Vidal y Plana. *Triangle: échanges artistiques: artistic exchanges, Henri Matisse, Georgette Agutte, Marcel Sembat*. Mercurol, France: Yvelinédition, 2006.

Charles Camoin: Rétrospective, 1879–1965. Exhibition catalog. Réunion: Réunion des Musées Nationaux, 1997.

Clandermond, Andrew, and Terence MacCarthy. *A Room with a View: A History of the Grand Hotel Villa de France*. Tangier: Minville, 2012.

Clement, Russell T. *Les Fauves: A Sourcebook*. Westport, CT: Greenwood, 1994.

Clévenot, Dominique. "Matisse au Maroc." *Horizons Maghrébins: Le droit à la mémoire*, no. 42 (2000).

Corbett, Rachel. *You Must Change Your Life: The Story of Rainer Maria Rilke and Auguste Rodin*. New York: W. W. Norton, 2016.

Correspondance entre Charles Camoin et Henri Matisse. Lausanne: Bibliothèque des Arts, 1997.

Correspondance Matisse-Sembat: Une amitié artistique et politique, 1904–1922. Lausanne: Bibliothèque des Arts, 2008.

Cottington, David. *Cubism in the Shadow of War: The Avant-Garde and Politics in Paris, 1905–1914*. New Haven, CT: Yale University Press, 1998.

Cowart, Jack. *Henri Matisse: The Early Years in Nice, 1916–1930*. Exhibition catalog. New York: Harry N. Abrams, 1986.

Cowley, Malcolm. *Exile's Return*. New York: Penguin, 1994.

Davenport, Guy. *A Balthus Notebook*. New York: David Zwirner, 2020.

Darwent, Charles. "The Moor in Matisse: Le Maroc de Matisse Institut du Monde Arabe, Paris." *The Independent*, November 28, 1999.

Delacroix, Eugène. *Eugène Delacroix: Selected Letters, 1813-1863*. Boston: MFA, 1970.

———. *Journal de Eugène Delacroix. Vol 3*. Paris: Plon, 1893.

———. *Journey to the Maghreb and Andalusia, 1832: The Travel Notebooks and Other Writings*. University Park: Penn State University Press, 2019.

Delacroix in Morocco. Exhibition catalog. Paris: Flammarion, 1995.

Danchev, Alex. *Georges Braque: A Life*. London: Hamish Hamilton, 2005.

Delaunay, Florence. *Le Fauvisme*. Collioure, France: Maison du Fauvisme Collioure, 2017.

Delocque-Fourcaud, André-Marc. "The Elderly Gentleman." In *Icons of Modern Art: The Shchukin Collection*. Paris: Editions Gallimard, 2022.

Djebar, Assia. *Women of Algiers in Their Apartment*. Charlottesville: University of Virginia Press, 1992.

Djemaï, Abdelkader. *Zorah sur la terrasse*. Paris: Seuil, 2010.

Drummond Hay, Sir John. *A Memoir of Sir John Drummond Hay*. London: John Murray, 1896.

Ducruet, César, et al. "Maghreb Port Cities in Transition: The Case for Tangier." *Portus Plus*, January 2011.

Dumas, Alexandre. *Tangiers to Tunis*. London: Peter Owen, 1959.

Elderfield, John. *Matisse: In the Collection of the Museum of Modern Art*. New York: Museum of Modern Art, 1978.

———. *The "Wild Beasts": Fauvism and Its Affinities*. Exhibition catalog. New York: Museum of Modern Art, 1976.

Entre Jaurès et Matisse: Marcel Sembat et Georgette Agutte, à la croisée des avant-gardes. Paris: Somogy, 2008.

Erbati, Elarbi, and Athena Trakadas. *The Morocco Maritime Survey: An Archaeological Contribution to the History of the Tangier Peninsula*. Oxford: British Archaeological Reports, 2008.

Escholier, Raymond. *Matisse from the Life*. London: Faber & Faber, 1960.

Félix Fénéon: The Anarchist and the Avant-Garde. Exhibition catalog. New York: Museum of Modern Art, 2020.

Finlayson, Iain. *Tangier: City of the Dream*. London: Tauris Parke, 2015.

Fisher, John. "The Bible Dream: Official Travel in Morocco, c. 1845–1935." In *The British Abroad since the Eighteenth Century, Volume 2: Experiencing Imperialism*, edited by Martin Farr and Xavier Guégan. London: Palgrave Macmillan, 2013.

Flam, Jack. *Matisse: A Retrospective*. Fairfield, CT: Hugh Lauter Levin, 1988.

———. *Matisse and Picasso: The Story of Their Rivalry and Friendship*. Cambridge: Westview, 2003.

———. *Matisse: The Man and His Art, 1869-1918*. Ithaca, NY: Cornell University Press, 1986.

Flanner, Janet. "King of the Wild Beasts—I". *New Yorker*, December 22, 1951.

———. "Letter from Paris." *New Yorker*, November 20, 1954.

Franck, Dan. *Bohemian Paris: Picasso, Modigliani, Matisse, and the Birth of Modern Art*. New York: Grove, 2001.

Fraser, John Foster. *Land of Veiled Women: Some Wanderings in Algeria, Tunisia and Morocco*. London: Cassell and Company, 1911.

Friedenthal, Richard. *Letters of the Great Artists*. New York: Random House, 1963.

From Russia: French and Russian Master Paintings 1870-1925 From Moscow and St. Petersburg. Exhibition catalogue. London: Royal Academy of Arts, 2008.

Fry, Roger. "Henri-Matisse in the Luxembourg." *Burlington Magazine*, May 1922.

Fulford, Robert. "The Painter We Weren't Ready For." *Maclean's*, April 25, 1959.

Gasquet, Joachim. Cézanne. Paris: Bernheim-Jeune, 1926.

Gide, André. *The Immoralist*. New York: Alfred A. Knopf, 1948.

Gilot, Francoise. *Matisse and Picasso: A Friendship in Art*. New York: Doubleday, 1990.

Giovannini, Joseph. "A Bridge from Moscow to Paris." *New York Times*, September 2, 2016.

Gowing, Lawrence. *Matisse*. London: Thames & Hudson, 1979.

Grammont, Claudine. *Charles Camoin: Un Fauve en liberté—The Free Fauve*. Paris: In Fine, 2022.

———. *Matisse in the Barnes Foundation*. New York: Thames & Hudson, 2015.

Grammont, Claudine, ed. *Matisse-Marquet: Correspondance 1898-1947*. Lausanne: Bibliothèque des Arts, 2008.

Grossman, Ron. "In 1913, a Culture War Erupted over an Exhibition of Modern Works at the Art Institute of Chicago." *Chicago Tribune*, April 16, 2023.

Groves, Robert. "Morocco as a Winter Sketching Ground." *International Studio*, November 1908.

Hamilton, Richard. *Tangier: From the Romans to the Rolling Stones*. London: Tauris Parke, 2019.

Harris, Walter. *Morocco That Was*. London: Eland, 2002.

Henri Matisse: Exhibition at the Museum of Modern Art. New York: Plantin, 1951.

Henri Matisse: Paintings and Sculptures in Soviet Museums. Leningrad: Aurora Art Publishers, 1978.

Henri-Matisse: Retrospective Exhibition. New York: Museum of Modern Art, 1931.

Herrera, Hayden. *Matisse: A Portrait*. New York: Harcourt Brace & Company, 1993.

Hilton, Alison. "Matisse in Moscow." *Art Journal* (Winter 1969–1970).

Holt, George Edmund. *Morocco the Piquant*. London: William Heineman: 1914.

Hook, Philip. *Breakfast at Sotheby's: An A–Z of the Art World.* London: Penguin, 2014.

———. *Modern: Genius, Madness, and One Tumultuous Decade That Changed Art Forever.* New York: The Experiment, 2022.

Hoorn, Jeanette. "Letters from Tangiers: The Creative Partnership between Elsie and Hilda Rix in Morocco." In *Impact of the Modern: Vernacular Modernities in Australia, 1870s–1960s*, edited by Robert Dixon and Veronica Kelly. Sydney: Sydney University Press, 2008.

———. *Moroccan Idyll: Art and Orientalism.* Victoria, Australia: Miegunyah Press, 2012.

Hughes, Robert. *Shock of the New: The Hundred-Year History of Modern Art.* London: Thames & Hudson, 1991.

Icons of Modern Art: The Shchukin Collection. Exhibition catalog. Paris: Gallimard, 2016.

"Ivan Morozov Talks to Félix Fénéon in 1920." *InCoRM Journal* 3 (Spring–Autumn 2012).

Jack Cowart Papers. MS.13. Matisse in Morocco. Archives and Manuscripts Collections, Baltimore Museum of Art.

Kean, Beverly. *All the Empty Palaces.* New York: Universe, 1983.

Kimmelman, Michael. "How the Spirit of Morocco Seized Matisse." *New York Times*, March 18, 1990.

Klein, John. *Matisse Portraits.* New Haven, CT: Yale University Press: Yale, 2001.

Kostenevich, Albert. "Sergei Shchukin: Modern Art Pioneer." In *Icons of Modern Art: The Shchukin Collection.* Paris: Gallimard, 2016.

Kostenevich, Albert, and Natalya Semyonova. *Collecting Matisse.* Paris: Flammarion, 1993.

Kropmanns, Peter. *Matisse à Issy: L'atelier dans la verdure.* Paris: L'Arche, 2010.

Labrusse, Rémi. "Deconstructing Orientalism: Islamic Lessons in European Arts at the Turn of the Twentieth Century." *Manazir Journal* 3 (2021).

———. *Matisse: La Condition de l'Image.* Paris: Gallimard, 1999.

Lavery, John. *Life of a Painter.* Boston: Little, Brown and Company, 1940.

Le Maroc de Matisse. Exhibition catalog. Paris: Institut du Monde Arabe/Gallimard, 2000.

Lefebvre, Denis. *Marcel Sembat—Franc-maçonnerie, art et socialisme à la Belle Époque.* Paris: Éditions Dervy, 2017.

Loti, Pierre. *Au Maroc.* Paris: Calmann Lévy, 1890.

Lyman, John. *Morrice.* Montreal: L'Arbre, 1945.

Lyon, Christopher. "Prelude to Morocco: Matisse in Moscow, 1911." *MoMA*, Summer 1990.

MacChesney, Clara T. "A Talk with Matisse." *New York Times*, March 9, 1913.

Martinent, Jean-Claude, and Guy Wildenstein. *Marquet: L'Afrique du Nord, Catalogue de l'œuvre peint*. Milan: Skira, 2001.

Matisse, Henri, et al. *The Vence Chapel, The Archive of a Creation*. Edited and with an introduction by Marcel Billot. Milan: Skira, 1999.

Matisse, Henri, with Pierre Courthion. *Chatting with Henri Matisse: The Lost 1941 Interview*. London: Tate, 2013.

Matisse. Edited by Caroline Turner and Roger Benjamin. Exhibition catalog. South Brisbane: Queensland Art Gallery and Art Exhibitions Australia, 1995.

Matisse, His Art and His Textiles. Exhibition catalog. London: Royal Academy of Arts, 2015.

Matisse in Morocco: The Paintings and Drawings, 1912-1913. Edited by Jack Cowart et al. Exhibition catalog. Washington, DC: National Gallery of Art, 1990.

Matisse on Art. Revised edition. Edited by Jack Flam. Berkeley: University of California Press, 1995.

Matisse: Radical Invention, 1913–1917. Exhibition catalog. New Haven, CT: Yale University, 2011.

"Matisse: Radical Invention, 1913–1917." Press release. Museum of Modern Art, 2010.

Maugham, W. Somerset. *The Magician*. New York: Penguin, 1992.

Maurois, Andre. *The Quest for Proust*. London: Constable, 1984.

McNeill, J.R. *The Mountains of the Mediterranean World*. Cambridge: Cambridge, 2003.

Mileeva, Maria. "Utopia in Retreat: The Closure of the State Museum of New Western Art in 1948." In *Utopian Reality: Reconstructing Culture in Revolutionary Russia and Beyond*, edited by Christiana Lodder, Maria Kokkori, and Maria Mileeva. Leiden: Brill, 2013.

Morrice and Lyman: In the Company of Matisse. Exhibition catalog. Richmond Hill, Ontario: Firefly, 2014.

"The National Gallery of Art to Present Paintings by Matisse." Press release. National Gallery of Art, October 28, 1986.

Olivier, Fernande. *Loving Picasso: The Private Journal of Fernande Olivier*. New York: Abrams, 2001.

Pennell, C.R. *Morocco since 1830: A History*. Oxford: Oneworld, 2003.

Porch, Douglas. *The Conquest of Morocco*. New York: Farrar, Straus and Giroux, 2005.

Potiron, Emmanuel. "Il faut sauver la villa Matisse." *Le Parisien*, August 6, 2002.

Poznanskaya, Anna, and Alexey Petukhov. "Sergei Shchukin: Outstanding Muscovite Collector." In *Icons of Modern Art: The Shchukin Collection*. Paris: Gallimard, 2016.

Proust, Marcel. *The Guermantes Way*. Translated by C. K. Scott Moncrieff. New York: Modern Library, 1925.

Read, Herbert. *The Meaning of Art.* London: Faber & Faber, 2017.
Reynolds-Ball, Eustace. *Mediterranean Winter Resorts.* Vol 1. South Europe. London: K. Paul, Trench & co., 1914.
Rix, Hilda. "Sketching in Morocco: A Letter from Miss Hilda Rix." *International Studio*, November 1914.
Roca, Juan Ramón. *Tangier: An Illustrated Guide.* Alicante, Spain: Roca Vicente-Franqueira, 2011.
Roe, Sue. *In Montparnasse: The Emergence of Surrealism in Paris, from Duchamp to Dali.* New York: Penguin, 2018.
Rogerson, Barnaby. *A Traveller's History of North Africa.* Gloucestershire, UK: Windrush, 1998.
———. "The Exploration of Light: European Painters in North Africa, from Delacroix to Klee." *Art Quarterly* (Summer 1999).
Rusakov, Yu A., and John E. Bowlt. "Matisse in Russia in the Autumn of 1911." *Burlington Magazine*, May 1975.
Russell, John. "Matisse and the Mark left on Him by Morocco." *New York Times*, June 22, 1990.
Schneider, Pierre. *Matisse.* New York: Rizzoli, 1984.
Shchukin, Sergei."Travel Diary." In *Icons of Modern Art: The Shchukin Collection.* Exhibition catalog. Paris: Gallimard, 2016.
Schwabsky, Barry. "Black Is Also a Color." *Nation*, June 21, 2010.
Selous, Gerald. *Appointment to Fez.* London: Richards Press, 1956.
Sembat, Marcel. *Les Cahiers Noirs: Journal, 1905-1922.* Edited and annotated by Christian Phéline. Paris: Viviane Hamy, 2014
Semenova, Natalya. *Morozov: The Story of a Family and a Lost Collection.* New Haven, CT: Yale University Press, 2020.
Semenova, Natalya, with André Delocque. *The Collector: The Story of Sergei Shchukin and His Lost Masterpieces.* New Haven, CT: Yale University Press, 2018.
Sijelmassi, Mohamed. *Moroccan Painting.* Paris: Jean Pierre Taillandier, 1972.
Sooke, Alastair. *Henri Matisse: A Second Life.* London: Penguin, 2014.
Spurling, Hilary. "Matisse and His Models." *Smithsonian Magazine*, October 2005.
———. "Matisse's Pajamas." *New York Review of Books*, August 11, 2005.
———. *Matisse the Master.* London: Penguin, 2006.
———. *The Unknown Matisse.* London: Penguin, 1998.
Spurling, Hilary, with Georges Bourgeois. *Henri Matisse, Man of the North: In the Footsteps of the Painter in His Native Picardy.* Cateau-Cambresis, France: Musée Matisse, 1999.
Stein, Gertrude. *The Autobiography of Alice B. Toklas.* New York: Vintage, 1990.
Stein, Leo. *Appreciation: Painting, Poetry, and Prose.* New York: Crown, 1947.

The Steins Collect: Matisse, Picasso, and the Parisian Avant-Garde. Exhibition catalog. New Haven, CT: Yale University Press, 2011.

Stewart, Natacha. "Matisse." *New Yorker*, April 5, 1982.

Stuart, Graham Henry. *The International City of Tangier.* Stanford, CA: Stanford University Press, 1955.

Taylor, Lance. *The Sultan's Gift: A History of St. Andrew's Church, Tangier, 1881-2006*. Tangier: Litograf, 2005.

Temkin, Ann, and Dorthe Aagesen. *Matisse: The Red Studio*. Exhibition catalog. New York: Museum of Modern Art, 2022.

"Testimony against Gertrude Stein." Transition Pamphlet no. 1 (supplement). Transition 1934-1935. The Hague: Servire, February 1935.

Tugendhold, Yakov. "S. I. Shchukin's French Collection (1914)." In *Icons of Modern Art: The Shchukin Collection*. Exhibition catalog. Paris: Gallimard, 2016.

Tyrwhitt Drake, CFT. "Notes on the Birds of Tangier and Eastern Morocco." *Ibis: A Quarterly Journal of Ornithology* (October 1867).

Vauxcelles, Louis. "The Art of J. W. Morrice." *Canadian Magazine*, December 1909.

Vincent, Hélène. *La Collection Agutte-Sembat*. Grenoble: Musée de Grenoble, 2003.

Vollard, Ambroise. *La vie & l'œuvre de Pierre-Auguste Renoir.* Paris: A. Vollard, 1919.

Ward, Vicky. "How a Russian Collector Changed the Course of Modern Art." *Town & Country*, September 10, 2016.

Watkins, Nicholas. "Matisse and Orientalism." *Burlington Magazine*, January 1998.

West, Shearer. *Portraiture*. Oxford: Oxford, 2004.

Wharton, Edith. *In Morocco*. Oxford: John Beaufoy, 2015.

Whitfield, Sarah. *Fauvism*. London: Thames & Hudson, 1991.

Woolman, David S. *Rebels in the Rif.* Stanford, CA: Stanford University Press, 1968.

Wright, Alastair. *Matisse and the Subject of Modernism*. Princeton, NJ: Princeton University Press, 2004.

Wullschlager, Jackie. "House of Modern Masterpieces: Shchukin at Foundation Louis Vuitton." *Financial Times*, October 21, 2016.

———. "Matisse: Inside His Private Universe." *Financial Times*, August 4, 2017.

———. "The Russians Are Coming." *Financial Times*, January 4, 2008.

INDEX

N

T